MATURE STUFF: Physical Activity for the Older Adult

David K. Leslie, Ed.

Sponsored by the
Council on Aging & Adult Development of the
Association for Research, Administration,
Professional Councils & Societies

An association of the
American Alliance for Health, Physical
Education, Recreation and Dance

Acknowledgements

Photos used at the beginning of each chapter were provided by:
Charles Daniel
Linda Napier
Wayne Osness
Jacki Robichoux

Cover photo by:
Jim Kirby

ISBN 0-88314-433-6

Purposes of the American Alliance for Health, Physical Education, Recreation, and Dance

The American Alliance is an educational organization, structured for the purposes of supporting, encouraging, and providing assistance to member groups and their personnel throughout the nation as they seek to initiate, develop, and conduct programs in health, leisure, and movement-related activities for the enrichment of human life.

Alliance objectives include:

1. Professional growth and development—to support, encourage, and provide guidance in the development and conduct of programs in health, leisure, and movement-related activities which are based on the needs, interests, and inherent capacities of the individual in today's society.

2. Communication—to facilitate public and professional understanding and appreciation of the importance and value of health, leisure, and movement-related activities as they contribute toward human well-being.

3. Research—to encourage and facilitate research which will enrich the depth and scope of health, leisure, and movement-related activities; and to disseminate the findings to the profession and other interested and concerned publics.

4. Standards and guidelines—to further the continuous development and evaluation of standards within the profession for personnel and programs in health, leisure, and movement-related activities.

5. Public affairs—to coordinate and administer a planned program of professional, public, and governmental relations that will improve education in areas of health, leisure, and movement-related activities.

6. To conduct such other activities as shall be approved by the Board of Governors and the Alliance Assembly, provided that the Alliance shall not engage in any activity which would be inconsistent with the status of an educational and charitable organization as defined in Section 501(c)(3) of the Internal Revenue Code of 1954 or any successor provision thereto, and none of the said purposes shall at any time be deemed or construed to be purposes other than the public benefit purposes and objectives consistent with such educational and charitable status.

Bylaws, Article III

Foreword

MATURE STUFF is the culmination of the ideas of many, and the dreams of a valiant group of pioneers from The American Alliance For Health, Physical Education, Recreation and Dance. AAHPERD is a voluntary professional education organization, made up of six national and six district associations with 54 state and territorial affiliates. The members are health and physical educators, coaches and athletic directors, and professional personnel in safety, leisure, education, and dance. AAHPERD is an umbrella for a number of allied disciplines and specialities within disciplines.

Over the years, since AAHPERD's founding in 1885, health educators, physical educators, coaches, dancers and choreographers, therapists, and recreation specialists have proposed many purposes for human movement to accomplish a variety of goals. Three categories of values have been described [Mosston, 1965]. The "Assigned" value belongs to the dancers and choreographers who attribute a feeling, an idea, or a mood to a movement. The "Functional" value is in the domain of the coaches where specific movements are required for particular sport skills. The "Intrinsic" value of movement is concerned with the intentional development of physical attributes or components required to develop and maintain a healthy mind and body. It would appear that, for those advancing in age, all three goals would be appropriate. To age successfully, an understanding of the components of total fitness is necessary. Extensive research has shown that the aged have the potential to improve work capacity and daily functioning, which makes the difference between remaining independent or becoming dependent.

Ideally, preparation for a fit old age should begin in youth in order that maximum benefits may accrue. We now know that the concept of trainability, even in old age, is valid. Exercise, good nutrition, and control of stress/relaxation is not necessarily to prolong life but to increase the years of feeling good. Chronological age is not a reliable barometer of physical condition, mental capacity, or behavior. Although we cannot stop the aging process, we can intervene to prevent or retard many of the disorders associated with aging.

For the majority of older people, especially women, education and trained leadership are essential. Many do not know what constitutes a safe and good exercise program to provide the amount of exertion necessary to obtain the desired physical changes. We may have missed this new clientele some 50 years ago or they may have missed opportunities due to leaving school early. Others may need to recall or refresh their physical skills. Members of our professions, all over the world, have the responsibility to help develop new roles, new careers, new techniques and processes, and new program materials for work with older people.

In order to respond to this challenge, the AAHPERD Committee On Aging was first appointed in 1974 by President Katherine Ley who reacted to research accomplished at The Andrus Foundation by Herbert deVries and a number of other research physiologists among our professional colleagues. In testimony before the United States Subcommittee On Aging in 1976, it was noted that, "training of older people requires instructors with highly specialized preparation and skills and this resource was lacking."

Early committees on Aging were small yet enthusiastic, hard working, and undaunted visionaries. During the years between 1974 and 1985, we believe we can safely say that an entire professional group became more aware of the needs of an older population with relation to health promotion and maintenance of fitness. A number of scholars, researchers, and practitioners from within The Alliance have updated their educational backgrounds and contributed to the literature concerning aging and health. A variety of print and media materials have been developed. Professional preparation for our students is moving forward and a number of varied and interesting programs, serving the older citizen, are in progress across the nation.

The Alliance has become affiliated with gerontological societies and has shared in conference programs with The American Association of Retired Persons, The National Council On The Aging/National Volunteer Organizations For Independent Living Of The Aged, The American Society On Aging, Elderhostel, Senior Games, and The Association For Gerontology in Higher Education, to mention a few. Members are active on the local level in the Aging Network. Leadership Workshops are being provided by way of District Conferences.

In 1985, The Board of Governors of The American Alliance For Health, Physical Education, Recreation and Dance saw fit to permanently structure a Council On Aging and Adult Development [CAAD] under the Association for Research, Administration, Professional Councils and Societies [ARAPCS]. The Council On Aging and Adult Development is growing rapidly and we are fortunate to have identified an enthusiastic and knowledgeable second generation of professional colleagues who have made this book and a number of other projects possible.

Grateful acknowledgement is due David Leslie, Charles Daniel, Helen Heitmann and Wayne Osness, who have edited and reviewed the manuscripts; Elinor Darland and Ray Ciszek, staff liaison over the years; and all of the chapter writers who have brought our dream to fruition.

To our students and readers, especially those in the wide range of health and caring professions, we hope this volume may serve as a timely and supportive base from which further ideas and applications may develop for the health and well-being of an ever growing older population.

Rosabel S. Koss
Professor Emeritus
Ramapo College
Ramapo, NJ

Preface

This book evolved out of recognition of the need for a resource that addressed the issue of aging from the perspectives of the subdisciplines represented by AAHPERD. First envisioned in the late seventies by the then AAHPERD President's Committee on Aging, action was initiated when the committee evolved into the Council on Aging and Adult Development (CAAD), a council in ARAPCS. Members of the new council approached the Alliance about the possibility of preparing a series of books or a book that met the growing need for HPERD material concerned with older populations. This book is the result of that effort.

A major concern of the editors was to provide material that would be of help to practitioners. The editors believed the most useful content would be that which reported current research findings as a knowledge base upon which practical applications would be based. This needed to be done in a way that retained the scholarly flavor but would be in a language that made content attractive to practitioners. The result is a book of thirteen chapters that is divided into three parts. The chapter authors were sought on the basis of their having practical experience with older adults and a scholarly background that includes the area of focus of their chapter.

The first part contains an introductory chapter that introduces the reader to the topic of aging in American society and ties in that topic to the interests of professionals in HPERD. Chapters two through six address the foundation areas of HPERD from the perspective of aging and include chapters that focus on the subdisciplines of biomechanics, exercise physiology, health, motor learning, and measurement. The second part of the book addresses aging from a programmatic perspective and includes chapters on the learning environment, programming, handicapping conditions and programming adjustments, and leisure activities. The third part of the book addresses program content and includes chapters on chair and standing exercises and their selection, aquatic exercises and dance.

The three parts are not totally exclusive in their content focus and coverage and there is some purposeful overlap and repetition. The intent is that the book can be used as a course text, in whole or in part, or as a reference for practitioners. It is directed toward upper division students and first year graduate students as well as practitioners working with older populations.

David K. Leslie
University of Iowa
Iowa City, IA

Table of Contents

PART I

FOUNDATION SCIENCES

1 CHARACTERISTICS OF OLDER ADULTS

Rosabel S. Koss, Professor Emeritus, Ramapo College

American society is aging. The future of our country will be shaped by trends and projections charted by the demographers.[1] Pifer and Bronte predict that, "in the decades to come, there will be fewer children and greatly increased numbers of elderly. Every aspect of American life will be affected, including: the family, women, intergenerational relationships, health care and ethical choices, minorities and the economy. Will we have a better society or a worse one? It depends on us."[2] The United States is not alone in this destiny. The entire world population is growing older, presenting a challenge to social policy worldwide. Drastic demographic changes in the European societies are said to have occurred 15 to 30 years ago, while the developing countries are just beginning to chart their older populations. There is an obvious need for increased international exchange of knowledge and expertise in the field of aging.

According to a United Nations report,[3] the number of persons in the world who are 65 or older will grow by 53.7 percent during the 20-year span between 1980 and 2000. The population over age 75 is experiencing especially rapid growth: by the year 2000, half of all elders will be 75 and older. The Abkhasians in Georgia of the Soviet Union refer to their older citizens as "Longer Living." In Sweden, they are the "Pensioner's." In Australia, it is "Aged Care." German research reports sports, games, exercises after age 40, for the "Older People." In China, it is "Elder Care" and everyone, including the elderly, seem to have a particular job to be done that is necessary for the good of the entire society.[4] Longevity rates vary among the nations and appear to be influenced by lifestyles.[5]

Gerōn is a Greek word with three meanings, like some of our English words. It can mean old man, *growing* older, or *awakening*. This is the root word for gerontology. Gerontology is the scientific study of the process of aging and the problems of aging people and is often confused with geriatrics, which is the subdivision of Medicare concerned with old age and its diseases.[6] It is a multi-disciplinary study that concerns itself with every aspect of human functioning in the later years, and has been developed to meet the needs of increasing numbers of older persons. According to Schwartz et al.[7] "The goal is not to extend life but to alleviate some of the personal, social, economic, and physical problems that afflict older citizens." The study of gerontology is a careful blending of the theoretical from the social and natural sciences, to produce new knowledge, information and understanding; with practical applications in the service of older people. The study of gerontology on the college and university campuses is a fairly recent development and has the potential of better preparing our future citizens for their own aging through increased sensitivity and awareness of their own aging process, their effectiveness as decision makers for families and communities, and the development of a cadre of knowledgeable care-givers for future older populations. The study of aging has a strong tradition of pragmatism so service learning or some sort of field experience is essential.[8] Multigenerational learning is also possible at all ages and needs wider development in the elementary and secondary schools. Health and physical educators can help meet this need by adjusting current curricular offerings to include units on lifecycle development, aging, and death and dying.

The terms: aging, older, elderly, golden agers, and senior citizens, must be qualified. Overnight, every night, approximately 5,000 Americans reach 65 years of age, the statutory limit for old age or "senility." Our government has ignored scientific evidence and arbitrarily accepted age 65 as the year when a person may receive full benefits for Social Security. Sixty-five was the age specified in Germany by Bismarck for retirement in his sweeping social reforms of the 1880s and it was politically convenient for us to copy that precedent. Today, in the United States, early retirement is possible with reduced benefits at age 62, while full benefits begin at age 65. In the future, retirement with full benefits is projected for age 67.[9] By law, there is no mandatory retirement age for workers (with the exception of pilots, police, and other safety workers), however, nearly half of all American men between the ages of 61 and 64 are retired.[10] "Many older workers have been pushed out of their jobs by forced retirement and others have been downgraded in the quality of work assigned to them."

In our society we might classify persons aged 50 to 60 as the very young olds, 61 to 70 the middle aged olds, 70 to 80 the old olds, and the 80 years on as very old olds and Centurians. Then again, there are the frail olds, the more able olds, and the vigorous super-olds! Some recent studies look at the population age 55 and older as the older population, the elderly as 65 and older, the aged as 75 and older and the very old as 85 and older. No two olds are alike. As to Centurians, Segerburg estimates that there were approximately 13,216 persons 100 years or older in 1979 in the United States. At this writing, the oldest documented person in the world was a Japanese lady who lived until age 113.[11]

When Does Aging Begin

Saxon and Etten[12] list seven reported hypotheses or theories of biological aging. "No one knows exactly how or why aging occurs. Although numerous theories have been proposed, no one theory is currently acceptable as an adequate explanation. Much of the available research involves sub-human species and cannot be generalized." Some scholars believe aging begins before birth. According to the Hayflick Genetic Factors Theory,[13] life span is determined by a fixed program in the genes or body cells, and is fixed from species to species; in humans it is estimated to be 110 to 115 years. Few live out their potential. The best single thing that one can do is to be born of long living parents. We do know that there is no disease produced solely by passage of time and that diseases associated with aging and degeneration can strike at any age.

Chronological age, or age in years, is not a good predictor of physical condition or behavior. Aging is a normal developmental process. *Primary aging* is the result of universal deficits which may occur at different times for different people as well as for different organs and systems within an individual. *Secondary aging* is the result of disease, crippling disability, poor lifestyle choices, or stress due to losses which may occur at varying ages among humans. One of the great challenges for gerontology today is to distinguish those changes which are "normal" aging from those that are pathological. Measurement of health entails looking at how well an individual copes with impairments and the extent to which life routines and homeostasis are maintained. There is no such thing as an old age personality. We age the way we live. There is a remarkable continuity of character and life styles. Old age is not a sudden and dramatic event, but merely a life cycle transition.[14]

Agism

In The United States, older persons suffer from a contagious disease found in no medical dictionary. It is an attitude called agism. Like racism and sexism, it is a collection of erroneous beliefs and attitudes concerning a mythical and stereotyped older person—sick, sad, tired, senile, dirty, ugly, and of no use to self or others. The American society is just beginning to learn that growing old is not considered to be a malediction everywhere in the world. A change in societal attitudes of Americans can help us increase the richness of our later years. Simple preventive measures can significantly reduce the negative impact that a poor lifestyle has on older adults. The U.S. Surgeon General in *Healthy People*,[15] suggested three reasons for increasing disease prevention and a *Health Promotion Initiative* for people of all ages. "Prevention saves lives; Prevention improves the quality of life; and Prevention can save dollars in the long run." We have succeeded as a society in helping people live longer. We should now concentrate on a better and healthier life for older people.

One of the problems each person faces is a reluctance to contemplate their own aging. People tend to avoid lectures, discussion, and serious study concerned with aging. When given a choice, only brave and serious students will select a course in gerontology, although careers of the future will require service to the older population. When one considers the alternative, becoming sensitized to one's own aging process and learning to age successfully should be highly desirable behaviors.

Characteristics of the Aged

For purposes of this introduction, an attempt is made to tease out from the statistics the characteristics of an aging population, both now and for the future. Aging can be defined as physiological, behavioral, sociological, and chronological phenomena.[16] Studies are usually attached to the chronological concept.

A number of models for assessing the elderly are reviewed and evaluated in a World Health Organization publication.[17] "Assessment should be multi-dimensional and in terms of functional status." There is general consensus that five basic dimensions should be included in any overall assessment of elderly individuals within a population; namely, activities of daily living, mental health, physical health, and social and economic functioning. For purposes of activity and independent living, we might divide our older population into three groups: The most able are super seniors, who can move freely and independently through space. The more able can move with some support, and the least able, or frail elderly, are mostly confined to chairs or beds. Statistics tell us that 80 to 85 percent of the elderly are fully independent and vigorous, 10 to 15 percent are less able and living with one or several disabilities, while 2 to 5 percent are least able and possibly institutionalized, at any given point of time. Piscopo describes the target population in four general groups: The well-aging, the ambulatory and wheel-chair elderly, the frail elderly, and the bed patients.[18] The greatest number of persons within the over 60 population are free of serious disabling disease and able to function without assistance.

Whatever model, concept, or statistical analysis the planner chooses to use, it is essential for program planning that we identify some of the more common and broadly applicable health characteristics and needs to be met for the target population. This is called "Fitting The Population." An example of this can be found in The Administration On Aging's, *A Healthy Old Age: A Source Book For Health Promotion With Older Adults.*[19]

Trends and Projections of the Aging Population

For a broad analysis of trends and projections, a recent edition of *Aging America: Trends and Projections,*[20] will be summarized.

There have always been a few individuals who have lived to an advanced age, but in the 20th century there has been a dramatic increase in the percentage of older persons in the population. Persons over 65 years numbered 29.2 million in 1986. They represented 12.1 percent of the U.S. population, about one in every eight Americans. By the year 2000, the projection is for 34.9 million in the over 65 age group. The older population itself is getting older. In 1986 the 65–74 age group [17.3 million] was eight times larger than 1900, but the 74–84 group [9.1 million] was 12 times larger and the 85+ group [2.8 million] was 22 times larger. (See Figures 1.1 and 1.2.)

In the United States the rate of change in the size of the population will be uneven. For the next 30 years there will be sustained but undramatic growth. With the aging of the "Baby Boomers", we will have become an older society whether or not we are prepared . The needs of the older population are already out-pacing public and private resources and the projected

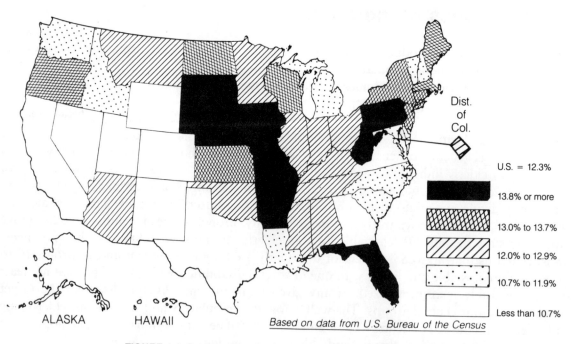

FIGURE 1.1. Persons 65+ as percentage of total population: 1987.

size of our older society by the year 2000 will challenge our capacity to adapt public policy.

The older population itself is aging. These are the high risk, frail elderly, who are 74 or older. Four generation families are becoming common and it is likely that older persons will have a surviving parent and great grand-children. While less than 5 percent of the population were 75 or older in 1982, by 2030, almost 10 percent of the population will be in that group.

The "dependency ratio" will become severely strained. This ratio represents the members or proportions of individuals in the dependent segment of the population [infancy to 18 and 65+] divided by the supporting or working population. Thus, in 1930, nine dependent individuals were supported by 100 workers. By 1980 18.6 dependents were supported by 100 workers and by 2020 the projection is for 29 dependents for every 100 workers.

The upward trend in life expectancy is continuing. A baby born in 1900 could expect to live an average of 47.3 years, while a baby born in 1985 could expect to live 74.7 years. The 1986 figure is 74.9 years. The life expectancy for men is less than that of women. The differential is seven to eight years and decreases after age 65. Life expectancy also differs with race. White women live the longest. Black males and males of other minority races have the lowest life expectancy rates. Reductions in the death rates of our population are thought to be due to increased food supply, development of the economy and transportation, changes in technology, and increased control over infectious disease.[21]

Older women outnumber older men and the ratio of females to males varies dramatically with age. At birth there are slightly more males than females but by age 65 in 1987 there were 83 men for every 100 women. This drops to 40 men for every 100 women at 85 plus years. Older women, living alone in the later years, on reduced income, with great risk of ill health, often

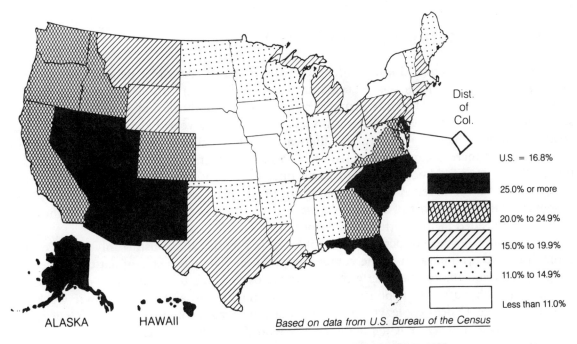

U.S. = 16.8%

25.0% or more

20.0% to 24.9%

15.0% to 19.9%

11.0% to 14.9%

Less than 11.0%

Based on data from U.S. Bureau of the Census

FIGURE 1.2. Percentage change in 65+ population: 1980 to 1987

suffer social and economic problems greater than those of the older male due to fewer years in the work force and unequal pay scales in the earlier years.

Geography makes a difference. In 1986, 49 percent of persons 65 and older lived in 8 states and of those that moved to another state, over one-third had moved from the Northeast or Midwest to the South or the West. Counties with large elderly populations are found across the country.

While the 1970 figures showed large numbers of elderly living in the Central City, it now appears that the average suburban population is 11.8% elderly and a decreasing proportion live in farm areas.

At the world level, the profile of the average elderly person is expected to change from rural to urban. Elderly women are becoming more urbanized than the general population in most countries. This "urbanization"[22] has serious implications with regard to social and economic development. Regions which had highly industrialized economies are now challenged with an aging population of vulnerable and frail persons who require increased resource allocations and new forms of service delivery.

Tne Veterans Administration operates the largest health care system in the United States because we have been involved in 10 major armed conflicts during 2 centuries of American history. In 1986, there were 5.5 million veterans age 65 plus. By the year 2000 there will be nine million elderly veterans. This number will drop back to 8.1 million in 2010. Over 95 percent of today's elderly veterans are men but the numbers of female aged veterans will double by the year 2000 due to women serving in World War II and the Korean conflict. Close to half of the veterans will fall into the 75 plus age range. This will seriously tax existing facilities.

It is imperative that planners and care-givers for the elderly check out the local statistics by way of the local planning authority and the Area Office On Aging so that they may have a clearer picture of the population to be served.

Economic Status of the Elderly

Although the 1981 White House Conference Report[23] states that older people in these United States are better off than they have been at any time in the history of our country, we still have some serious problems. The Gray Panthers report that, "One-third of all elderly Americans are struggling to feed and house themselves on less than $4,000 a year; Health care for the elderly costs four times what it does for other Americans; Forty percent of those consigned to nursing homes are not there because of illness but because they cannot care for themselves and have nowhere else to go; Almost one-third live alone, too many in shabby hotels, broken down tenements or on the street. A large percentage of the homeless are over 65; Most elderly live in desperate fear that the cost of a major illness will rob them of what meager savings they have. Some avoid needed medical attention because of cost."[24]

The economic position of persons 65 or older is, in general, at a considerably lower level and is much less secure than that of the younger population. There is a strong pattern of declining incomes with age among the elderly due to factors over which they have little control such as sex, race, health, survival of spouse, and their own health and ability to continue work at an acceptable wage. Older people who work full-time have wages comparable to a younger person of the same race and sex. For the many elderly who do not work, social security benefits that keep pace with the cost of living are vital.

Age and sex are important factors in income level. For males, income tends to increase with age until about 55 years. Many retire or are retired early and the steady decline of income begins. Median income levels for women begin lower, are often interrupted, and start to decline at age 50.

The impact of taxes on the incomes of all age groups is an unknown variable. Charts on income distribution show the after-tax income of the elderly to remain clustered at the lower end, with smaller numbers of elderly people in middle and high income brackets. The recent law requiring income tax on part of the social security for elders in middle and high income brackets will have a serious impact for those seniors who have worked hard and long for economic security.

The "Cost of Living Adjustment," [COLA] enacted in 1972,[25] is sometimes withheld, seemingly as a result of compromise or at the whim of our two-party governmental system. Older people had been led to believe that there was a social compact or promise that is now being broken. If the "COLA's" do not continue, inflation will have dire results on the incomes of the elderly, and women will have the most to lose.

There are striking differences between the incomes of elderly men and women and between elderly whites, blacks and other minorities. Elderly white men tend to have the highest median income, while elderly black women have the lowest. This is in contrast to the stereotype of the older rich widow.

Elderly persons who live alone receive much less income than those who live as a part of a family or as members of a multi-person household. Black, unrelated families are the poorest, with a median income well below the poverty level. Women who did not work outside the home receive half of the spouse's benefit as long as the spouse lives. When they are widowed, there is only one check.[26]

A Harris survey in 1981 showed heavy reliance on the Social Security benefit. Sixty-six percent of those over 65 received no interest from savings accounts; 78 percent had no investment income; 68 percent no pension income; 87 percent no wages; 95 percent received no money from their children.[27]

Social Security benefits are the single largest source of income and go to 91 percent of all elderly. More than half of the elderly depend on Social Security for over half of their income and one-fifth receive 90 percent or more of their income from this source. The third day of any month is the prime shopping day for seniors. Social Security high's, low's and median's are seldom quoted in the literature as they are quickly out-dated and dangerous. Benefits are determined by a formula which takes into account a number of individualized circumstances.[28] The best advice for those under 65 years of age, who would like to plan for their future, is to visit the local Social Security office, file a card of inquiry to be sure the employer has been making contributions regularly, and that you are identified correctly on the computer. Applications for benefits to begin should be made three months prior to retirement. Seniors with concerns about their Social Security benefits should contact their local social security office for advice. Also, the Office On Aging in the area may be a source of advocacy for a senior with problems.

Many persons face poverty for the first time in their lives after they retire. In 1986, about 3.5 million elderly persons were below the poverty level. Another 2.3 million or 8 percent of the elderly were classified as "near poor" (income between the poverty level and 125 percent of this level). In total, one fifth of the older population was poor or near poor in 1986. One of every nine elderly whites was poor in 1986, compared to one-third of elderly blacks and about one-fourth of elderly Hispanics.[29] Although there has been an improvement since 1970, poverty rates are high during older age due to a substantial reduction in income which is not compensated for by changes in lifestyle and the likelihood of major expenditures for health care which is not fully covered by Medicare. Almost half of the poor receive no public assistance of any kind. Some receive Supplementary Security Income, food stamps and energy assistance while others live in government subsidized housing. The high cost of energy has eaten into the food budgets of the elderly. Between 25 and 30 percent of the total federal budget is spent in programs directly assisting the elderly. With the exception of Social Security, this money does not go directly to meet the needs of the elderly but is used to operate Aging Network programs mandated by the Older American's Act. This is not direct assistance but salaries to employ people to assist the elderly.

Retirement and Education:

People in the recent past worked until they were no longer able. Even though there is no legal mandatory retirement age for most workers today, the average age of retirement is 62 years, so it is now possible to spend almost one-third of one's life in this changed life situation.

Retirement is often a severe life crisis because social status, as seen by self and others, is related to productivity. Men especially have a difficult transition because they are likely to have fewer interests or social contacts outside their jobs. Women generally find the transition easier because they are used to domestic activity whether or not they have worked outside the home and are more likely to have social ties outside the workplace.

In our society it appears that the better educated professionals and executives from business and industry have an easier and more gradual transition into retirement than do blue collar workers. Discarding one's past obligation to work and building a new life outside the workplace is never easy. However, with our new understanding of retirement as part of the life cycle, it becomes obvious that education can no longer be reserved for the young. We are all "unfinished people" and training and development of the total individual, mental, physical, social, and spiritual beings is a continuous life long process.

It is well to remember that the aged have typically not completed as many years of education as younger groups, although the educational level of the older population has been steadily increasing. Between 1970 and 1986, their median level increased from 8.7 years to 11.8 years. The percent who had completed high school rose from 28 to 49 percent. About 10 percent had four or more years of college. The median numbers of years of school completed varied considerably by race and ethnic origin. In 1986 it was 12.1 years for whites, 8.3 years for blacks, and 7.2 years for Hispanics.[30]

Adult education is one the rise for both job related and enrichment purposes. The 1981 White House Conference Report recognizes the value of education for the aging and recommends free access to education at all levels for the over 65 population. Education is seen as a valuable and worthwhile process that can make lives more enjoyable, useful, and functional at all ages.[31]

Studies indicate that the elderly are capable of learning,[32] although they may be educationally handicapped through lack of basic skills and/or rusty in literacy skills due to nonuse. Pacing, or time required to sort out responses, is important. Some find the academic setting threatening; have a lack of motivation; are disengaged[33] or have some personal problems such as poor health, finances, or lack of transportation. The vast majority have the ability to participate and could benefit by helping to solve personal problems, preparing for new careers, personal enrichment, or self actualization. A number of structured arrangements, both formal and informal, at a variety of sites, for individuals and groups and sponsored by a partnership of the public and voluntary sectors from among health providers, consumer organizations, and the older consumers will be necessary.[34]

The behavior patterns of some older citizens, particularly those who did not continue education or do not mingle in the multi-generational society, express viewpoints and values that are obsolete and contrary to those held by modern society. Modernization theory states that the older person suffers declining status unless intervening variables such as education, social mobility, volunteering or returning to the workplace, new interests etc. become a part of the life experience. Generation gaps exist usually with relation to money, religion, parenting, morality, and prejudice.[35]

Work Patterns:

Most older persons say they would like to work, but the labor force participation of men and women drops rapidly with increasing age. In 1986, 88.9 percent of men age 50 to 54 and 62 percent of women in this age group were in the labor force. By age 60 to 64, only about 55 percent of men and 33 percent of women were working. Among those 70 or older, only 10 percent of men and 4 percent of women were at the work place.[36] This is due to voluntary early retirement, mergers and closing of industries, decrease of self-employment, and inability of older people to find employment for a variety of reasons. As more women have entered the work force, a drastic increase has taken place in the portion of their time spent outside the home. However, while men tend to work straight through the working years, women go in and out of the labor force. This can prove to be a disadvantage as to possible retirement benefits.

Part-time work is increasingly important as an economic resource. With fewer younger people projected for the work force, part-time work by seniors can help with labor shortages. Close to 50 percent of older men and 60 percent of older women who work are part-time employees. Most of this employment is service oriented or involves professionals who manage to carry on some part of a former practice. A group of large business employers, identified by the American Association For Retired Persons, are changing workplace policies and practices to accommodate an older work force.[37]

Older people offer their time and abilities to volunteer to a wide variety of organizations across the nation. This is a valuable economic resource as hours served provide an "in kind" payback to the society for services enjoyed throughout a lifetime. Programs are administered by the Federal Agency for Volunteerism, ACTION. In a given year ACTION sponsored 332,000 Retired Senior Volunteer Program Participants, 18,000 were Foster Grandparents, and 4,800 were Senior Companions. Countless others participate by becoming involved in charitable and voluntary organizations on the community level. Volunteerism is one way to perpetuate the time and place structure and worthwhile use of time and abilities for the older person.

Satisfying use of leisure time is a challenge for most retirees. Upon retirement there are 50 more hours per week to fill in order to compensate for the time spent at the workplace and in grooming and commuting.

The work ethic of the past creates problems with seniors who do not enjoy education for leisure or leisure counseling, or have not developed hobbies or avocations. They tend to perceive recreation, exercise, crafts, music, films, and other enriching experiences as time wasting and nonproductive. Pre-retirement planning materials challenge individuals to reconstruct life experiences and patterns as they search for new ideas and new ventures.

Religion:

Religion is as diverse as the population. Most people identify with some religion. According to a U.S. Census figure, only two to three percent report no religious affiliation. However, only half of the general population attends religious services regularly. An analysis of church attendance shows a steady increase from the late teens until it peaks in the late 50s to early 60s. Supposedly the decline in later years is related to ill health, disability, and transportation difficulties. There is little or no evidence to support the myth that older people tend to become more religious as they age.[38] Religious attitudes tend to remain stable throughout a lifetime depending on early religious training. It is difficult to establish operational definitions of the religious experience. For older Americans religious institutions have traditionally served as a focal point for both spiritual and social activities. Religious groups provide numerous services in the areas of counseling, education, transportation, recreation, nutrition, fellowship, health care and housing assistance, home visiting, and volunteer service opportunities. Religious groups often provide senior housing and long-term care facilities. The mission to the elderly is growing as more clergy and lay people develop greater awareness of the needs of the older population. Most nationally organized religious groups are developing programs to more fully serve the elderly. While relatively new, these ventures look most promising.[39] For the nonwhite elderly, who are not participating in federally supported programs, they can often be reached when the local church becomes the focal point of contact.

Crime:

Older persons list crime as one of their greatest fears and limit travel to avoid specific areas and times of day. State Divisions On Aging have provided grants for a Home Protective Program where the homes of clients will be made more secure against burglary. Neighborhood watch programs have also been established. When the elderly do become victimized the impact on their lives is apt to be greater than for a younger person. However, criminal victimization rates for the elderly are lower than those for other age groups. The nonwhite aged are more vulnerable. Some elderly do not report crimes for fear of repercussion. Special legal services and advocacy may be required. Retired lawyers and paralegal personnel are often organized, at the local level, to assist seniors with problems.[40]

Voting Power:

Older persons are more likely to vote than members of younger age groups. Indications are that the future older population will be much more politically astute, articulate and assertive. As a special interest group they are linking up with minority and women's groups. AARP (The American Association For Retired Persons) with 27 million members, and NCOA (The National Council On The Aging) have joined with over two dozen other senior citizen organizations to form The Leadership Council of Aging. The 1986 NCOA Conference sent more than 19 bus loads of seniors to lobby "On The Hill." In this effort every congressional office was visited. In spite of changing patterns in the profile of older Americans, public policy regarding the aging remains ambiguous in definition and scope and, at best, uneven and inconsistent in implementation and enforcement.[43] This fact alone makes it difficult for seniors with diversified backgrounds and interests to fully utilize their voting potential.

Housing:

Seniors live, for the most part, in single family dwellings in their own community, in Senior Citizen Housing, in rented apartments, in segregated adult town-houses, condominiums, trailer parks, resort settings, single room occupancy in shabby hotels, and "on the street." The more fortunate travel a great deal, as long as they are able, and those who have funds follow the sun.

Of the 18.2 million households headed by older persons in 1985, 75 percent were owner occupied and 25 percent were rental units. Eighty-three percent of these owner occupied properties were owned free and clear. Those 75 years or older were more likely to rent. Males were more likely than females to own their own homes and persons living alone were more likely to rent than those living with spouses. Over a third of the owner-occupied households were occupied by men or women living alone, while two-thirds of the rental units were maintained by those living alone. The elderly are most likely to live in older homes of lower value and a significant number live in inadequate housing and do not have telephones.[42] Significant proportions of renters and owners live in housing with flaws, such as incomplete kitchens, open cracks and holes, and incomplete plumbing facilities. There is no information available on the number of elderly persons on waiting lists to get into subsidized housing and funds for housing have been cut back during the '80s. The recent trend to convert apartments and trailer camp sites to condominiums has dislocated many of the elderly, and local zoning laws usually do not permit alternative housing choices, although some states are more liberal than others. Florida, for example, allows groups of nonblood relatives to purchase property and live together as "families of choice." Relatively small numbers of the elderly live in intergenerational households with children and other relatives. This percentage increases with advanced age, particularly for older women.

Most older people enjoy living close to one or more of their children and contacts are frequently on a daily or weekly basis. Neighbors and other relatives provide substantial support and daily help for seniors living alone.

Changing Life Styles:

More than one half of the elderly are married and live together but most older men are married and most older women are widowed. Differences in marital status for most women are due to greater longevity of women and the fact that men tend to marry younger women. The average widow, who is not remarried, has been widowed six years and can expect to live an additional 24 years, in all, as a widow.

There are growing trends toward divorce, separation, and re-marriage in the total population. Some seniors cohabit for companionship and economic reasons. When the baby boom generation reaches old age, one half of the persons over 65 will have been divorced. This will mean extended families, increasing numbers of nonblood relatives, and more individuals seemingly cut loose from family support.

Changing family structure due to increased longevity means that four-generation families are increasingly more common. A large number of older persons live alone rather than in families. Some of this is due to mobility of offspring, smaller family housing, and greater expectations of seniors for comfort and independence.

Health:

Older persons have a positive view of their personal health. Seventy percent who live in the community describe their health as excellent, very good, and good, as compared to others their age. Only 30 percent report that their health is fair, or poor.[43] Self perception of health varies with income, sex, race, marital status, education, and employment. After 65, women report more positively than men, and whites more favorably than blacks. The never marrieds report more favorably than the marrieds, divorced, widowed, and separated. Those with higher education are more likely to view health as good. Older persons who are employed report better health status. Chronic conditions, not necessarily limiting, are a burden of old age.

The pattern of illness and disease has changed over the years. Acute conditions used to be the cause of death at the turn of the century while chronic conditions are now more prevalent. More than four of every five persons over 65 have one chronic condition and multiple conditions are commonplace. The leading chronic conditions are arthritis, hypertension disease, hearing impairments, and heart conditions. Most hospitalization for older persons is for heart disease, circulatory problems, diseases for the respiratory and digestive systems, and cancer. Older men are more likely than women to suffer acute illnesses, while elderly women are more likely to have chronic illnesses that cause physical limitations. Elderly blacks generally have poorer health than whites and hypertension among blacks 65 to 74 years of age is a challenging problem. Heart disease is the leading health problem for the elderly. Heart disease, cancer, and stroke together account for three-quarters of the deaths of the elderly.[44]

Severe chronic illness can prevent individuals from functioning on their own in life situations and brings about the need for long-term care services. A study with relation to the future growth of long-term care shows that 5.2 million persons over 65 were mildly to severely disabled in 1985. This figure is expected to reach 7.3 million in 2000, 10.1 by 2020, and 14.4 by 2050.[45] There is some hope, however, that certain chronic diseases may be reduced by new technologies. Must we continue to build more nursing home beds or can we become more creative and develop a comprehensive home health care policy? "Too often, Medicare and Medicaid regulations force people to enter hospitals and nursing homes in order to receive any help at all."[46] With the frail elderly the need for assistance is essentially personal care and home management, and friends, spouses, relatives, and others can provide valuable unpaid assistance.

"Mental health problems of the elderly are significant in their impact on mental status and emotional status in later life. Between 15 and 25 percent have serious symptoms due to mental disorders."[46] Mental health problems can be early or late in onset. About one-quarter of state mental hospital patients are 65 or older. The number of persons with mental disorders in nursing homes continues to rise.

"Alzheimer's disease is the leading cause of cognitive impairment in old age. This disease has an insidious onset and a gradually progressive course."[47] It brings a loss of intellectual abilities, including memory, judgement, abstract thought, as well as changes in personality and behavior. At the present time there is no cure, and positive diagnosis, before autopsy, is not conclusive. Other organic mental disorders such as depression, dementia, fever, trauma, and drug reactions, present many of the same symptoms and there is reliable evidence that Alzheimer's disease is over diagnosed. Drug compliance, drug interaction, and alcoholism are serious problems for the elderly.[48] [49] There is a growing body of knowledge pointing out the adverse effects of mental health problems on the course of illness in later life.[50]

The elderly use mental health facilities at half the rate of the general population although it is generally assumed that they have the same prevalence of mental health or psychiatric problems as the rest of the population.

Utilization of physician services increases with age and medical doctors and allied health professionals are currently estimated to spend increasing amounts of time with the aged. This is projected to rise to 75 percent by the turn of the century. Much remains to be done relating to the education of medical doctors and health professionals in geriatrics and gerontology.

Problems exist in the use of health care services and hospitalization. Medicare covers fewer of the expenses incurred. Eye examinations and dental visits are without coverage. Dentures must be paid for out-of-pocket. The new Catastrophic Coverage Act will cause a monthly increase in the basic premium, the part B premium, and a supplemental premium based on federal income tax liability. The new law does not cover hospital or doctor deductibles or physicians' charges above what Medicare recognizes as reasonable and allowable when physicians do not accept assignment. It does not cover long-term custodial care either in a nursing home or at home and it does not provide routine physical examinations, eyeglasses, hearing aids, dentures and routine foot care.[51]

The emerging change in morbidity charts to a "Rectangular Survival Curve" would appear to show the possibility of natural death and the compressing of the so-called "terminal dip" into a shorter span of the life cycle. This is advanced by Fries and discussed in the *New England Journal of Medicine*.[52] Many ethical questions concerning longevity and the treatment of the terminally ill are emerging. It appears that some limits may have to be set with relation to health costs for the terminally ill and the elderly.[53] Debate continues concerning policy issues and the rationing of medical care.

Misconceptions about health and senility of the elderly exist. Many seniors suffer severe feelings of loss, grief, anger, and depression due to life events, income reduction, and physical limitations. These problems may be seen as transitory and not irreversible mental disorders. Poor health and loneliness, not enough money or job opportunities, and fear of crime are the same problems identified by Americans of all ages.

Havighurst says: "The elderly have three pressing needs; Safety, Identity, and Stimulation."[54] Transportation is a major problem and Sunday is the most difficult day of the week. The fears and anxieties about possible future health difficulties are greater than the actual state of health and well-being.

A longitudinal study at Duke University[55] showed that far from conforming to any depressing stereotype of decline, the majority of older persons remained in good health, socially and sexually active, with reasonable financial security and good mental acuity until the final weeks of life. They have an enormous store of unused potential for contributing to contemporary society. Only five percent are in need of custodial care. The rest of the aging population are fairly healthy and capable of independent living. Even though some have chronic maladies they are able to live active and involved lives.

Lifetime Fitness, Exercise and Activity:

Fitness, exercise and leisure activity have the potential to improve the health and quality of life at all ages, including today's and tomorrow's elderly. Studies show a startling difference between active and inactive seniors. Active seniors show an increase in vitality, less dependence on laxatives, fewer visits to the physician, and improved general functioning.[56] Research into the effects of exercise on the elderly must take into account those age-related physical changes that are due to lifestyle and degenerative diseases as against those that are the result of the aging process. Ostrow warns that the improved status of older adults may be due to elimination of weaker individuals by death and disease, and to the fact that those in the research population are healthier older people.[57] However, research does show change in oxygen consumption, blood pressure, muscle strength and endurance, and greater flexibility in range of motion.[58–62] Spirduso notes changes in the neuromuscular system[63] while Smith et al.[64] report that when stress is placed on bone through weight-bearing exercise, calcium content and resistance to fracture are increased. The bone mineral content increased thus retarding osteoporosis. Psychological effects, such as reduced anxiety and tension, less depression, improvement in body image, greater self-sufficiency, self-satisfaction, and a general improvement in mood have been reported.[65–67] People are trainable at all ages.[68] It would appear, from the research evidence, that exercise for the elderly can improve physical and psychological health. All movement counts as exercise. Almost anyone, regardless of age, sex, income level, education, living circumstances, or health or functional status, can find some form of physical activity that is comfortable, enjoyable, and within his/her own limits. Being fit is being able to do the things one wants and needs to do. (See Chapter 4 on motor learning.)

Attitudes toward fitness, exercise and aging pose barriers to program development and to the participation of older people. Conrad[69] found: "The frail barrier is the negative public image of older people as feeble, frail, over-the-hill, and unable to compete with or keep up to younger people. The second barrier is the common myth that the older one gets, the less there is need for exercise. The third barrier is the negative attitudes of older people who feel their abilities are limited and exercise might be dangerous. They overrate the benefits of light and sporadic exercise and underrate their abilities and capacities." Physicians rarely prescribe exercise for patients of any age who are considered to be healthy. Physicians are sometimes biased against exercise for older people, advising them to "take it easy" or to avoid climbing stairs, and by adapting the drug approach to most of their symptoms. (See chapters on exercise and chapter on leisure and recreation.)

In testimony before the Senate Subcommittee on Aging[70] deVries stated: "In view of the many benefits likely to result from the physical fitness in the elderly, it seems desirable to begin the implementation of programs of exercise, nutrition and stress reduction or relaxation procedures. However, training of older people in these areas requires instructors with highly specialized preparation and skills. At the present time it is this resource that is lacking." In the hearings, he and others sounded the call for professional preparation in working with older adults in programs of health, fitness and leisure services.

Since that time much has been accomplished. Many of the experts already in our profession are updating their present knowledge and applying their specialties to gerontology, and professional preparation is underway at a number of colleges and universities across the nation. *Guidelines For Exercise Programs For Older Adults*, have been developed by The American Alliance for Health, Physical Education, Recreation and Dance.[71] A sample medical report form is also available.

Model exercise programs for the older adult can be low impact for the development of strength, flexibility, agility, sociability, and self satisfaction, or high intensity programs to include cardiopulmonary change. Older participants in high intensity programs should learn heart monitoring and understand Prescriptive Exercise as described elsewhere in this book. Programs of exercise for older adults can be designed to fit the needs of the least able, sitting in chairs; the more able, moving around a strong base of support; and the most able, who can move freely through space.

Ideally, preparation for a fit old age should begin in youth in order that maximum benefits accrue. When such activity has not occurred we now know that the concept of trainability, even in old age, is valid. Exercise is not necessarily to prolong life but to increase the years of feeling good.

Future Projections:

The world is changing so fast that each generation is different than those who came before. In the past 50 years we have experienced the atomic age, the space age, and the computer age. Life expectancy has increased and the very old are living longer. More than 80 new nations have appeared worldwide and the global population has more than doubled. It is estimated that 75 percent of all information ever known in the history of the world has been discovered in the past 25 years. "The aged are among the true pioneers of our times and pioneer life is notoriously brutal."[72] While modern society makes longevity possible, there are few models or maps to guide us toward quality life in the later years. The old have been shaping the world for the young but as America grows older, much that we have in place will no longer fulfill the needs or expectations of a changing older population.

The era of the United States as a youth-oriented culture is coming to an end. With each passing day the average older American grows healthier, better educated, more politically wise, more accustomed to lifestyle changes, more mobile, more youthful in appearance, more comfortable with technology, and more outspoken. Tomorrow's elderly will have traveled to more places, will have read more books and magazines, will have met more people, will have lived through more world changes, will have experienced more sexual and lifestyle experimentation, will have lived longer, and will be a part of a more powerful "elder culture" than any previous cohort.[73]

The New York Times reports the first comprehensive statistical portrait of Americans 85 and older as emerging from new research.[74] This group is the old old, the oldest old, and the extreme aged, which numbers about 2.6 million and is increasing. As a group these 85 and older are less frail, less likely to be institutionalized, and more independent than previously believed. They are apprehensive of their impact on the economy, the health care system, and the family of the future. They have new appreciation for their powers of survival and are being studied to provide clues to aging that may benefit younger generations.

The over 85s have unique characteristics, yet there is also diversity among the extremely old. Twenty-three percent are in nursing homes or mental hospitals, but the great majority live at home. About 11 percent live with their children, but most who live alone are in daily contact with their children. They are householders or spouses who value living independently as long as they can. Nearly 70 percent were widowed by age 85 and 14 percent had at least one year of college. Many are poor as they may have outlived their savings and most of their income is from Social Security. They may be cash poor with equity in a home. Some states have "reversed mortgage programs" which allow seniors to draw an income from home equity.

With this age group care is expensive as it involves a complex management process rather than a cure. Cancer is less important at extreme old ages. The same causes of death are operational. Both the potential, as well as the burden of growing older deserve recognition as we should not gloss over the part of aging which involves loss and inevitable decline in function. Butler says: "Although increasing longevity is a blessing, something we shouldn't be despairing about, we must focus on the cost of caring for the very old in the future when the baby boom reaches Golden Pond."[75]

Along with all the changes in the aging of America is the need for our people to grow older with the highest level of health, vitality, and independence possible. In the past, most of our funding has been focused on health care delivery for those who are ill. Education for wellness, health promotion, and disease prevention for an entire American population would appear to assist in cutting costs for the future.

Binstock and Pepper see a tremendous demand for public and private insurance by older children who look forward to caring for their parents.[75] Binstock believes that the rapidly aging American population may demand a mandatory National Health Insurance Program. "The real problem is to avoid intergenerational conflict in the transitional period, between now and the time when the younger generation realizes what is happening to them."

Notwithstanding the above health care delivery problem, it is clear that older people will have higher expectations for their retirement years and will demand better "elder care" services and more sophisticated and educationally sound programming in Senior Centers, Nursing Homes, and the community-at-large. Bingo, busy work for crafts, kitchen orchestras, and comic quartets will not be enough. They will seek and deserve professional caregivers who are not only compassionate but knowledgeable and creative.

Future hiring practices and guidelines for a variety of preventive programs in both mental and physical health will require the services of professionals who are adequately prepared, beyond the para-professional level.[76]

The challenge is one we cannot fail to meet. The aged are sensitive barometers of how well our society handles the basic problems of living. An analysis of the trends and projections with relation to the characteristics of an aging population is essential. New specialties can be developed. Greater understanding and sensitivity will grow among the young while those who are aging can utilize education for the necessary adaptation to new lifestyles, better health, and more joy in living.

References

[1]U.S. Senate Special Committee On Aging in conjunction with the American Association of Retired Persons, the Federal Council On The Aging and the U.S. Administration On Aging, *Aging America: Trends and Projections*, 1987–1988 Edition, Washington, D.C. U.S. Department of Health and Human Services. 186 pp.

[2]Pifer and Bronte (1986). *Our Aging Society: Paradox and Promises*. NY: W.W. Norton.

[3]United Nations, Department of International, Economic and Social Affairs, *Selected Demographic Indicators*, 1950 to 2000, Demographic Estimates, 1980.

[4]Missine, Leo E. (1982, Nov.–Dec.). "Elders Are Educators," Perspectives On Aging. NCOA, Washington, D.C. pp. 5–7.

[5]Elrick, Harold, M.D. et al. (1978). *Living Longer and Better*. Mountainview, CA: World Publications.

[6]Schwartz and Peterson (1979). *Introduction To Gerontology*. New York, NY: Holt, Rinehart, Winston.

[7]Schwartz, Snyder and Peterson (1984). *Aging and Life, An Introduction To Gerontology*, 2nd. edition. New York, NY: Holt, Rinehart, Winston.

[8]NCOA (1984). *Service Learning In Aging: Implications For Health, Physical Education, Recreation and Dance*. NCOA: Washington, D.C.

[9]Smith, Lee, "Social Security, Will you get yours?" Fortune Magazine, Time Inc. New York, N.Y. July 20, 1987.

[10]AARP, Worker Equity, "Age Discrimination In Employment Act" Pamphlet, AARP, Worker Equity, 1909 K. St. N.W. Washington, D.C.

[11]Segerburg, Osburn (1982). *Living To Be 100: 1200 Who Did And How They Did It*. New York, NY: Scribners, 406 pp.

[12]Saxon, S. and Etten, M.J. (1987). *Physical Change and Aging: A Guide For The Helping Professional*, 2nd. ed. New York, NY: Teresias Press.

[13]Hayflick, Leonard (1977). "The Cellular Basis For Biological Aging," in Finck and Hayflick, eds. *Handbook Of The Biology Of Aging*. New York, NY: Van Nostrand, Rinehard, Co.

[14]Schaie, K.W. and Willis, S.L. (1986). *Adult Development and Aging*, 2nd. ed. Boston, MA: Little, Brown.

[15]U.S. Department of Health, Education and Welfare (1979). *Healthy People: The Surgeon General's Report On Health Promotion and Disease Prevention*. Washington, D.C. Public Health Service, #79-55071.

[16]Op. Cit. U.S. Senate, Special Committee On Aging.

[17]Fillenbaum, Gerda (1984), *The Well-being Of The Elderly, Approaches To Multi-dimensional Assessment*. World Health Association, Geneva, Switzerland.

[18]Piscopo, John (1985). *Fitness and Aging*. New York, NY: John Wiley and Sons, pp. 153-154.

[19]Fallcreek and Mettler (1984). *A Healthy Old Age, A Sourcebook For Health Promotion With Older Adults*, Washington, D.C.: U.S. Dept. of Health and Human Services, 33 pp.

[20]Op. Cit. U.S. Senate, Special Committee On Aging.

[21]Kart, Metress and Metress (1988). *Aging, Health and Society*. 2nd. Ed. Boston, MA: Jones and Bartlett.

[22]Weeks, John R. (1984). *Aging Concepts and Special Issues*. Belmont, CA: Wadsworth, p. 302.

[23]White House Conference On Aging (1981). *A National Policy On Aging*, Washington, D.C.: G.P.O., 3 vol.

[24]Gray Panthers (1984). *Two Portraits Of Old Age In America*, Brochure, Gray Panthers Project Fund, PA. Philadelphia, 3700 Chestnut St. 19104, 1984.

[25]Mathews and Berman (1983). *Sourcebook For Older Americans*. Berkeley, CA: Nola Press.

[26]Op. Cit. Mathews and Berman

[27]NCOA (1981). Harris Poll. *Aging In The Eighties, America In Transition*. Washington, D.C.: NCOA.

[28]Op. Cit. Mathews and Berman

[29]AARP, *A Profile Of Older Americans*, 1987, AARP and AoA. Washington, D.C.: Program Resource Department, AARP, 1909 K. Street, N.W. Washington, D.C. 20049.

[30]Op. Cit. AARP, *Profile Of Older Americans*.

[31]Op. Cit. *White House Conference On Aging*, 1981.

[32]Botwinick, J. (1977). "Intellectual Abilities," in Birren, J. and Schaie, K. eds. *Handbook of Psychology Of Aging*. New York, NY: Van Nostrand, Rinehold.

[33]Cummings and Henry (1961). *Growing Old: The Process of Disengagement*. New York, NY: Basic Books.

[34]McClusky, Howard (1974). "Education For Aging: The Scope Of The Field and Prospects For The Future." In Grabowski and Mason, eds. *Learning For Aging*, Washington, D.C.: Adult Education Association, pp. 324–355.

[35]Cowgill, D. (1974). "Aging and Modernization: A Revision of The Theory." Gubrium, J. Ed. *Late Life: Communities and Environmental Policy*. Springfield, IL: Thomas.

Cowgill and Holmes (1972). *Aging and Modernization*. New York, NY: Appleton, Century, Crofts.

[36]Op. Cit. U.S. Senate, Special Committee On Aging.

[37]Op. Cit. AARP, Worker Equity.

[38]Fecher, Vincent J. (1982). *Religion and Aging*, An Annotated Bibliography. San Antonio, TX: Trinity University Press.

[39]Chiaventone and Armstrong, Eds. (1985). *Affirmative Aging: A Resource For Ministry*. Minneapolis, MN: Episcopal Society For Ministry On Aging.

[40]Barkas, J.L. *Protecting Yourself Against Crime*. Booklet #504. New York, NY: Public Affairs Committee, Inc.

[41]Estes, C.L. and Edmonds, B.C. (1981). "Symbolic Interaction and Social Policy Analysis." *Symbolic Interaction* 4, no. 1.

Estes, C.L. (1979). *The Aging Enterprise*. San Francisco, CA: Jossey-Bass.

[42]Op. Cit. U.S. Senate, Special Committee On Aging.

[43]National Center For Health Statistics, "Current Estimates For The National Health Interview Survey, U.S. 1986," Vital and Health Statistics Series 10, No. 164, Oct. 1987.

[44]Op. Cit. U.S. Senate, Special Committee On Aging.

[45]Op. Cit. U.S. Senate, Special Committee On Aging.

[46]Op. Cit. U.S. Senate, Special Committee On Aging.

[47]Op. Cit. Kart, Metress, Metress, p. 49–50.

[48]Simonson, William (1984). *Medications and The Elderly*. Rockville, MD: Aspen.

[49]Buys and Saltman. *The Unseen Alcoholics-The Elderly*. Booklet #602. New York, NY: Public Affairs Committee, Inc.

[50]Fries and Crapo (1981). *Vitality and Aging*. Boston, MA: W.H. Freeman.

Schneider and Brady (1983, Oct. 6). "Aging and The Nature Of Death." *New England Journal Of Medicine,* Vol. 309, H-14.

[51]The Prudential Insurance Co. (1988, Summer). *AARP Health Insurance News,* Vol. 5 No. 3.

[52]Op. Cit., Fries and Crapo, Schneider and Brady.

[53]Callahan, Daniel. (1987). *Setting Limits: Medical Goals In An Aging Society*. New York, NY: Simon and Shuster.

[54]Havighurst, Robert J. (1976). Aging In America: Implications For Education. Washington, D.C.: NCOA.

[55]Palamore, Erdman (1981). *Social Patterns In Normal Aging: Findings From Duke University Longitudinal Studies*. Durham, NC: Duke University Press.

[56]National Association For Human Development (1976). *Basic Exercises For People Over Fifty*. Washington, D.C.

[57]Ostrow, A.C. (1984). *Physical Activity And The Older Adult*. Princeton, NJ: Princeton Book Co.

[58]deVries, H.A. "Physiological Effects Of An Exercise Training Regimen On Men Aged 52 to 88," *Journal Of Gerontology,* 25: 325–336.

[59]Buccola and Stone, "Effects of Jogging and Cycling Programs On Physiological and Personality Variables In Aged Men," *The Research Quarterly,* 46: pp 134–139.

[60]Moritani, T. (1981). "Training Adaptations In The Muscles Of Older Men." In Smith and Serfass, eds. *Exercise And Aging*. Hillside, NJ: Enslow.

Sidney, K.H. (1981). "Cardiovascular Benefits of Physical Activity In The Exercising Aged." in Smith and Serfass, eds. *Exercise And Aging.* Hillside, NJ: Enslow.

Shepard, R.J. (1978). *Physical Activity And Aging.* Chicago, IL: Yearbook Publishers.

[61]Serfass, R.C. (1980). "Physical Exercise And The Elderly." in G.A. Still, ed., *Encyclopedia Of Physical Education, Fitness and Sports.* Salt Lake City, UT: Brighton.

[62]Adrian, M.J. (1981). "Flexibility With The Aging Adult." in Smith and Serfass eds., *Exercise and Aging.* Hillside, NJ: Enslow.

Munns, K. (1981). "Effects Of Exercise On The Range Of Joint Motion In Elderly Subjects." Smith and Serfass, Eds. *Exercise and Aging.* Hillside, NJ: Enslow.

[63]Spirduso, W.W. "Physical Fitness, Aging and Psychomotor Speed," *Journal Of Gerontology,* 35: pp 850–865.

[64]Smith E. and Redden W. (1976). "Physical Activity A Modality For Bone Accretion in The Aged." *American Journal Of Roentgenology, 126, 1297.*

Smith E. and Smith P. (1981). "Physical Activity And Calcium Modalities For Bone Mineral Increases In Aged Women." *Medicine and Science In Sports and Exercises,* 13, pp. 80–84.

[65]Op. Cit., Ostrow.

[66]Blumenthal, J., Schoken, D., Needels, T., and Hindle, P. (1982). "Psychological and Physiological Effects Of Physical Conditioning In The Elderly." *Journal Of Psychosomatic Research,* 26: pp. 505–510.

[67]Op. Cit. Buccola and Stone.

[68]Op. Cit. deVries, H.A.

[69]Conrad, C.C. (1977, April). The President's Council On Physical Fitness and Sports. *Physical Fitness Research Digest,* Series 7, No. 2.

[70]deVries, H. "Testimony Before Senate Sub-Committee On Aging, March 3, 1976, p. 718, 55–648, 075–46.

[71]The Council On Aging And Adult Development, ARAPCS, AAHPERD, 1900 Association Drive, Reston, VA., 22091.

[72]Silverman, P. ed. (1987). *The Elderly As Modern Pioneers.* Bloomington, IN: Indiana University Press.

[73]Dychtwald, Ken. (1985). *Wellness And Health Promotion For The Elderly.* Rockville, MD: Aspen.

[74]Collins, Glenn, "First Portrait Of The Very Old: Not So Frail," New York, N.Y., The New York Times, Thurs. Jan. 3rd. 1985, p. A1 and C8.

[75]Op. Cit. The New York Times.

Butler, Robert N.M.D. Brookdale Professor Of Geriatrics, Mount Sinai School Of Medicine, New York, N.Y.

Binstock, Robert H., Henry R. Luce Professor Of Aging, Case Western Reserve University, Ohio, Cleveland.

Pepper, Claude, House Of Representatives, U.S. Congress, [Dem.] Florida, Former Chairman Of House Sub-committee on Health and Long-term Care.

[76]Association Gerontology In Higher Education and University Of Southern California, *Employment In The Field Of Aging, The Supply and Demand In Four Professions,* AoA Grant, Peterson, D., Bergstone, D., and Douglass, E., July 1988.

2 HEALTH ASPECTS OF AGING

Edited by Gene Ezell, University of Tennessee

Contributing authors:
  David J. Anspaugh, Memphis State University
  Gene Ezell, University of Tennesse
  Barbara Rienzo, University of Florida
  Jill Varnes, University of Florida
  Hollie Walker, Jr., Memphis State University

Introduction

There is a great need for a number of preventive and educational services among the elderly in this country. For example, there is a need for health education in such diverse settings as the home, hospital, and community agencies. Programs that provide information concerning hypertension, diabetes, alcoholism, arthritis, and drug abuse are needed, as are educational programs on consumer information and medical programs and services. Educational planners must provide understanding in the above-mentioned areas so the quality of life can be enhanced for the growing numbers of elderly within the United States. As we age, education can help to change lifestyle habits and promote behaviors which can help prevent illness, negative health behaviors, and provide much-needed information on health care resources.

In this chapter, the reader is provided, from a health perspective, a review of theories of aging, changes in selected physiological systems, changes in psychological and sociological influences, and a section on health care delivery systems for the aged.

Theories of Aging

The process of aging is not completely understood. Various theories may explain what happens to our bodies as we age. The genetic theory implies that the aging process is programmed from birth. In other words, everything that occurs to the cell happens as a consequence of genetics. According to this theory, there is a "biological clock" which keeps track of elapsed time and initiates the aging sequence when certain limits are reached. The genetic program of the life span operates differently among individuals and within the various species. Variations in the environment may affect one's life span, but these factors do not outweigh the genetic factors in determining how long one will live. Obviously, the genetic makeup one inherits from his/her parents are major factors in the determination of how one ages.

The mutation theory builds on the genetic theory by adding the possibility of mutations in the genes due to environmental factors, such as irradiation, which cause improper messages to be communicated, leading to the dysfunction of cells that make up vital organs. Chemicals, such as cancer-causing substances, can also cause such mutations.

The "wear and tear" theory refers to use and abuse of all biologic structures, including molecules and cells. According to this theory, every molecule in our body has a pre-determined life and its continued use will wear it down. The wear and tear on physical molecules therefore will eventually lead to irreparable damage in the body. This theory is closely related to Hans Selye's Stress theory which states the continued stress upon any part of the body, such as the heart, will eventually lead to the exhaustion and gradual destruction of that part of the body.

The error catastrophe theory of aging states that every biological function can lead to certain statistical errors. Metabolic reactions are not always perfect, and defective cells may be produced within the body as a result of these abnormalities. An error can have a "snow-ball" effect where one wrong message triggers another. The result of accumulating a large number of errors may result in a major insult, or death.

The autoimmune theory is based on the observation that immunity against oneself can develop. Immunity is a mechanism whereby the recognition of self and foreign objects is maintained. In autoimmune cases, such a recognition system becomes confused. For example, the products of an error in translation of genes may result in the production of cancer cells. Usually, this sort of a modification of cell surface is recognized and consequently, the transformed cell is killed so that it is no longer a threat to the host. A confused lymphocyte, however, can and does produce antibodies against self and thereby destroys normal cells of the body. A continued reduction in the functioning of lymphocytes over time can produce a variety of autoimmune diseases. For this reason, autoimmune diseases have an increased incidence among the elderly.

It is clear that any one theory cannot account for the complex process of human aging. Interactions of biologic changes, plus the emotional makeup and social environment in which we live, are all critical factors which cannot be separated, and all of these factors must be taken into account when explaining the aging process.

Aging is a natural process which begins with conception, although we usually describe the years prior to 30 (years of age) as growth rather than aging. Hopefully as the body ages one will continue to grow. This continuous growth or aging process is a shared experience enjoyed by those who have demonstrated the ability to survive. Individuals are unique in the manner in which they age as well as how they accept the aging process. However, there are some general characteristics of aging which can be observed as people grow older.

There is a general, overall decline in physical capacity as one ages. The rate of this decline is affected by a variety of lifestyle factors as well as inherited abilities. As one ages there is a decreased functional ability in the major body systems which may contribute to a delay or masking of the usual signs and symptoms of disease; this decline also influences the ability of the individual to adapt to environmental or other changes. Most older people report feeling capable of doing everything they have always done, it merely takes longer.

Changes in Sensory Functions:

Aging individuals demonstrate a decline in all of the five senses which means it is necessary to increase the level of stimulation in order for the sense organ to respond. The need for increased stimulation has very real implications for health and safety because of the extent to which people rely on the senses to serve as an early warning system to avoid dangerous situations.

Skin

The skin which contains touch sensors also serves as one of the body's first lines of defense against disease. Any break in this barrier allows an infecting organism to enter and infection will result. The skin becomes more fragile with age and is more easily cut, reacts more slowly to irritants, and may be easily damaged by heat. Care should be taken to ensure that hot water is not too hot (lukewarm is sufficient), and gloves should be worn when using cleaning solutions to prevent chemical burns or irritation. Dry skin may also affect aging skin and may be aggravated by exposure to soaps, cleaning products, or dry air in heated rooms. This dryness results in itching skin (winter itch) which when scratched may contribute to infection or long term skin irritation. Frequent use of lotions (lard or shortening are great and less expensive) will help prevent severe itching and dryness.

Vision

Changes in visual acuity (eyesight) frequently occur with aging; the most noticeable change is in the ability to adapt to darkness, caused by the inability of light to penetrate the lens and cornea. Older people need brighter lights for most activities and regular light bulbs are better than fluorescent lights. Because of the decline in night vision, older drivers should be encouraged to limit their night driving as much as possible.

Some common complaints associated with the eyes include floaters which are tiny specks that "float" across the field of vision; dry eyes which may require the use of artificial tears, or excessive tears which may result from an increased sensitivity to light, wind, or dust. Wearing sunglasses usually solves the problem.

Eye diseases which are common to the elderly include cataracts and glaucoma. Cataracts develop gradually, usually without pain or other noticeable discomfort. A cloudy or opaque area forms on the lens inside the eye and may or may not impair vision. Glaucoma results when there is too much fluid pressure within the eye. This pressure causes internal eye damage and may gradually destroy vision. This condition develops without warning, although it may be more common in those who also have hypertension. Periodic glaucoma tests are recommended for anyone over the age of 35 years.

Hearing

Hearing loss affects 30 percent of adults ages 65 through 74 years, and 50 percent of those ages 75 through 80 years, but is more common in men than in women. Individuals of average or above intelligence and those who over the years have paid close attention to others' speech patterns seem to exhibit the least hearing loss as they age. Hearing difficulties range from the inability to understand certain words or sounds, to total deafness, and affect over 10 million people in the U.S. Individuals with a hearing impairment are at a tremendous disadvantage when trying to communicate with others. Individuals with hearing impairments often will limit social activities and desirable leisure pursuits to avoid the frustration and embarrassment of not being able to understand what is being said. The feelings of frustration over a declining ability to communicate may lead to withdrawal and depression.

Some common types of hearing loss associated with aging include presbycusis, conduction deafness, and central deafness. Presbycusis results from changes in the delicate inner ear that lead to difficulties in understanding the spoken word and an intolerance for loud noises, but the individual is not totally deaf. This condition is usually attributed to aging but is viewed by some researchers as a disease. It is not curable or correctable.

Conduction deafness is another type of hearing loss frequently experienced by the elderly. This condition causes sounds and others' voices to seem muffled, although ones own voice may sound louder than normal. In conduction deafness the sound waves do not travel properly through the ear. In some instances this type of hearing loss can be corrected by merely flushing out the ear or using a medication. Surgery is used as a last resort, but usually restores any hearing loss.

Central deafness is a rare occurrence resulting from damage to the nerve centers in the brain. The sound levels are not affected, but the understanding of language is; this condition cannot be corrected but therapy may be helpful.

Taste

The sensation of taste alters somewhat with age, as does one's sense of smell. As one ages, stronger flavored foods become more acceptable as does the desire for saltier foods due primarily to the decrease in functioning taste buds. Secretion of saliva is reduced; the oral mucosa becomes thinner and is more easily injured if coarse foods are eaten. The desire for sweets frequently declines with age. The alteration in the sense of smell probably has some effect on the enjoyment of foods as these two senses are closely allied. These physiological changes, coupled with alterations in the preparation of foods, frequently lead to complaints about food prepared for older individuals.

Changes in the Digestive Process and the Gastrointestinal Tract

The various enzymes necessary for digestion of food are released in lesser amounts due, it is believed) to a wasting away of the secretion mechanisms. Thus the ability of the body to break down foods for its use is decreased. This decreased ability begins in the mouth where the teeth initiate the breakdown of foodstuffs. Missing or decayed teeth or improperly fitting dentures interfere with the first step of digestion. The jaw shrinks with age which can contribute to ill fitting dentures; but regular dental visits continue to be necessary whether one has dentures or not.

As age increases, esophageal pain may result from inflammation, postural changes (lying down or stooping), or even ingestion of too much food. Hiatal hernias are not uncommon in advanced years. The hiatus is the opening for the esophagus in the diaphragm and if herniated, a portion of the stomach protrudes into the chest cavity. Symptoms include difficulty in swallowing and pain beneath the lower end of the sternum (breastbone). This pain can sometimes be confused with the pain of a heart attack.

The digestive enzymes which act upon the food once it enters the stomach are decreased in amount, but remain adequate for digestion. Little absorption of nutrients occurs in the stomach.

The amount of time needed for the small intestine to absorb nutrients is increased but so is the time needed for the food to move through the alimentary or digestive tract. There is a general loss of muscle tone throughout the tract which indicates a need for special thought when planning and preparing foods. High fiber foods and raw or slightly cooked vegetables provide an opportunity for the digestive system to "exercise." There is a decline in the ability of the individual to absorb calcium and iron, which may necessitate an increase in calcium rich foods such as dairy foods and green leafy vegetables, and iron rich foods, such as organ meats and some fruits.

Older people are five times as likely to report problems with constipation than are younger people. Frequently this is an overemphasized ailment resulting from the individual's preoccupation with having a daily bowel movement. Overuse of convenience foods which are low in fiber, and limiting intake of fluids, due sometimes to incontinence, may contribute to infrequent bowel movements. Frequent use of laxatives can become habit forming and result in the loss of normal bowel functioning. In general, attention to regular exercise (walking) and fiber in the diets will help the individual to maintain regularity.

Successful control of elimination is essential to a healthful and socially active life. The inability of the elderly person to predict when urination (voiding) will occur is a major cause of embarrassment and causes a fear of socialization. Incontinence (inability to contain urine) is viewed as undesirable in an adult in our society and can lead to feelings of hopelessness and despondency. Any interruption of cerebral control such as a stroke, brain damage, or loss of muscular control may result in urinary incontinence. This frequently results in the individual decreasing fluid intake in an attempt to control the problem. Retraining and certain drugs are sometimes used to control the problem of incontinence, but these treatments are not always effective. Use of adult forms of diapers are an acceptable solution, but care must be taken to protect the skin from breaking down due to the constant exposure to urine.

Neurologic Changes

Aging brings about changes in the nervous system both in structure and function; generally there is a decrease in the ability to receive and transmit neural impulses which has an effect upon sensory perception. Coordination of eyes and limbs is diminished and may increase the possibility of accidents. In addition there is a decreased vibratory sense below the knee which makes detection of uneven surfaces more difficult.

Mental functioning does change with aging, but most changes are not observed before the age of 70 years and this is not true in all cases. Some older individuals maintain the same mental functioning abilities as they had as young adults. Studies indicate maintaining mental activity helps to keep the mind functioning well. Problem solving may require longer to process all the information but the ability is not diminished with normal aging. Good mental functions should last until about the age of 80 years, unless affected by disease.

Emotional problems, acute illness, adverse drug reactions, poor nutrition, or injuries may result in temporary mental impairments. If not treated these "minor" medical emergencies can result in permanent damage to the sensitive cells of the brain.

The two most common forms of permanent mental impairment in old age are multi infarct dementia and Alzheimer's disease. Multi infarct dementia is the result of a series of minor strokes which kills brain tissue. About 20 percent of the irreversible cases of mental impairment are the result of this condition. In Alzheimer's, changes in the nerve cells of the outer layer of the brain result in the large scale death of brain cells. Individuals suspected of having a permanent loss of mental function should have a complete medical evaluation with all the necessary physiological, neurological, and psychiatric tests.

Individuals with irreversible disorders should be encouraged to maintain their previous lifestyles as much as possible. Use of notes and written instructions can be helpful and may be effective in maintaining brain function for a longer period of time. Families of individuals with Alzheimer's and similar disorders need considerable support and understanding.

Practicing good lifestyle habits, including developing leisure skills, may be the best way to avoid those disorders which can mimic irreversible brain disorders. Senility is not a part of the "normal" aging process.

Cardiovascular Changes

As age increases, the heart muscle decreases in size and strength. It does not fill as readily with blood nor does it squeeze the blood out with as much force. By the age of 65 years, cardiac output (blood pumped out) has decreased by 30 to 40 percent. The heart rate remains fairly stable but if one performs strenuous activity the heart rate does not speed up as fast as it did when the individual was younger. Other cardiovascular changes which are observed are an increase in the likelihood of the blood vessel to rupture or blood clots to form; increased possibility of varicose veins; and a decrease in blood formation.

The elderly person with a less functional heart and circulatory system does not adjust to extreme temperatures of hot and cold. This includes internal as well as external temperature changes; an above normal body temperature reading is cause for immediate concern in the elderly.

Respiratory System

Environmental conditions may have the greatest impact on the respiratory system, with cigarette smoking being the most significant. It is the major cause of lung disease and premature aging of the system. Specific identifiable structural changes can be seen as a result of smoking. If one stops smoking the lungs will return to the healthy state of a nonsmoker providing no permanent damage has occurred. Not smoking and regular exercise will assist this system to stay healthy.

If the respiratory system becomes less functional than normal there is an increased risk of respiratory infections and they are more dangerous than in a normal lung. Prolonged bed rest may result in complications such as bronchitis and pneumonia.

Musculoskeletal System

Muscles

The muscles lose strength and size with age; thus the overall muscle mass is reduced. The response to nerve stimulation is slower; and the muscle reflex becomes less efficient. Allowing more time to complete a task or not imposing a time limitation may be desirable.

Osteoarthritis

The joints are less flexible and a wearing out of the joints, or osteoarthritis, may occur. Osteoarthritis allows bone to rub on bone and can cause swelling around the joints with considerable discomfort. Heat and moderate exercise can be used as a self-care measure to ease the discomfort of arthritis. Heat may relieve pain and stiffness and restore some of the mobility. Warm baths or heating pads (set on low, wrapped in a towel) or hot wet cloths are best. Spandex type garments, such as gloves, knee braces or ankle braces, may be worn at night to decrease stiffness. Use of assistive devices for mobility and household uses is recommended.

Between arthritic flare-ups, mild forms of range of motion exercises should be done once per day. Isometric muscle strengthening exercises will result in less strain on arthritic joints but are contraindicated if cardiovascular problems are present. A minimal increase in pain may be noticed when first beginning an exercise program, but it should last no longer than two hours. Aspirin or an aspirin substitute is the usual pain reliever.

Osteoporosis

After the age of 50 in women and 70 in men the amount of calcium deposited in the bones is less. About 25 percent of postmenopausal women are affected by bone loss (osteoporosis). This is a disease which develops over time taking 10 to 20 years to become obvious. There is some question as to whether or not this bone loss can be replaced. Bones of the legs, arms, and spine are usually affected and frequently led to a condition termed "dowager's hump." Hip fractures are also quite common in osteoporotic women.

Although everyone will experience a degree of bone loss if they live long enough, there are factors which place some people more at risk than others. Some of these risk factors can be controlled.

Those which cannot be controlled include the age at which the woman experiences menopause. The earlier the onset of menopause, the greater the risk of bone loss. Genetic factors influence the amount of bone one has at maturity and the speed at which bone is lost with age. Black women seem to be at lesser risk, although the reasons why are still unclear. Some possible reasons include larger bones in the black female at maturity. Black women lose bone at a slower rate, probably due to hormonal differences between white women and black women. Small women are at greater risk because bone loss will occur at the same rate as for larger women and the small woman has less to lose at the outset. The development of osteoporosis is one area where having some excess body weight can be beneficial. This is somewhat related to the excess weight placing more stress on the bones, thus the bone adapts to the greater stress by producing more bone. Prior to menopause, estrogen, progesterone, and small amounts of androgens are produced by the ovaries. After menopause, very small amounts of estrogen and progesterone are produced, but the ovaries and the adrenal glands continue to produce the same amount of androgens. The androgens can be chemically converted to estrogen in fat tissue. The greater the amount of fat, the more estrogen produced. The downside is that this places women with more body fat at greater risk for cancer of the endometrium.

The use of oral contraceptives over a long period of time; the number of children (more can be better); daily nutrition practices; calcium rich foods; regular exercise; being a nonsmoker; moderate use of alcohol; and fluoridated water can all prove beneficial in decreasing the risk of osteoporosis. (See Chapter 1.)

The female hormone estrogen plays a significant role in calcium storage, and estrogen therapy should be used if the ovaries have been removed or the woman has experienced menopause. Women who have been physically active place stress on the bones and joints which encourage calcium production.

Selected Drug and Dietary Concerns

Diet

The physiological changes which occur with aging require some dietary modifications for good health. The elderly frequently eat less food due to the fact that the food does not taste as good and dental difficulties may make eating unpleasant. Because of eating less food, fewer vitamins and minerals and less protein are taken in. High quality proteins and calcium in the form of milk, eggs, and meats should be eaten (these are also good sources of B-12 and iron). If the individual is eating less than 1200 calories per day in a well balanced diet, a multiple vitamin should be taken. Care should be taken to be sure the individual understands his/her dietary needs and why changes may be necessary.

Drugs

Age is also a factor in the body's response to different drugs which is compounded by the fact that many elderly take a variety of different drugs. Resistance to the expected effect, sensitivity to specific drugs, and the ability of the body to absorb or circulate medications are altered. The liver and kidneys are less efficient, making it more difficult to metabolize and excrete drugs. There is potential for drug build up which complicates the use of drug therapy. These basic problems, coupled with the tendency to overmedicate, may result in severe side effects. The side effects include nausea, vomiting, changes in pulse rate and rhythm, dizziness, and visual disturbances. Dramatic mood swings, increased irritability, and insomnia may also be the result of drug reactions or interactions.

Use of nontoxic drugs which are not usually addicting and are the least expensive available are the best for the elderly. Individuals should be carefully instructed in the correct way to take any prescribed medicines; all medications should be clearly labeled as to what it is, its purpose, and when to take it. These labels should be large enough to be easily read. Also, associating the taking of the drugs with a daily event will help assure proper dosage and time spacing.

Sensory

Changes in sensory awareness (vision, hearing) and impaired coordination and balance can contribute to an increased number of accidents in older adults. Some diseases, medications, and other drug use may increase impaired coordination and balance. Individuals should be advised to change body positions more slowly to prevent dizziness or faintness, and should be fully informed as to the possible effects of various drugs upon their ability to function. Injuries to older adults can at best result in a slow recovery and at worst permanent impairment or death.

Implications of Aging for Human Sexuality

Sexuality is the sum of physical, mental, and emotional factors surrounding a physiological need. It encompasses our relationship with ourselves as well as with others. It is influenced by genetic, in-utero developmental, and sociocultural-learning factors. This chapter will discuss the impact of aging on one's sexuality in the present American culture.

Negative attitudes seem to prevail in this society about sexuality and the aging population.

Generally, older people are seen as asexual. This phenomenon is attributed to the general discomfort felt by Americans both toward sexuality and toward the process of aging. As a result, various myths perpetuate among persons of all ages regarding sexuality and elders. These are summarized as follows: 1) Elderly people do not have sexual desires; 2) Elderly people are not able to make love, even if they wanted to; 3) Elderly people are too fragile and might hurt themselves if they attempt to engage in sexual relations; 4) Elderly people are physically unattractive and therefore sexually undesirable; and 5) The whole notion of older people engaging in sex is shameful and perverse. (Kay and Neeley, 1982.) All the above beliefs are predicated upon notions that are not based on fact and tend to hurt the elderly by negating their feelings, causing guilt, creating barriers to a fulfilling relationship, and limiting their ability to obtain the assistance they need to adjust to the changes that inevitably take place as the body ages. As will be shown, there is no "natural" age limitation to expression of sexuality in all its forms. Greater understanding among the elderly themselves and those who work and interact with them will help to dispel myths and create an atmosphere that allows individuals to make more personal, independent decisions which fit their particular needs and values regarding sexual expression.

In order to appreciate the changes that may impact sexuality with aging, the physiological changes that occur during the climacteric must be understood. The "climacteric" is generally thought of as the "change of life"—a time period in which many changes, physical, mental, and social, are happening in the lives of most persons. It is marked physically by the menopause in women and a more subtle, but definite, reduction in the hormonal production of the reproductive organs in men. The age range of the climacteric is 35 to 65 years of age. Most of the discussion in this chapter is limited to those changes which are physiologically based that impact sexuality.

Physiological Changes in the Female

About the age of 50, but any time between the ages of 40 through 55, the female will experience the "menopause," the cessation of ovarian functioning and, therefore, the end of her fertility. Although many symptoms are associated with the menopause, hot flushes (brief periods of warmth involving blood capillary expansion in the face, neck, and chest) and night sweats have been found to be the only true symptoms. These are thought to be related to irregularity of hormonal production and are more severe in women when the rate of ovarian involution is more rapid. (Pearson, 1982.) Since the ovaries' decreasing hormonal production is gradual, the menopause involves about a year of varying menstrual irregularity, alternate scanty and heavy bleeding. Other conditions which have been identified by women and researchers as associated with the menopause and which may interfere with sexual expression, but which have not been shown to be caused by the cessation of ovarian function include: aches in the back of neck and head, breast pains, constipation, diarrhea, skin crawls, rheumatic pains, numbness and tingling in extremities, weight gain, dizzy spells, headaches, blind spots before the eyes, tired feelings, pounding of the heart, pressure or tightness in the body, feelings of suffocation, feeling blue or depressed, feeling excitable, inability to concentrate, trouble sleeping, crying spells, feelings of panic, worry about body, worry about nervous breakdown, irritability and nervousness, forgetfulness, and loss of interest in most things. (Kaufert and Syrotuik, 1981.) These latter "symptoms" are thought to be related to life changes happening at the same time as the menopause, such as children leaving home or a divorce. Poor marital adjustment is one factor that has been found to be associated with more frequent and more severe menopausal symptoms. (Uphold and Susman, 1981.) Kaufert and Syrotuik (1981) found that women in the menopause are no more or less likely to be depressed or have negative self-perception than women in other stages in life. However, women and their physicians tend to share the mistaken view that depression is concomitant of the menopause. Women are cautioned against accepting medication for the menopause before having other possible causes of such symptoms checked.

Changes in ovarian production of estrogen do affect several reproductive organ tissue characteristics, with a wide range of individual differences in the severity of such changes. The vagina undergoes atrophy; it does not expand as much in length nor width upon sexual stimulation as it had in younger years. There is a reduction in the amount and length of time involved in production of lubrication with stimulation. Severity of either of these changes can result in painful intercourse (termed "dyspareunia") or involuntary constriction of the outer third of the vagina (termed "vaginismus"). Women may need to use a water soluble lubricant, estrogen cream, or estrogen therapy in order to correct this problem.

Another effect of decreased estrogen levels on the vagina is less acidic secretions, which increases the chance of developing vaginal infections. Other problems related to decreased elasticity and thinner vaginal walls include bladder and urethral irritation during intercourse and the development of cystitis (bladder infection) or urinary incontinence (losing control of urination, for instance when sneezing or laughing). (Hogan, 1980 and Yoselle, 1981.) One of the treatment regimens for these problems are the Kegal exercises. These involve the contraction and release of the muscles around the vaginal opening (the pubocongeal muscles). This exercise has been found not only to maintain vaginal shape and size, increase lubrication, and decrease incontinence, but also to increase feelings of sexual pleasure for both the woman and her partner. (Hartman and Fithian, 1974.)

It has been found that those women who maintain regular (approximately once a week or more) level of sexual activity (specifically, intercourse) retain vaginal muscle tone and lubrication capacity and have less dysfunction. (Masters and Johnson, 1982) Estrogen replacement therapy is also effective in curing more severe dysfunctions.

Other changes in the reproductive system tissue include thinning of the labia majora and minora, the folds of tissue which become engorged with blood and contain many sensitive nerve endings for sexual stimulation. As a result, the clitoris, whose only function is to receive and transmit sexual stimulation, may become more exposed. For some women direct stimulation of this organ, pleasurable in the past, may become painful. Communication with a partner in this case is of the utmost importance to avoid misunderstanding and resulting sexual problems for the couple.

The uterus can also undergo some change in response to this aging process. During orgasm, uterine contractions may become spasmotic instead of rhythmic, and feel painful. This condition is readily treatable with estrogen therapy. The contractions during orgasm may not be as numerous nor as intense as in younger years. However, most women who continue sexual relations have reported that orgasm is no less satisfying than it was previous to the menopause.

Physiological Changes in the Male

As men age, from about 55 or 60 onward, levels of testosterone production gradually decrease. Most men, as they move through their 50s, will probably have noticeable changes surface in sexual response patterns and in the intensity of that response. If men and their partners do not understand that these are "normal" results of the aging process, dysfunction and premature cessation of sexual activity may occur.

The engorgement of blood which causes an erection may take longer to occur, and full penile erection may necessitate more direct stimulation than in younger years. An erection may be more difficult to reattain after loss during preorgasmic stages, yet older men are able to maintain an erection for a longer period of time before orgasm than in their younger years. The latter change, for many couples, is a positive one—since the female partner generally takes longer to orgasm and the more lengthy "foreplay" is enjoyed. Another related change is the need to ejaculate and orgasm. For older men, ejaculation may occur every second or third coital experience, resulting in more numerous erections. Ejaculation may also be less forceful and reduced in volume. The feeling of "ejaculatory inevitability," present in younger years, may disappear. Contractions of the penis and rectum accompanying ejaculation decrease. However, as with women, it must be noted that those men who report continued sexual activity through their older years have also reported continued satisfaction with sexual response. It is a sexual myth that the aging process *per se* causes erectile incompetence or sexual dysfunction of any type in the male. (Charatan, 1982 and Driver & Detrick, 1982.)

The Psychology of Aging

The aged have an advantage over other groups in that they have had more experience with coping, problem solving, and stress management. Most older individuals have no delusions regarding their present lifestyle. They have integrity based on the knowledge of where they have been, what they have accomplished, and who they really are. The experiences of life provide the elderly with a unique emotional strength which should not be underestimated.

Sociological Theories of Aging

Psychological and social changes during the aging process are closely related and have a significant impact on each other. It is difficult to explain mental processes, behaviors, and feelings without considering the social rules, positions, and norms associated with aging. Consequently, it is wise to approach aging theories as an aspect of psychosocial theories.

Disengagement Theory

Probably the most controversial theory is the disengagement theory. This theory views aging as a process whereby society and the aging person gradually withdraw or disengage from one another, to the mutual satisfaction and benefit of both. This theory states that the aging individual is freed from societal roles and thus can reflect and be centered upon themselves. "Disengagement" means an orderly method for the transfer of power or authority from the old to the young. For many older individuals, disengagement from the mainstream is not desired, nor should it be expected from all aged persons. Critics of this theory point out that if the health and the financial means are available, there is no reason why the elderly should not remain in the mainstream of society. Mental health experts realize that depression in the aging may be caused by a lack of daily responsibility.

Activity Theory

In direct opposition to the disengagement theory is the activity theory. Advocates of this theory believe that an older person should continue a middle-aged life style, denying the existence of old age as long as possible. This theory suggests ways of maintaining activity in the presence of the losses associated with aging. For example, replacing the work role with other roles when retirement occurs or establishing new friendships when old ones are lost. Unfortunately, many of the aged lack the physical, emotional, social, or economic resources to continue active roles in society.

Developmental Theory

The developmental or continuity theory states that the factors of personality of each person predisposes them toward actions in old age similar to actions followed during earlier phases of their life cycle. For example, an activist at age 20 will likely be an activist at age 70. However, concepts and patterns which develop over a lifetime will influence whether an individual remains engaged and active or becomes disengaged and inactive. This particular theory is unique in that it recognizes that there are multiple adaptations to the complex process of aging.

Mental Health and Aging

There are many myths which prevail concerning mental health and the aged. For example, there is a popular belief that with age there is a decline in mental functioning. There is a loss of neurons with age, but there is little correlation between the number of neurons lost and impaired mental function. Other misconceptions are that the elderly are "childlike," "senile," or "rigid" in their behavior: certainly, aging alone does not necessitate a significant change in personality and, in fact, several studies have demonstrated personality to be stable over a lifetime. Every part of the life cycle presents new emotional challenges to each person, and old age is no exception. One's history of adjustment to these challenges can influence mental health during old age. A person who has successfully coped with problems in the past will more likely maintain mental health during the aging process; however, a series of unsuccessful emotional adjustments may result in severe emotional problems in an elderly person.

Due to a feeling of alienation, some elderly people react by isolating themselves emotionally and physically from others. Others react to such alienation by becoming combative, noisy, or very critical and demanding of those around them. Further, many elderly people experience a loss of self-esteem because society is "telling" them through their attitudes and actions that old people are no longer wanted or needed. The older person's sense of worth and value, therefore, diminishes drastically as they perceive the uncaring or negative attitudes of younger people. A common reaction to alienation and the accompanying stress is depression. (See Chapter 13.)

Other personality changes occur to the elderly due to organic brain disorders and senile dementia. These disorders affect social and psychological function. Some of these disorders are caused by specific degenerative disease such as diabetes, emphysema, arteriosclerosis, or stress. The disorders caused by disease are sometimes irreversible. Other organic brain disorders are brought on by malnutrition or infection and are considered to be reversible. The decline in psychological function due to organic brain disorders is very gradual in some cases, while others appear to have a sudden onset. An important fact to remember about these disorders is the conditions are not inevitable for every aging person, even though other relatives might have experienced one of the disorders. Organic brain disorders typically affect memory and perception. The person displays anxiety, confusion, and time disorientation with previous personality traits possibly exaggerated by the illness. The person may also experience a deterioration in intellectual function, judgement, and memory. Some elderly persons with organic brain disorders experience hallucinations and delusions.

Alzheimer's Disease

The term "Alzheimer's" refers to a presenile dementia in which there can be rapid mental deterioration over three or four years, or slow progression over a number of years. In the early stages, symptoms include forgetfulness, memory loss, impaired judgement, inability to do routine tasks, disorientation and depression. In the second stage, the symptoms progress. Symptoms during this stage include increased disorientation, agitation, restlessness (especially at night), loss of sensory perceptions, muscle twitching, and repetitive action. In the final stage, the person becomes completely dependent on others. The person suffers identity loss, speech problems, and loss of control of body functions.

Several theories as to the cause of the disease have been suggested. The theories being considered include exposure to an inordinate amount of aluminum, chromosomal or genetic defects, a slow acting virus, an immune system malfunction, and physical trauma to the head.

Researchers at Harvard Medical School have identified that in Alzheimer's disease the brain loses it s usual ability to produce brain protein. Researchers feel the reason for this deficiency is that the brain cells have only half as much RNA as normal. When the brain cells are deficient in RNA, it follows that brain protein cannot be produced. This represents the "tip of the iceberg" in solving the problems of Alzheimer's diseases with much more research needed to solve the mystery.

Mental Health and Retirement

Retirement necessitates a major reorganization of life's activities. Research has indicated that the loss of the work role does not inevitably lead to adjustment problems. Many retirees expand their activities into other roles, such as being a volunteer, grandparent, or friend. Significant others in the individual's life which serve as reference givers (family, friends, cliques at work) are significant in the adjustment in retirement. If the individual begins the process for retirement with preparations and support, the transition is not necessarily a painful one. It is imperative that preparation be made by the individuals so that they have something to retire *to*, and not just retire *from* their workplace.

Awareness of Mortality

Regardless of age, death is a fact of life. Although in the first phase of old age the majority of the elderly live with spouses, widowhood increases as aging occurs. This creates further challenges and adjustments.

Some of the severe emotional problems the elderly may be confronted with include the following:

1. *Grief:* Grief can be the result of a loss and can occur at any age. Usually, grief is associated with death, but can also result from such losses as bodily function, appearance, housing, emotional or psychological, or a pet.

2. *Depression:* Depression is a most frequent problem in the elderly. Although depression can be experienced at any age, it is not uncommon for it to be a new problem in old age. Some of the life events which may trigger depression include retirement, independence of children, reduced income, a changing body image, death of family and friends, and the message that one's worth is declining because of age.

   Depression may manifest itself through insomnia, weight loss, apathy, constipation, boredom, hostility, and loss of self esteem. The suicidal rates for the elderly are alarmingly high and any threat of such an act should be taken seriously. Starvation, misuse of medication, intoxication, or overt expression of the desire to die may be indications of suicidal desires.

3. *Other Concerns:* Unhealthy responses to the challenges of aging may result in several emotional disorders. When the stress of a particular situation is perceived as overwhelmingly painful, the elderly person may regress to childhood days when things were more simple. This behavior may be evidenced in an inappropriate dependency upon others to help them with simple tasks, such as eating or bathroom habits, while some others react to stressors by becoming restless. Others become disoriented and confused, losing touch with time, place, and sometimes reality. Paranoid delusions may be observed in some elderly through a drastic change in behavior and/or mood. Hypochondriasis (an unusual obsession with one's physical well-being) is another emotional disorder that is used by older people to displace anxiety.

Health Care Issues

Besides those mentioned previously, there are many ways in which older persons can take care of themselves and their partners in adapting to the changes which are related to their sexuality. Being able to recognize these as natural developments which may change the way in which they have been sexual and being able to communicate differences and alternative preferences with a partner are two of the most vital of self-care techniques. Individuals must also be able to recognize when expert help is necessary, how to seek out that help, and how to ascertain the quality of such professionals.

Birth control is one personal health concern which many couples must face. The birth control pill is no longer prescribed for women close to 40, especially those who smoke. If an IUD has been in place, it can be left, but new IUDs are not recommended for peri-menopausal women. The diaphragm, condom, and spermicides remain safe, acceptable, relatively effective methods. However, some couples find these unsatisfactory for aesthetic or disruptive reasons. One newer method, the contraceptive sponge, seems to be a more acceptable method because it is relatively effective (83–88%) and not as messy or disruptive as other barrier methods. The rhythm method, of course, is more unreliable than in younger years because of the variability of the menstrual cycle as the ovaries gradually cease functioning. As a result, many couples turn to sterilization at this time if they have not done so sooner.

It should be noted that hysterectomy is not a recommended procedure solely for the purpose of birth control, although that reason has been used by some physicians for prescribing it. Hysterectomy, the removal of the uterus and sometimes the fallopian tubes and ovaries, should be performed when these organs are diseased. It is recommended that, if possible, patients seek a second opinion prior to such surgery.

Heart disease affects many older individuals today and has been shown to interfere with sexual relations for as long as a year after recovery. (Green, 1975 and Mahta and Krop, 1979.) Although physically, sexual relations are considered safe when two flights of stairs can be climbed, many couples are afraid to resume because they are fearful of bringing on a second attack. Actually, sexual relations may be beneficial for cardiac health after it is safe to resume again.

Cancer of the prostate is another common problem for older men. If surgical removal of the prostate is necessary, erectile problems often result because nerves to the penis are damaged. If surgery on the prostate is necessary for reasons other than cancer, dysfunction with erection is less common. However, "retrograde ejaculation" (ejaculate enters the bladder instead of coming out the penis) often results.

Medication for high blood pressure interferes with the sexual response cycle. Erectile dysfunction in men, lower sexual drive and arousal, or inhibited ejaculation are some side effects. If such problems develop, it is usually possible to change prescriptions to one which controls blood pressure without these undesirable effects. (Masters and Johnson, 1982.)

The loss of a sexual partner through sickness or death can result in a long period of time for no sexual relations. Individuals can then suffer from what Masters and Johnson have termed "Widow's or Widower's Syndrome" if they desire sexual relations after a period of a year or so has passed without sexual relations. An understanding partner and gradual return to sexual activity through masturbation and other noncoital activity are sometimes effective in their cure. However, some individuals may require professional assistance in resolving such dysfunction. Couples can inquire about reputable sex therapists through their family physician or through the local medical society. The American Association of Sex Counselors, Educators, and Therapists (AASECT) certifies professionals in this area.

A Final Word about Sexuality

It must be noted again that many of the changes affecting sexuality result from psychological reactions to perceived biological changes. Properly interpreted, biological changes may result in less pressure to perform and a more satisfying sensuality coupled with sexuality for many aging couples. It must also be stated that the decision regarding sexual activity must remain with the individual or couple. The purpose of education for older clients and gerontological professionals is to assist them in making satisfying personal choices.

Remaining healthy and fit through good nutritional practices and exercise seems to be valuable in maintaining a healthy, active sexual life. There are no magic devices or formulas, vitamins or minerals, or chemicals which are effective aphrodisiacs. The most important sexual organ is between the ears; the best predictor of a healthy, satisfying sexual life is the younger years. "If you don't use it, you'll lose it" seems to apply as much to sexuality as to other areas of life.

Health Care Delivery Services and the Elderly

The full range of services described below constitutes the "Continuum of care." Unfortunately, while each of these services is available in some communities across the country, the full range is rarely available in any one community. And even in those communities which may have all services represented, the demand for some services is certain to exceed available capacity. Many of the services described may be provided by formal service agencies, but mixed with ongoing informal care.

The elderly person presents the care giving professional with a variety of value conflicts and ethical dilemmas. Medicine's orientation has been focused on arriving at a diagnosis of a condition and then proceeding with a treatment procedure aimed at its cure. Efforts are usually geared toward the identification of a single dysfunction. However, among elderly patients a single problem is not the rule. There are certain degenerative changes that occur and certain diseases that increase in incidence with age. Thus elderly patients may be suffering from many physical conditions superimposed one upon the other rather than from a single problem. These multiple physical changes and disorders can lead to confusion in arriving at an accurate diagnosis. For instance, chest pain is a symptom that can accompany a variety of conditions that increase in incidence with age. Chest pain can signal conditions such as heart disease and a potential attack, stomach disorders, and esophageal problems. The presence of nonspecific symptoms can cause one to overlook a specific disease state. Additionally, the aged individual is at a much higher risk of suffering an illness which may temporarily or permanently change cognitive and thus decision-making ability. Finally, we live in a society which holds certain negative attitudes and beliefs about the elderly, limiting the range of options for older people and at times hindering their access to the best care and life quality.

Functional Status

Functional status represents the level of an individual's behavioral capabilities in a variety of areas including 1) physical health, 2) quality of self-maintenance, 3) quality of role activity, 4) intellectual status, 5) social activity, 6) attitudes toward the world and toward self and 7) emotional status. Functional status, independent of existing pathology, is clearly important in representing an individual's state of health. Persons who exhibit similar clinical symptoms may vary widely on functional measures. Thus, functional status represents something more than clinical and physical health status.

From a practical point of view, measurement of functional status is a difficult but important element in the planning and development of services. Its importance lies in the fact that it is an indicator of need. How people behave—that is, whether they actually seek the services they require, and if they do, what kind of services they seek and how often—is a more useful variable to the health planner than a detailed description of clinical pathology.

Functional Assessment

The growing interest in functional assessment and its value for the overall measurement of health status of the elderly reflects a variety of concerns. It has become increasingly apparent that, given the many chronic conditions of the aged, narrowly focused physical measures are not enough and that the interaction of aging with illness—or secondary age—requires the use of many broader measures.

Because older people make up a varied group with very different lifelong habits and behaviors, we are coming to realize that it is nearly impossible to predict future behavior. It is also difficult to devise a "normal range" within which people will adapt to chronic illnesses and disabilities.

It appears, then, that how older people behave and perform in the face of a chronic illness or disability is determined by a number of things, including overall lifestyle and attitudes toward health and aging, coping with abilities, the expectation of (important) others, and those geriatric health services that are available and economically feasible.

Increased emphasis on functional assessment measures comes from those interested in making better predictions about the types of health services needed and their anticipated use and from those concerned with improving the quality and efficiency of treatment through more accurate and complete diagnostic procedures.

Health care services may be delivered in three settings: home, community, and institutional. Home services are: monitoring, homemaking, health care, and nutritional services. Community services are: Senior Centers, Community Medical Services, dental services, community mental health, adult day care, respite care, and hospice care. The institutional services are: Intermediate Care, Skilled Nursing Care, and Acute Care Hospitals. Many of the services described may be provided by formal services agencies or integrated into ongoing informal care.

Monitoring services are intended to supervise or keep in touch with chronically impaired or frail persons living alone. They include organized, active services such as telephone networks and friendly visiting as well as more "passive" services such as alert apartment managers, friendly neighbors, and alarm systems. A variety of innovative monitoring programs have been developed such as using mailmen who are instructed to stop and knock at the door of an older person who has failed to activate a signal that all is well.

Homemaker services are the general housekeeping services needed to keep someone at home (e.g. house cleaning, shopping, meal preparation, minor repairs, financial management, laundry and errands). Both the types and quality of services provided, as well as the public funding available to pay for these services, vary widely from state to state. Information regarding access to this type of service is available through family service, home health or aging agencies.

Home health care includes skilled nursing services (medical services furnished or directed by a licensed nurse), rehabilitation services (improving function in activities of daily living through physical, occupational and speech therapies), and personal care service. Home health care, as an alternative to long-term institutional care, has become a valuable resource in many communities.

Chronic conditions such as arthritis or diabetes can cause functional impairment, but is usually not enough to indicate the need for long-term institutional care. The degree of functional impairment is determined by the elderly person's ability to handle daily activities and moving about without assistance. Elderly who are functionally disabled are often bedridden, need assistance with dressing and bathing, or need help in moving around outside the home. These people are typical candidates for home health care and do not necessarily require institutionalization. Availability or lack of institutional facilities, willingness of family or friends to care for the person, costs of care, the person's reluctance to enter an institution, and availability of home care are all important variables to consider when deciding whether a person should enter an institutional facility. Home health services are provided by both nonprofit (e.g. Visiting Nurse Associations) as well as proprietary organizations and private individuals.

Nutrition programs are an important resource for a wide spectrum of older individuals. These programs include congregate dining and home-delivered meals programs, such as "Meals on Wheels," to an estimated 2.85 million elderly each year. These programs are important not only for providing an important portion of the daily nutritional requirement five times each week, but also because of the opportunity provided for social contact, recreation, education, health screening, and outreach programs. Home delivered meals are an important resource for housebound individuals who are unable to shop, prepare meals, or follow special dietary regimens.

Senior centers provide opportunities for important social contact and recreational activities. They also serve as a convenient site for health screening, nutrition programs, education programs and outreach activities. Support for senior centers varies among communities, with government, charitable organizations, and private philanthropy contributing varying shares.

Community medical services provided by private physicians, in clinics, or in Health Maintenance Organizations (HMOs) are a crucial component of the continuum of care. These visits are more likely to be for chronic conditions, and tend to be with general practitioners and internists. In the current organization of care, the physician is often placed in the role of "gatekeeper," certifying that such services are necessary.

Community dental services are an often overlooked, but extremely important aspect of care for older people. Dental problems are correlated with nutritional deficits and ill health, and have a direct impact on quality of life by changing enjoyment of food and altering communication and social contact. Serious misconceptions about adequate dental care (for example, many believe that elderly persons with full dentures need not visit the dentist) contribute to continuing problems of dental health for older people.

Adult day care in the U.S. is available in two types. The first, a "day hospital" program, typically has rehabilitation as its goal. It provides more "medically" oriented services, and is generally affiliated with a health care institution. The second type, a "multi-purpose program," focuses more on social programs and activities, and is more likely to be affiliated with a community service agency.

There are two basic reasons for providing day care: 1) to avoid or prevent admittance to a nursing home for any patient who can live at home but needs a variety of health related services for health maintenance and rehabilitation, and 2) to ensure that the elderly frail will enjoy a better quality of life. Day care emphasizes health maintenance, health restoration, and rehabilitation of physical ailments.

Respite care refers to a range of services which allows care providing family members time away from caretaking responsibilities. The services may range from an in-home visit of a few hours by a volunteer or paid worker, through an institutional stay of many weeks for the client. The importance of this service, given the considerable stress of providing care to an aged spouse, sibling, or parent, cannot be underestimated.

The *hospice* concept offers a set of services intended to improve the quality of life of terminally ill patients. While some hospice care is provided in institutional settings such as hospitals and nursing homes, the major focus has been on home care. In both settings the family is included in planning and providing care. Interdisciplinary care teams are emphasized. The overall goal of the hospice is to avoid suffering and pointless "heroic" interventions, while offering support to the patient and family.

Acute care hospitals are an important source of care for older patients. The elderly have more hospital days per year than the general population. However, as many as 18 percent of the elderly are "misplaced" in acute care hospitals, often awaiting placement in nursing homes.

Nursing homes are defined as facilities which provide nursing care as their primary and predominant function. Intermediate care facilities (ICF) and skilled nursing facilities (SNF) differ in their nursing staffs. This difference is based on the assumption that a higher level of nursing skills is needed to provide the treatments required by SNF patients but not by ICF residents. However, differences in regulations among states lead to widely differing distributions of patients between the two levels of care. The consensus is that for some patients, a long-term care facility is the most appropriate and humane setting for care.

Medicare

Medicare is a federal insurance program financing a portion of the health care costs of persons aged 65 and older. In October 1983, the Federal Government instituted a prospective payment system call Diagnosis Related Groups (DRGs) for hospital payment under Medicare. Due to this program, hospitals are discharging Medicare recipients earlier. Because of this earlier hospital discharge, we are seeing more utilization for Extended Care programs.

Extended care facilities are of two types: 1) hospital based and 2) nursing home based. The extended care program is designed as a short-term rehabilitation/recuperative program for extended care after hospital confinement.

The Medicare benefits for extended care are very limited and have several requirements that must be met for coverage. The Medicare recipient must also require a skilled service on a daily basis as an inpatient.

Medicaid

Medicaid is a public welfare program for persons of all ages paid with matching federal and state funds. As has been true of other categorical assistance programs, states set their own eligibility requirements. Generally speaking, persons who were eligible for Old Age Assistance are eligible for Medicaid, although in some states, such as Massachusetts, eligibility standards for Medicaid are less strict than those for other welfare programs. Medicaid provides long-term, unlimited nursing home care without requiring previous hospitalization. Not surprisingly, Medicaid has become the principal public mechanism for funding nursing home care.

Bibliography

A Long Goodbye—Coping With Alzheimer's Disease and Other Forms of Dementia. (1988). Medical Essay, Mayo Clinic Health Letter.

American Hospital Association (1985). *Health Promotion for Older Adults: Planning for Action*. Chicago, IL: Center for Health Promotion.

Besdine, Richard W., Bennett, G., Terry, T., and Wetle, T. (1982). *Handbook of Geriatric Care*.

Brody, E.M. (1985). *Mental and Physical Health Practices of Older People*. New York, NY: Springer Publishing Company.

Caldwell, E. and Hegner, B.R. (1975). *Geriatrics: A Study of Maturity*. Albany, NY: Delmar Publishers.

Charatan, F.B. (1982). Sexual Function in Old Age. *Journal of the Florida Medical Association, 69*, No. 4, 305–309.

Driver, J.D. and Detrick, D. (1982). Elders and Sexuality. *Journal of Nursing Care, 15*, No. 2, 8–11.

Dychtwald, K. (1986). *Wellness and Health Promotion for the Elderly*. Rockville, MD: Aspen Publications.

Hogan, R. (1980). *Human Sexuality—A Nursing Perspective*. New York: Appleton Century Crofts.

Green, A.W. (1975). Sexual Activity and the Post-myocardial Infarction Patient. *American Heart Journal, 89*, 246–252.

Hartman, W. and Fithian, M. (1974). *Treatment of Sexual Dysfunction*. New York: Jason Aronson.

Kaplan, M. (1979). *Leisure: Lifestyle and Lifespan*. Philadelphia: W.B. Saunders Company.

Kaufert, P. and Syrotuik, J. (1981). Symptom Reporting at the Menopause. *Social Science Medicine, 15E*, 173–184.

Kay, B. and Neeley, J.N. (1982). Sexuality and Aging: A Review of Current Literature. *Sexuality and Disability, 5,* No. 1, 38–46.

Kermis, M.D. (1986). *Mental Health in Late Life—The Adaptive Process.* Boston, MA: Jones & Barlett Publishers, Inc.

Mahta, J. and Krop, H. (1979). The Effect of Myocardial Infarction on Sexual Functioning. *Sexuality and Disability, 2,* 115–121.

Masters, W.H. and Johnson, V.E. (1982). Sex and the Aging Process. *Medical Aspects of Human Sexuality, 16,* 40–57.

Masters, W.H., Johnson, V.E., and Kolodny, R.C. (1982). *Human Sexuality.* Boston, MA: Little, Brown and Company.

National Institute of Aging, National Institutes of Health, Public Health Service (1984). *Help Yourself to Good Health.* Washington, D.C.: Department of Health and Human Services and Pfizer Pharmaceuticals.

National Institutes of Health (1980). *Our Future Selves.* Washington, D.C., Department of Health and Human Services.

Notelovitz, M. and Ware, M. (1982). *Stand Tall.* Gainesville, FL: Triad Publishing Company.

Pearson, L. (1982). Climacteric. *American Journal of Nursing, 82,* No. 7, 1098–1102.

Pelletier, K.R. (1981). *Longevity.* New York, NY: Delacorte Press.

Pfeiffer, E. (1974). Sexuality and the Aging Individual. *Journal of the American Geriatric Society, 22,* No. 11, 481–484.

Piscopo, J. (1985). *Fitness and Aging.* New York, NY: John Wiley & Sons.

Schwartz, A.N., Snyder, C.L., and Peterson, J.A. (1979). *Aging and Life.* New York, NY: Holt, Rinehart, and Winston.

Seefeldt, Vern, (ed.) (1986). *Physical Activity and Well Being.* Reston, VA: AAHPERD.

Teague, M.L. (1987). *Health Promotions: Achieving High-Level Wellness in the Later Years.* Indianapolis, IN: Benchmark Press Inc.

Uphold, C.R. and Susman, E.J. (1981). Self-Reported Climacteric Symptoms as a Function of the Relationships Between Marital Adjustment and Childrearing Stage. *Nursing Research, 30,* No. 2, 84–88.

Wantz, M.S. and Gay, J.E. (1981). *The Aging Process.* Cambridge, MA: Winthrop Publishers, Inc.

Warner-Reitz, A. (1981). *Healthy Lifestyles for Seniors.* New York: Meals for Millions/Freedom from Hunger Foundation.

Wells, Thelma (ed.) (1982). *Aging and Health Promotion.* Rockville, MD: Aspen Publications.

Wolford, R.L. (1983). *Maximum Life Span.* New York, NY: Avon Books.

Yoselle, H. (1981). Sexuality in the Later Years. *Topics in Clinical Nursing, 3,* No. 1, 59–70.

3 BIOLOGICAL AGING AND THE BENEFITS OF PHYSICAL ACTIVITY

Everett L. Smith, University of Wisconsin
Catherine Gilligan, University of Wisconsin

Introduction

All living creatures age. Aging is species-specific and controlled by the genetic makeup of the cell. Aging can be defined chronologically or physiologically. Physiological aging is the loss of the ability to adapt to one's environment. Peak physiological function is reached at approximately age 30, after which, in sedentary persons, physiological capabilities decline. Average functional declines are evident in work capacity, cardiac output, heart rate, blood pressure, respiration, basal metabolic rate, musculature, nerve conduction, flexibility, and bone. Two factors in addition to age contribute to these average declines. One is occult disease. We will refer to the changes with age in the absence of disease as normal aging. The second is disuse. The average person decreases in physical activity with age, but regular physical activity can reduce or reverse age-related declines in function.

This brief overview of biological changes with age and the benefits of physical activity for the older adult only introduces the subject. For an in depth review the reader is referred to Shephard (1987), Smith and Serfass (1981), Spirduso & Eckert (1989), and *Topics in Geriatric Rehabilitation,* Volume 1, Number 1 (1985).

Metabolic Rate and Thermal Regulation

The average 70-year-old has a lower resting metabolic rate and daily energy expenditure than a 30-year-old (Astrand, 1970). As a result, weight and fat increase while muscle mass declines. Tzankoff and Norris (1977) indicated that the decline in basal metabolic rate is directly related to the decline in muscle mass. Total body water also declines, which is related to the loss of muscle mass. Physical activity helps to counteract most of these body composition changes. On the average, thermal regulation is compromised in the sedentary older adult, particularly in subjects over 70. However, active subjects have better thermal regulation than inactive subjects at any age (Dill et al., 1967). These changes in body composition and thermal regulation make the older adult less able to adapt to both heat and cold stresses. Older adults participating in a physical activity program should be aware of the necessity of remaining hydrated and of avoiding excessively hot or cold environments. The average older adult is more susceptible to hypothermia. Cold-induced vasoconstriction and increased blood pressure may strain the heart during physical activity.

Muscle and Strength

Age-related decreases in muscle mass and strength are well documented. Muscle mass, power, strength, and endurance all decline with age. Power, which includes components of strength, fiber type, and neural factors, shows the most pronounced decline. Endurance during low and moderate intensities decreases the least and latest. Steen (1988), reviewing the literature, reported that total muscle mass decreased approximately 40 percent by the age of 70. In men, strength is maximal between 30 and 35 years of age and remains relatively constant until about age 50. Strength then declines approximately 20 percent by the mid-60s and continues to decline after this age (Buskirk & Segal, 1989). The decline is more pronounced in the lower back and legs (large muscle groups) than in the arms (small muscle groups) (Cress & Schultz, 1985). Muscle mass was 11.4 percent lower in older men (mean age 69) than middle-aged men (mean age 46) studied by Borkan et al. (1983). Campbell et al. (1973) found that muscle mass and strength of the extensor digitorum brevis was lower in 28 healthy older subjects (ages 60–69) than in subjects under 60. No decline in motor units occurred up to age 58. Similarly, Brown (1973) found that the number of motor units decreased only slightly between the ages of 9 and 60. The number of motor units dropped sharply after age 60. An increase in motor unit size compensated for the decrease in motor unit number. This compensatory mechanism, while helping to maintain strength, could decrease fine motor control (Buskirk & Segal, 1989). Sperling (1980) reported that hand grip strength was 21 percent lower in old (70 years) than in young (20 to 30 years) men and women. Grimby et al. (1982) reported a similar difference of 23 percent between men 30 and 80 years of age in hand grip strength, but a greater difference of 40 percent in leg and back muscle strength. McDonagh et al. (1984) also showed that the age-related decline depended on the muscle group studied. Older men (mean age 71) were 41 percent lower in maximum voluntary contraction of the triceps surae (gastrocnemius and soleus) than younger men (mean age 26), but only 20 percent lower in the elbow flexors. Murray et al. (1980) measured static and dynamic contractions for knee flexion and extension in men aged 20 to 86. Knee strength was 35–55 percent lower in 70–86-year-old men than in 20–35-year-old men. Young et al. (1984) compared quadriceps strength and cross-sectional area in young (20–29) and elderly women (71–81). The differences in strength and size of the muscle were proportional. Davies et al. (1983) assessed power in old (mean age 60) and young (mean age 22) men. Maximal force production of the triceps surae was 40–50 percent lower in the older men. Makrides et al. (1985) reported that maximum power during ergometer cycling decreases approximately 6 percent per decade. Larsson et al. (1979) found that both strength and velocity of contraction of the lower body were lower in subjects over 50, but endurance relative to maximal strength did not change. Isometric strength, extension velocity, and dynamic strength of the knee extensor changed little between the ages of 29 and 40 and then declined.

Skeletal muscle consists of both slow and fast twitch fibers. Several researchers have reported that with age, the ratio of fast twitch to slow twitch muscle fibers declines, depending on the site. The ratio of Type II/I fibers in the quadriceps decreased from approximately 1.28 in 20–29-year-old men to 0.99 in 60–65-year-old men (Larsson, 1978) and to 0.77 in 78–81-year-old men (Grimby et al., 1982). Larsson et al. (1979) reported that Type II fiber area was highly correlated with strength in the vastus lateralis in subjects aged 20 to 65. Parallel to the pattern of loss in strength, the alteration in Type II fiber area was greater in the vastus lateralis than biceps brachii, which did not change significantly in fiber distribution with age (Grimby et al.,

1982). In contrast to these needle biopsy studies, Lexell et al. (1983) found no significant change in fiber type distribution in whole vastus lateralis preparations. Fiber size also did not differ. Muscle size was 18 percent lower in an old age group (mean age 71) than in a young age group (mean age 30), and fiber number was 25 percent lower.

Research on the effects of physical activity on neuromuscular changes in the aging population is sparse. McCafferty & Edington (1970) hypothesized that there may be an age beyond which training no longer stimulates muscle hypertrophy in either the skeletal muscle or the heart. However, Petrofsky & Lind (1975) observed no difference in muscular strength or endurance of the arm in men between 25 and 65 performing similar work activities in an aircraft corporation machine shop.

Suominen et al. (1977b) studied 69-year-old men and women who completed an 8 week physical activity program held for 1 hour, 5 times a week. They concluded from their study that fitness and strength improve similarly with exercise in both young and old adults.

Larsson (1982) studied the influence of high repetition, low resistance training on quadriceps strength and muscle morphology in 18 men aged 22–65. With 15 weeks of training, strength tended to increase regardless of age, with a greater increase in subjects aged 56–65. Subjects aged 20–39 did not change significantly in Type I or Type II fiber area. The middle age group (40–55) increased significantly in Type II fiber area, while the oldest age group (56–65) increased significantly in both Type I and Type II fiber areas.

De Lorme & Watkins (1951) hypothesized a two-stage process for strength gain: increased nerve activity followed by muscle hypertrophy. Moritani (1981) trained both young and old men in an eight-week isotonic strength regimen. Young subjects increased both neural activity and muscle mass, while older subjects increased only in neural function. Further research is necessary to determine if muscle hypertrophy can be induced in the older adult with different training techniques or longer exercise regimes.

Agre et al. (1988) studied elderly women (63–88 years of age, mean age 71) to determine the effect of a 25-week light resistance and aerobic exercise program upon arm and leg strength. Exercise subjects (n=35) attended physical activity sessions one hour, three times per week. Exercise subjects improved 11–25 percent in elbow extension, shoulder internal rotation, shoulder external rotation, and knee flexion strength, significantly more than control subjects (n=12). Elbow flexion and knee extension changes did not differ between exercise and control subjects.

Aniansson and Gustafsson (1981) examined men 69–74 years of age and found that leg muscle strength increased during a 12-week strength training program. Maximal knee extension torque increased 9–22 percent. The relative area of Type IIa fibers also increased with training.

The research reviewed indicates that on the average muscle mass, strength, and Type II fibers decrease with age. Regardless of age, however, physical activity improves strength and Type I and Type II fiber areas.

Reaction Time

Nerve conduction velocity is approximately ten percent lower in the average older adult (Shock, 1962) due to metabolic and synaptic changes. Impulses from the nerve to the muscle cell membrane and therefore muscle contraction in response to stimuli are slowed.

In humans, a high physical activity level appears to promote better reaction times in both young and old adults. Spirduso (1975) reported that inactive men had slower reaction times than active men in both young and old age groups. Similarly, women (mean age 53) who ran at least 30 minutes a day, five days a week had significantly faster reaction times than sedentary women (mean age 54) (Baylor & Spirduso, 1988). Several cross-sectional studies show a similar association between physical activity and reaction time (Baylor & Spirduso, 1988; Rikli and Busch, 1986). A few intervention studies support this correspondence between physical activity and reaction time. Spirduso & Farrar (1981) found that reaction time was faster in aerobically trained than untrained old rats. Dustman et al. (1984) evaluated reaction time in three groups of older adults (ages 55–70): an aerobic exercise group, a strength and flexibility exercise group, and a non-exercising control group. The two exercise groups met three days per week for four months. Subjects in the aerobic exercise group improved significantly in reaction time and work capacity, while the strength and flexibility exercise group and the control group did not change significantly.

Flexibility

Flexibility tends to decline with age and this decline is related to changes in connective tissues in muscle, ligaments, joint capsules, and tendons (Johns, 1962). These connective tissue changes increase the resistance to movement. Disease is also an important factor in the average flexibility decline. More than 80 percent of people over the age of 55 have signs of osteoarthrosis (Kellgren and Lawrence, 1957). The relative contributions of disuse, disease, and age to flexibility changes are unknown.

Estimates of the decline in flexibility with age vary widely with the sites measured, the measurement method, and the subject screening process. Ahlback and Lindahl (1964) reported that 70–79-year-old men had hip flexibility approximately 25 percent lower than men aged 20–29. Allander et al. (1974) evaluated wrist, hip, and metacarpophalangeal flexibility in 309 women aged 33–70. Flexibility was 3.7–9.9 percent lower in the oldest age group (mean age 56) than in the youngest age group (mean age 35). In another part of this study, comprising 208 women and 203 men, flexibility declined 0–14.7 percent between the 45–49 and 65–69 year age groups, with a mean change of 7.7 percent. Boone and Azen (1979) evaluated 23 movements of the shoulder, elbow, forearm, wrist, hip, knee, ankle, and foot in male subjects 18 months to 54 years of age. While subjects over 19 had significantly less flexibility than younger subjects on 15 of the motions, only two motions (elbow extension and wrist flexion) were significantly different between age groups over 20. In contrast, Einkauf et al. (1987) found that spine mobility was 29–50 percent lower in healthy women aged 70–79 than in 20–29-year-old women. Smith & Walker (1983) studied knee and elbow flexion and extension in 60 healthy men and women aged 55–84. Ten year age groups did not differ significantly except for knee flexion in the women. Range of motion of the shoulder, elbow, forearm, wrist, hip, knee, ankle, foot, and first metatarsal were evaluated by Walker et al. (1984) in subjects aged 60–69 and 75–84. As in the study by Smith & Walker (1983), flexibility did not differ significantly between the two age groups. Germain & Blair (1983), on the other hand, reported a greater decline in flexibility after the age of 70. Subjects aged 50–70 were six percent lower in shoulder flexibility than subjects aged 20–30, while subjects over 70 were 11 percent lower in flexibility than the 50–70 year age group. Shoulder flexion was greater in subjects classified as active than for inactive subjects in the same age group. Similarly, Rikli & Busch (1986) found that shoulder and trunk flexibility were higher in active women in both young (mean age 22) and old (mean age 69) age groups.

Murray (1985) evaluated shoulder motion in 40 men and women aged 25–36 and 55–66. Older men (mean age 62) had inward rotation 10 percent higher than younger men (mean age 31). Younger men, however, had five percent greater shoulder flexion and six percent greater shoulder extension. Younger and older women differed significantly for only one of the six movements, glenohumeral abduction, by five percent. A later study from the same laboratory (Sepic et al., 1986) reported that younger subjects (ages 25–35) had plantar flexion approximately 10 percent higher than older subjects (ages 50–60).

Few research programs have tested the effects of physical activity on flexibility in older adults. Chapman et al. (1972) studied joint stiffness in 20 young (ages 15–19) and 20 old (ages 63–88) adults. After a six week training program both groups showed the same amount of improvement. Lesser (1978) studied 60 elderly subjects who exercised for 10 weeks. Flexibility improved at two-thirds of the sites measured, but no statistical significance levels were reported. Buccola & Stone (1975) measured trunk and leg flexibility by the sit and reach test in 36 men, ages 60–79. Subjects who participated in a 14-week walk-jog program (n=16) improved significantly in flexibility, but subjects who participated in a 14-week cycling program (n=20) did not change significantly. Frekany & Leslie (1975) evaluated ankle flexibility and sit and reach flexibility in 15 women, aged 71–90, recruited for a 7-month exercise program. Left and right ankle flexibility and sit and reach flexibility improved significantly during the study. Gutman et al. (1977) studied elderly men and women divided into conventional exercise, Feldenkrais exercise, and control groups. After six weeks, rotational flexibility was improved, but there were no significant differences between groups. Munns (1981) worked with 40 elderly subjects (mean age 72), 20 of these serving as controls. After 12 weeks, the exercise group had improved at all sites (neck, shoulder, wrist, knee, hip, and ankle) by 8–48 percent, while the control group declined. Raab et al. (1988) evaluated flexibility of the shoulder, ankle, hip, wrist and neck in elderly women (mean age 71). Subjects in the exercise groups (n=33) improved significantly in ankle plantar flexion, shoulder flexion, shoulder abduction, and left cervical rotation. Hip flexion improved in both exercise and control groups.

Bone

Bone loss presents a significant problem for women over 60 and men over 80. More than six million elderly men and women in the U.S. have a significant degree of bone loss. Men over 50 lose about 0.4 percent/year in bone mass. Women, however, lose approximately one percent/year after age 35. This loss accelerates to two–five percent/year in the period immediately following menopause. The decreased mass and thus strength of the bone results in approximately 1.3 million osteoporotic fractures annually. Vertebral wedge and crush fractures and Colles' fractures start at about age 50. By age 80, 40–90 percent of women have one or more spine fractures (Cummings, 1987; Kelsey, 1984). Hip fractures are fairly uncommon before age 65, but the risk increases exponentially with age, doubling every 6–10 years (Melton et al., 1986; Scott, 1984). In the U.S., there are approximately 267,000 hip fractures per year (Johnston & Slemenda, 1987; Martin and Houston, 1987) at a cost of 7.2 billion dollars per year (Cummings, 1987). Five to 15 percent of hip fracture patients die within a year of the injury. Of the survivors, only one-quarter regain their ability to perform the activities of daily living independently, while one-quarter are totally disabled (Martin & Houston, 1987).

The role of physical activity in the prevention of bone loss with age has yet to be delineated.

Mechanical forces, i.e. gravity or weight bearing and muscle contraction, are important in the maintenance of bone. If either gravity or muscle contraction is significantly reduced or increased, bone formation and removal are affected. For example, subjects at bedrest or in weightlessness lose bone mineral of the calcaneous and spine. Athletes generally have greater bone mineral content (BMC) than sedentary subjects. Evidence that this difference is not solely due to genetic differences is provided by studies of tennis players. Tennis players have 8–35 percent greater bone mineral content in their dominant arm than in their nondominant arm (Smith & Gilligan, in press (b)).

Physical activity can affect bone mineral mass regardless of age. Aloia et al. (1978) reported that total body calcium increased in nine postmenopausal women exercising three times/week for one year relative to control subjects. Krolner et al. (1982) studied 27 women, aged 50–73 with previous Colles' fracture. Lumbar spine BMC increased 3.5 percent after 8 months in exercising subjects while decreasing 2.7 percent in control subjects. The exercise programs in these two studies, which were not designed to specifically stress the arms, had no significant effect on radius BMC. Exercise programs which included specific upper body work, however, decreased bone loss in the arm. Simkin et al. (1986) studied 40 postmenopausal osteoporotic women. Exercise subjects (n=14) met 45–50 minutes, three times per week for five months. Fifteen minutes of each exercise session consisted of dynamic forearm loading exercises. Exercise did not significantly affect BMC (measured by single photon absorptiometry) but mass density (measured by Compton scattering) increased 3.8 percent in the exercise group while declining 1.9 percent in the control group. Chow et al. (1987b) evaluated the calcium bone index (CaBI) in osteoporotic patients on fluoride treatment. Twenty subjects who exercised regularly had a significantly higher CaBI after 12.5 months than subjects who exercised less than three times per week (n=18). Smith et al. (in press) also reported that bone loss was slowed in an exercise program which combined arm work with aerobic activities. Women (ages 35–65) in the exercise program participated three times/week, 45 minutes/session for four years. The exercise group (n=80) had significantly lower bone loss rates in the radius, ulna, and humerus than the control group (n=62). Dalsky et al. (1988) evaluated lumbar spine BMC in 35 postmenopausal women (ages 55–70). Seventeen subjects exercised for nine to 22 months, and 18 subjects served as controls. All subjects received 1500 mg calcium supplementation per day. Spine BMC increased significantly with nine months training (5.2 percent) and 22 months training (6.1 percent), while it did not change significantly in the control group. Fifteen subjects in the exercise group were re-evaluated after 13 months of detraining. Spine BMC decreased significantly with detraining, and final spine BMC measurements did not differ significantly from values prior to the exercise program. White et al. (1984) compared the effects of aerobic dance and walking for 26 weeks on distal radius BMC in recently postmenopausal women. BMC declined significantly in the control and walking groups, but did not change significantly in the aerobic dance group. Both exercise groups increased significantly in bone width. Chow et al. (1987a) divided postmenopausal women into a control group and two exercise groups—aerobic and aerobic plus strengthening exercise. At the end of one year, both exercise groups had a significantly higher CaBI than controls, but there was no significant difference between the two exercise groups. While the control group declined in CaBI, both exercise groups increased. Smith et al. (1981) studied radius BMC in elderly women (mean age 81). Radius BMC change was significantly higher in subjects who exercised for three years (+2.3 percent) than in control subjects (−3.3 percent).

These exercise intervention studies show that physical activity can play an important role in maintaining bone or reversing bone loss, regardless of age or initial bone status. A recent prospective study on 3,110 men and women over 65 (mean age 73) indicated that fracture risk in this age group was reduced by regular physical activity (Sorock et al., 1988). Subjects who participated in moderate physical activity, such as walking, three or more times a week had a lower rate of reported fractures in the subsequent year. Subjects who had experienced fractures within four years prior to the study were excluded from the analysis. Relative risk ratios were 0.41 for active men and 0.76 for active women, although inactive and active subjects did not differ significantly in fracture risk based on 95 percent confidence intervals.

Cardiovascular

Decrease in maximum heartrate (6–8 beats/decade) and maximum stroke volume contribute to a 30 percent decline in cardiac output between ages 30 and 70. This decline results from changes in both the heart and vascular system. The heart muscle is weaker and maximum heartrate lower. Blood vessels lose elasticity and narrow, increasing the resistance to blood flow. Systemic pressure is approximately 20 percent higher in an elderly person than a young person at half the cardiac output (Shephard, 1987). On the average, both systolic and diastolic pressure increase with age both at rest (10–40 mm Hg systolic, 5–10 mm Hg diastolic) and during exercise. Environmental and disease factors contribute to this increase.

During mild exercise, the cardiac output of the average older adult is adequate, but the average older adult cannot maintain adequate blood flow to tissues for intense exercise.

Part of the average decline in cardiac output may be due to occult disease. Lakatta (1986) suggested that occult coronary heart disease and atherosclerosis may be present in up to 60 percent of people over 50. He found that cardiac output declined less with age in 61 men who were carefully screened and found free of occult coronary disease. Maximum cardiac output did not differ significantly between the young (25 to 44) and old (65 to 80) groups. While maximum heart rate was lower in the older subjects, cardiac output was maintained by increased end diastolic volume and stroke volume.

Work Capacity

The ability to exercise and do physical work is one of the first to show obvious decline. In cross-sectional studies, VO2 declines approximately 0.4–0.5 ml/kg/min per year of age in men and 0.20–0.35 in women (Smith & Gilligan, in press (a)). The work capacity of inactive and active groups declines at about the same rate, although active subjects have greater work capacity than inactive groups of the same age. The loss of work capacity is related to declines in numerous body functions, including cardiovascular, respiratory, and muscular changes. In a review of both cross-sectional and longitudinal studies, Buskirk & Hodgson (1987) found rates of change varying from 0.04 to 1.43 ml/kg/min per year of age. Fardy et al. (1976) reported a decrease of 25 percent in estimated maximum VO2 (ml/kg/min) between healthy men aged 25–34 (n=106) and 55–74 (n=58). Resting systolic blood pressure was 12 mmHg higher and diastolic pressure 5 mmHg higher in the older age group. Drinkwater et al. (1975) reported that VO2 (ml/kg/min) declined approximately 0.338 ml/kg/min per year of age in a cross-sectional study of 109 women aged 10–68. Both maximum cardiac output and VO2 declined with age in a study of 54 sedentary men and women aged 18–68 (Julius et al., 1967). Age did not, however, affect the relationship between cardiac output and VO2. Sheffield et al. (1978) studied women ages 19–69, and did not find a statistically significant decrease in treadmill exercise time with age. Maximum heart rate, however, declined 0.88 beats/minute per year of age. Siconolfi et al. (1985) evaluated men and women aged 18–65 without overt coronary disease. Maximum VO2 (mg/kg/min) was almost 50 percent lower in 60–65 year olds than 18–29 year olds. Systolic pressure was 17 mmHg higher in older men and 28 mmHg higher in older women than in the youngest age group. Diastolic blood pressure was 9 and 13 mmHg higher, respectively.

Several researchers have evaluated changes over time in work capacity. Plowman et al. (1979) evaluated 36 women between the ages of 18 and 68 after an average of 6.1 years. Subjects in their 20s did not change significantly in aerobic work capacity, while subjects 30 and older declined at approximately the rate predicted by the original cross-sectional study (Drinkwater et al., 1975). Maximum heartrate declined by 2–4 beats/minute in age groups under 50 and over 60, while it declined by 7.6 beats/minutes in the 50–59 year age group. Ericsson & Irnell (1969) studied 42 men and 42 women aged 57–71. They reported that maximal work capacity declined an average of 12 percent in men and 19 percent in women after five years. Robinson et al. (1975) retested former college students after 22 years. Maximal heartrate declined 15 beats/minute and maximal VO2 25 percent during this period.

Kasch (Kasch, 1976; Kasch et al., 1985) demonstrated that most of the age-related decline in fitness could be averted by consistent exercise. Two groups of formerly sedentary men exercised for six (n=17, mean age 48) and seven years (n=10). One group of habitually active men continued training for ten years (n=16, mean age 45). The first two groups trained an average of two sessions per week including 20 minutes of calisthenics and 30–35 minutes of interval and continuous running at 65–92 percent of heart rate reserve. The chronic exercise subjects ran an average of 59 minutes, three times per week, at 60–93 percent of heartrate reserve. The first intervention group improved in maximal VO2 by 23 percent in six weeks, while the second intervention improved 10 percent in seven years. Maximal oxygen uptake plauteaued after one year of exercise. The habitually active men did not change significantly in maximum VO2 in ten years. Fifteen of the habitually exercising men continued to exercise for an additional five to eight years, an average of 3.3 days/week for 45 minutes at 77 percent of heartrate reserve. The 15 men who exercised for 15 years increased slightly from 44.6 to 45.2 ml/kg/min during the first ten years and decreased in the following five years to 40.2 ml/kg/min. In the 13 men who exercised 18 years, work capacity decreased only slightly from 44.6 to 43.1 ml/kg/min in 18 years.

Physical activity can improve work capacity at any age, although some researchers have reported that the training effect may be less pronounced in older adults. In several exercise intervention studies, improvements in work capacity were smaller in older age groups (Kilbom, 1971; Pollock et al., 1971; Roskamm, 1967; Wilmore et al., 1970). In contrast, Suominen et al. (1977a) reported that eight weeks of training improved maximal oxygen uptake by 11 percent in 27 previously sedentary men, ages 56–70, divided into 3 5-year age groups. These subjects, none of whom had participated in regular physical activity for at least 20 years, trained 3–5 times per week for 45–60 minutes. Work capacity increased by a similar amount in all three five-year age groups.

Other researchers have studied the effect of exercise training on work capacity and cardiovascular function in the elderly. deVries (1970) trained 68 men (mean age 70) for 6 weeks, 45–60 minutes per session. Changes in estimated maximal VO2 (ml/kg/min) did not differ significantly between exercise and control groups. Exercise subjects, however, improved significantly in oxygen pulse and physical work capacity at a heartrate of 145, while control subjects did not change significantly. Adams & deVries (1973) studied 23 women aged 52–79 from a retirement community. Exercise subjects (n=17) trained 3 months, 40–60 minutes per session. Work capacity was evaluated on a submaximal bicycle ergometer test. Control subjects did not change significantly in physical work capacity, oxygen uptake, or oxygen pulse, while the exercise subjects increased significantly. Buccola & Stone (1975) studied 36 men aged 60–79 participating in walk-jog and cycling training programs. After 14 weeks of training, exercise subjects decreased significantly in resting systolic and diastolic blood pressure and improved significantly (12 percent) in estimated maximum VO2.

Cunningham et al. (1987) studied blood lipids and fitness in 200 men at retirement (ages 55–65). One hundred men randomly assigned to an exercise group trained 3 times/week at 60–70 percent of maximum work capacity, 50–55 minutes/session including warm-up and cooldown. After one year, maximum VO2 increased 10.9 percent in the exercise group, a significantly greater increase than in the control group. Cholesterol and HDL levels did not differ between exercise and control groups at either the beginning or the end of the study.

Kiessling et al. (1974) compared the fitness of previously sedentary men (ages 46–62, n=10) participating in a 10–13 week endurance training program with that of 9 chronic runners (ages 43–66). Work capacity increased 8 percent with the training program, but was still 23 percent lower than in the chronic runners. Schocken et al. (1983) studied 24 men and women without cardiovascular disease (mean age 72) who participated in 3 exercise sessions weekly for 12 weeks. Maximum work load increased approximately 10 percent. Suominen et al. (1977b) trained 14 men and 12 women, all aged 69. The exercise program took place five days per week, one hour per session, for eight weeks. Estimated maximal oxygen uptake improved 11 percent in men and 12 percent in women. Thomas et al. (1985) randomly assigned 224 recently retired men (mean age 63) to exercise groups. Exercise subjects trained at 60 percent of maximum heartrate reserve 3 days/week for one year. Sessions were 50–55 minutes long, including 30 minutes of walking or jogging. Maximum VO2 increased significantly by 12 percent in 88 subjects who completed the training program, and did not change significantly in the 100 control subjects. Improvement in exercise subjects was negatively correlated with initial work capacity and positively correlated with the intensity of training.

Tzankoff et al. (1972) studied work capacity and serum cholesterol in 15 men, ages 44–66, who participated in a 25-week training program. Subjects participated an average of 55 minutes per session and 2.3 sessions per week. Maximum work capacity increased significantly by 21.6 percent while maximal heartrate did not change significantly. Serum cholesterol declined in both exercise and control groups. Morse & Smith (1981) evaluated the effect of a fitness trail for older adults. Seventeen subjects (mean age 71) participated in a three-month exercise program and 10 subjects (mean age 70) served as controls. Both the exercise and control groups improved significantly in fitness by 32 percent and 27 percent respectively. Improvement did not differ significantly between groups, but was significantly higher than in a test-retest group. The authors hypothesized that the control group increased because of increased activity during the summer months. Both the intensity and frequency of exercise may affect the response of older adults to training. Badenhop et al. (1983) studied 32 healthy subjects (mean age 68) assigned randomly to high intensity (HI, 60–75 percent heartrate reserve, n=14), low intensity (LI, 30–45 percent, heartrate reserve, n=14) and control groups (n=4). Exercise groups trained 25 minutes/day, 3 days per week for 9 weeks. Both exercise groups improved similarly in maximal VO2 (ml/kg/

min), the high intensity group by 16 percent and the low intensity group by 14.8 percent. deVries (1971) studied 52 men aged 60–79 before and after a six-week exercise program. Increases in fitness were negatively correlated with initial work capacity, and positively but weakly correlated with intensity of training.

Niinimaa & Shephard (1978a; 1978b) evaluated fitness changes in 19 elderly subjects (mean age 65) who participated in an 11-week exercise program. Training sessions were held four times per week for one hour. Nine subjects exercised at heartrates between 145 and 155 beats/minute and improved significantly in maximum VO2 (10 percent). Ten subjects who exercised at lower heartrates did not change significantly in maximum VO2. Seals et al. (1984) evaluated the effects of six months of low intensity training followed by six months of high intensity training. Subjects performed the aerobic training 20–30 minutes per sessions, three times per week. Maximum VO2 (ml/kg/min) improved a total of 30 percent, and increased significantly during both training periods. Maximal cardiac output did not change significantly, while arteriovenous 02 difference increased. At submaximal work loads, stroke volume increased, heart rate, blood pressure, and systemic vascular resistance decreased, and cardiac output and arteriovenous oxygen difference did not change significantly.

Sidney & Shephard (1978) studied men and women aged 60–83 in an exercise program held four times per week. Subjects were assigned to frequency and intensity categories based on attendance and exercise heartrates. After 7 weeks of exercise, the low frequency/low intensity group had lower maximum VO2 (ml/kg/min) than the other three groups. Maximum VO2 increased significantly in the other groups, with the greatest improvement in the high frequency/high intensity group. In the following seven weeks, the two high intensity groups did not change significantly but the high frequency/low intensity group improved significantly in maximum VO2 (ml/kg/min). Twenty-two subjects who completed a year of training increased 24 percent in maximum VO2, and most of the improvement occurred during the first seven weeks.

Respiratory

Total lung capacity does not change appreciably with age, but vital capacity declines 40–50 percent and residual volume correspondingly increases 30–50 percent between the ages of 30 and 70. Changes in the lung tissue decrease the availability of oxygen to the cardiovascular system. The lung exhibits decreased elasticity in the average older adult, resulting in a decrease in the capacity to expire and an increased residual volume. The total surface area of the lung decreases 25–30 percent between 30 and 70 years. This in conjunction with and other alterations in the thorax result in decreased Pa02.

Conclusion

The benefits of physical activity programming for the older adult are clear. Proper programming must be devised that avoids injury and is based upon an understanding of the needs and limitations of the individual and group participants. The general declines with age provide only rough guidelines. Assessment of physical capabilities and of the goals of the individual is necessary to design appropriate physical activity programs for older adults. Two older adults of the same age can vary widely in their fitness. One 65 year old may still be participating in Master's races, while another is a resident of a nursing home. No one program will be appropriate for both these people. The first priority for exercise programs for sedentary older adults is to achieve and maintain fitness sufficient to perform the activities of daily living independently. Morse & Smith (1981) reported that maximum work capacity in 24 subjects over age 75 was less than 10 ml/ kg/min. This means that subjects would be at their maximum capacity simply walking at about 2.5 mph.

Bibliography

Adams, G.M. & deVries, H.A. (1973). Physiological effects of an exercise training regimen upon women aged 52 to 79. *Journal of Gerontology, 28*, pp. 50–55.

Agre, J.C., Smith, E.L., Pierce, L.E., McAdam, M., & Raab, D.M. (1988). Light resistance and stretching exercise in elderly women: effect upon strength. *Archives of Physical Medicine & Rehabilitation, 69*.

Ahlback, S.O., & Lindahl, O. (1964). Sagittal mobility of the hip joint. *ACTA Orthopedica Scandinavica, 34*, pp. 310–322.

Allander, E., Bjornsson, O.J., Olafsson, O., Sigfusson, N., & Thorsteinsson, J. (1974). Normal range of joint movements in shoulder, hip, wrist and thumb with special reference to side: a comparison between two populations. *International Journal of Epidemiology, 3*, pp. 253–261.

Aloia, J.F., Cohn, S.H., Ostuni, J., Cane, R., & Ellis, K. (1978). Prevention of involutional bone loss by exercise. *Annals of Internal Medicine, 89*, pp. 356–358.

Aniansson, A., & Gustafsson, E. (1981). Physical training in elderly men with special reference to quadriceps muscle strength and morphology. *Clinical Physiology, 1*, pp. 87–98.

Astrand, P.O. & Rodahl, K. (1970). *Textbook of Work Physiology*. New York: McGraw Hill.

Badenhop, D.T., Cleary, P.A., Schaal, S.F., Fox, E.L., & Bartels, R.L. (1983). Physiological adjustments to higher- or lower-intensity exercise in elders. *Medicine and Science in Sports and Exercise, 15(6)*, pp. 496–502.

Baylor, A.M. & Spirduso, W.W. (1988). Systematic aerobic exercise and components of reaction time in older women. *Journal of Gerontology, 43*, pp. 121–126.

Boone, D.C. & Azen, S.P. (1979). Normal range of motion of joints in male subjects. *Journal of Bone and Joint Surgery, 61A*, pp. 756–759.

Borkan, G.A., Hults, D.E., Gerzof, A.F., Robbins, A.H., & Silbert, C.K. (1983). Age changes in body composition revealed by computed tomography. *Journal of Gerontology, 38*, pp. 673–677.

Brown, W.F. (1973). Functional compensation of human motor units in health and disease. *Journal of the Neurological Sciences, 20*, pp. 199–209.

Buccola, V.A. & Stone, W.J. Effects of jogging and cycling programs on physiological and personality variables in aged men. *Research Quarterly, 46(2)*, pp. 134–139.

Buskirk, E.R., & Hodgson, J.L. (1987). Age and aerobic power: the rate of change in men and women. *Federation Proceedings, 46*, pp. 1824–1829.

Buskirk, E.R., & Segal, S.S. (1989). The aging motor system: Skeletal muscle weakness. In W.W. Spirduso & H.M. Eckert (Eds.), *Physical Activity and Aging*. Champaign, IL: Human Kinetics, pp. 19–36.

Campbell, M.J., McComas, A.J., & Petito, F. (1973). Physiological changes in ageing muscles. *Journal of Neurology, Neurosurgery & Psychiatry, 36*, pp. 174–182.

Chapman, E.A., deVries, H.A., & Swezey, R. (1972). Joint stiffness: effects of exercise on young and old men. *Journal of Gerontology, 27*, pp. 218–221.

Chow, R.K., Harrison, J.E., & Notarius, C. (1987). Effect of two randomised exercise programmes on bone mass of healthy postmenopausal women. *British Medical Journal, 292*, pp. 607–610.

Chow, R.K., Harrison, J.E., Sturtbridge, W., Josse, R., Murray, T.M., Bayley, A., Dornan, J., & Hammond, T. (1987). The effect of exercise on bone mass of osteoporotic patients on fluoride treatment. *Clinical and Investigative Medicine, 10*, pp. 59–63.

Cress, M.E. & Schultz, E. Aging muscle: functional, morphologic, biochemical and regenerative capacity. (1985). *Topics in Geriatric Rehabilitaton, 1(1),* pp. 11–19.

Cummings, S.R. (1987). Epidemiology of osteoporotic fractures. In H.K. Genant (Ed.), *Osteoporosis Update 1987.* San Francisco: Radiology Research & Education, pp. 7–12.

Cunningham, D.A., Rechnitzer, P.A., Howard, J.H., & Donner, A.P. (1987). Exercise training of men at retirement: a clinical trial. *Journal of Gerontology, 42,* pp. 17–23.

Dalsky, G.P., Stocke, K.S., Ehsani, A.A., Slatopolsky, E., Lee, W.C., & Birge, S.J. (1988). Weight-bearing exercise training and lumbar bone mineral content in postmenopausal women. *Annals of Internal Medicine, 108,* pp. 824–828.

Davies, C.T.M., White, M.J., & Young, K. (1983). Electrically evoked and voluntary maximal isometric tension in relation to dynamic muscle performance in elderly male subjects, aged 69 years. *European Journal of Applied Physiology, 51,* pp. 37–43.

de Lorme, T.L. & Watkins, A.L. (1951). *Progressive Resistance Exercise.* New York: Appleton Century.

deVries, H.A. (1970). Physiological effects of an exercise training regimen upon men aged 52 to 88. *Journal of Gerontology, 25,* pp. 325–336.

deVries, H.A. (1971). Exercise intensity threshold for improvement of cardiovascular-respiratory function in older men. *Geriatrics, 26,* pp. 94–101.

Dill, D.B., Horvath, S.M., Van Beaumont, W., et al. (1967). Sweat electrolytes in desert walks. *Australian Journal of Sports Medicine, 23,* pp. 746–751.

Drinkwater, B.L., Horvath, S.M., & Wells, C.L. (1975). Aerobic power of females, ages 10 to 68. *Journal of Gerontology, 30(4),* pp. 385–394.

Dustman, R.E., Ruhling, R.O., Russell, E.M., Shearer, D.E., Bonekat, H.W., Shigeoka, J.W., Wood, J.S., & Bradford, C. (1984). Aerobic exercise training and improved neuropsychological function of older adults. *Neurobiology of Aging, 5,* pp. 35–42.

Einkauf, D.K., Gohdes, M.L., Jensen, G.M., & Jewell, M.J. (1987). Changes in spinal mobility with increasing age in women. *Physical Therapy, 67,* pp. 370–375.

Ericsson, P. & Irnell, L. (1969). Effect of five years' ageing on ventilatory capacity and physical work capacity in elderly people. *ACTA Medica Scandinavica, 185,* pp. 193–199.

Fardy, P.S., Maresh, C.M., Abbott, R., & Kristiansen, T. (1976). An assessment of the influence of habitual physical activity, prior sport participation, smoking habits, and aging upon indices of cardiovascular fitness: preliminary report of a cross-sectional and retrospective study. *Journal of Sports Medicine & Physical Fitness Quarterly Review, 16,* pp. 77–90.

Frekany, G.A. & Leslie, D.K. (1975). Effects of an exercise program on selected flexibility measurements of senior citizens. *The Gerontologist, 4,* pp. 182–183.

Germain, N.W. & Blair, S.N. (1983). Variability of shoulder flexion with age, activity and sex. *American Corrective Therapy Journal, 37(6),* pp. 156–160.

Grimby, G., Danneskiold-Samsoe, B., Hvid, K., & Saltin, B. (1982). Morphology and enzymatic capacity in arm and leg muscles in 78–81-year old men and women. *ACTA Physiologica Scandinavica, 115,* pp. 125–134.

Gutman, G.M., Herbert, C.P., & Brown, S.R. (1977). Feldenkrais versus conventional exercises for the elderly. *Journal of Gerontology, 32,* pp. 562–572.

Johns, R.J. & Wright, U. (1962). Relative importance of various tissues in joint stiffness. *Journal of Applied Physiology, 17,* pp. 824–828.

Johnston, C.C. & Slemenda, C. (1987). Osteoporosis—An Overview. *The Physician and Sportsmedicine, 15,* pp. 64–69.

Julius, S., Amery, A., Whitlock, L.S., & Conway, J. (1967). Influence of age on the hemodynamic response to exercise. *Circulation, 36,* pp. 222–230.

Kasch, F.W. (1976). The effects of exercise on the aging process. *Physician & Sportsmedicine, 4(6),* pp. 64–68.

Kasch, F.W., Wallace, J.P., & Van Camp, S.P. (1985). Effects of 18 years of endurance exercise on the physical work capacity of older men. *Journal of Cardiopulmonary Rehabilitation, 5,* pp. 308–312.

Kellgren, J.H. & Lawrence, J.S. (1957). Radiological assessment of osteoarthrosis. *Annals Rheum Dis, 16,* pp. 494–502.

Kelsey, J.L. (1984). Osteoporosis: Prevalence and incidence. In (Ed.), *Osteoporosis: National Institutes of Health Consensus Development Conference, April 2–4, 1984. Program and Abstracts.* Washington, D.C.: NIH, pp. 25–28.

Kiessling, K.H., Pilstrom, L., Bylund, A.C., Saltin, B., & Piehl, K. (1974). Enzyme activities and morphometry in skeletal muscle of middle-aged men after training. *Scandinavian Journal of Clinical & Laboratory Investigation, 33,* pp. 63–69.

Kilbom, A. (1971). Physical training in women. *Scandinavian Journal of Clinical and Laboratory Investigation, 28,* pp. S1–S34.

Krolner, B., Toft, B., Nielson, S.P., & Tondevold, E. (1983). Physical exercise as prophylaxis against involutional vertebral bone loss: a controlled trial. *Clinical Science, 64,* pp. 541–546.

Lakatta, E.G. (1986). Hemodynamic adaptations to stress with advancing age. In P.O. Astrand & G. Grimby (Eds.), *Physical Activity in Health and Disease.* Uppsala, Sweden: Almqvist & Wiksell Tryckeri, pp. 39–52.

Larsson, L. (1978). Morphological and functional characteristics of the aging skeletal muscle in man. *ACTA Physiologica Scandinavia, 457S,* pp. 1–36.

Larsson, L. (1982). Aging in mammalian skeletal muscle. In F.J. Pirozzolo & G.J. Maletta (Eds.), *The Aging Motor System.* New York: Praeger, pp. 60–98.

Larsson, L. (1982b). Physical training effects on muscle morphology in sedentary men at different ages. *Medicine & Science in Sports & Exercise, 14,* pp. 203–206.

Larsson, L., Grimby, G., & Karlsson, J. (1979). Muscle strength and speed of movement in relation to age and muscle morphology. *Journal of Applied Physiology, 46,* pp. 451–456.

Lesser, M. (1978). The effects of rhythmic exercise on the range of motion in older adults. *American Corrective Therapy Journal, 32(4),* pp. 118–122.

Lexell, J., Henriksson-Larsen, K., Winblad, B., & Sjostrom, M. (1983). Distribution of different fiber types in human skeletal muscles: Effects of aging studied in whole muscle cross sections. *Muscle & Nerve, 6,* pp. 588–595.

Makrides, L., Heigenhauser, G.J., McCartney, N., & Jones, N.L. (1985). Maximal short term exercise capacity in healthy subjects aged 15–70 years. *Clinical Science, 69,* pp. 197–205.

Martin, A.D. & Houston, C.S. (1987). Osteoporosis, calcium and physical activity. *Canadian Medical Association Journal, 136,* pp. 587–593.

McCafferty, W.B. & Edington, D.W. (1970). Skeletal muscle and organ weights of aged and trained male rats. *Gerontology, 20,* pp. 44–50.

McDonagh, M.J.N., White, M.J., & Davies, C.T.M. (1984). Different effects of ageing on the mechanical properties of human arm and leg muscles. *Gerontology, 30,* pp. 49–54.

Melton, L.J., Wahner, H.W., Richelson, L.S., & O'Fallon, W.M., & Riggs, B.L. (1986). Osteoporosis and the risk of hip fracture. *American Journal of Epidemiology, 124,* pp. 254–261.

Morse, C.E. & Smith, E.L. (1981). Physical activity programming for the aged. In E.L. Smith & R.C. Serfass (Eds.), *Exercise and Aging: The Scientific Basis.* Hillside, NJ: Enslow, pp. 109–120.

Munns, K. (1981). Effects of exercise on the range of joint motion in elderly subjects. In E.L. Smith & R.C. Serfass (Eds.), *Exercise and Aging: The Scientific Basis.* Hillside, NJ: Enslow, pp. 167–178.

Murray, M.P. (1985). Shoulder motion and muscle strength of normal men and women in two age groups. *Clinical Orthopedics & Related Research, 192,* pp. 268–273.

Murray, M.P., Gardner, G.M., Mollinger, L.A., & Sepic, S.B. (1980). Strength of isometric and isokinetic contractions. Knee muscles of men aged 20 to 86. *Physical Therapy, 60,* pp. 412–419.

Niinimaa, V. & Shephard, R.J. (1978a). Training and oxygen conductance in the elderly. I. The respiratory system. *Journal of Gerontology, 33,* pp. 354–361.

Niinimaa, V. & Shephard, R.J. (1978b) Training and oxygen conductance in the elderly. II. The cardiovascular system. *Journal of Gerontology, 33,* pp. 362–367.

Plowman, S.A., Drinkwater, B.L., & Horvath, S.M. (1979). Age and aerobic power in women: a longitudinal study. *Journal of Gerontology, 34,* pp. 512–520.

Pollock, M.L., Miller, H.S., Janeway, R., Linnerud, A.C., Robertson, B., & Valentino, R. (1971). Effects of walking on body composition and cardiovascular function of middle-aged men. *Journal of Applied Physiology, 30(1),* pp. 126–130.

Raab, D.M., Agre, J.C., McAdam, M., & Smith, E.L. (1988). Light resistance and stretching exercise in elderly women: effect upon flexibility. *Archives of Physical Medicine & Rehabilitation, 69,* pp. 268–272.

Rikli, R. & Busch, S. (1986). Motor performance of women as a function of age and physical activity level. *Journal of Gerontology, 41,* pp. 645–649.

Robinson, S., Dill, D.B., Tzankoff, S.P., Wagner, J.A., & Robinson, R.D. (1975). Longitudinal studies of aging in 37 men. *Journal of Applied Physiology, 38(2),* pp. 263–267.

Roskamm, H. (1967). Optimum patterns of exercise for healthy adults. *Canadian Medical Association Journal, 96,* pp. 895–900.

Schocken, D.D., Blumenthal, J.A., Port, S., Hindle, P., & Coleman, R.E. (1983). Physical conditioning and left ventricular performance in the elderly: assessment by radionuclide angiocardiography. *American Journal of Cardiology, 52,* pp. 359–364.

Scott, W.W. (1984). Osteoporosis-related fracture syndromes. In (Ed.), *Osteoporosis: National Institutes of Health Consensus Development Conference, April 2–4, 1984. Program and Abstracts.* Washington, D.C.: NIH, pp. 20–24.

Seals, D.R., Hagberg, J.M., Hurley, B.J., Ehsani, A.A., & Holloszy, J.O. (1984). Endurance training in older men and women. I. Cardiovascular responses to exercise. *Journal of Applied Physiology, 57(4),* pp. 1024–1029.

Sepic, S.B., Murray, M.P., Mollinger, L.A., Spurr, G.B., & Gardner, G.M. (1986). Strength and range of motion in the ankle in two age groups of men and women. *American Journal of Physical Medicine, 65(2),* pp. 75–84.

Sheffield, L.T., Maloof, J.A., Sawyer, J.A., & Roitman, D. (1978). Maximal heart rate and treadmill performance of healthy women in relation to age. *Circulation, 57(1),* pp. 79–84.

Shephard, R.J. (1987). *Physical Activity and Aging, Second edition.* Rockville, MD: Aspen.

Shock, N.W. (1962). The physiology of aging. *Scientific American, 206,* pp. 100–108.

Siconolfi, S.F., Lasater, T.M., McKinlay, S., Boggia, P., & Carleton, R.A. (1985). Physical fitness and blood pressure: the role of age. *American Journal of Epidemiology, 122,* pp. 452–457.

Sidney, K.H. & Shephard, R.J. (1978). Frequency and intensity of exercise training for elderly subjects. *Medicine & Science in Sports, 10(2),* pp. 125–131.

Simkin, A., Ayalon, J., & Leichter, I. (1986). Increased trabecular bone density due to bone-loading exercises in postmenopausal osteoporotic women. *Calcified Tissue International, 40,* pp. 59–63.

Smith, E.L. & Gilligan, C. Health related fitness of the older adult. In T.F. Drury (Ed.), *Assessing Physical Fitness and Activity in General Population Studies.* Washington, D.C.: NCHS, in press (a).

Smith, E.L. & Gilligan C. Exercise and bone remodelling. In W.A. Peck (Ed.), *Bone and Mineral Research/ 6.* Amsterdam: Elsevier, in press (b).

Smith, E.L., Gilligan, C., Shea, M.M., Ensign, C.P., & Smith, P.E. Exercise reduces bone involution in middle-aged women. *Calcified Tissue International,* in press.

Smith, E.L., Reddan, W., & Smith, P.E. (1981). Physical activity and calcium modalities for bone mineral increase in aged women. *Medicine and Science in Sports and Exercise, 13,* pp. 60–64.

Smith, E.L. & Serfass, R.C. (1981). *Exercise and Aging: The Scientific Basis.* Hillside, NJ: Enslow.

Smith, J. & Walker, J.M. (1983). Knee and elbow range of motion in healthy older individuals. *Physical & Occupational Therapy in Geriatrics, 2,* pp. 31–38.

Sorock, G.S., Bush, T.L., Golden, A.L., Fried, L.P., Breuer, B., & Hale, W.E. (1988). Physical activity and fracture risk in a free-living elderly cohort. *Journal of Gerontology, 43,* pp. M134–M139.

Sperling, L. (1980). Evaluation of upper extremity function in 70-year-old males and females. *Scandinavian Journal of Rehabilitative Medicine, 12,* pp. 139–144.

Spirduso, W.W. (1975). Reaction and movement time as a function of age and physical activity level. *Journal of Gerontology, 30,* pp. 435–440.

Spirduso, W.W. & Eckert, H.M. (1989). *Physical activity and aging.* Champaign, IL: Human Kinetics.

Spirduso, W.W. & Farrar, R.P. (1981). Effects of aerobic training on reactive capacity: an animal model. *Journal of Gerontology, 35,* pp. 654–662.

Steen, B. (1988). Body composition in aging. *Nutrition Reviews, 46,* pp. 45–51.

Suominen, H., Heikkinen, E., Liesen, H., Michel, D., & Hollman, W. (1977a). Effects of 8 weeks endurance training on skeletal muscle metabolism in 56–70 year old sedentary men. *European Journal of Applied Physiology, 37,* pp. 173–180.

Suominen, H., Heikkinen, E., & Parkatti, T. (1977b). Effects of eight weeks' physical training on muscle and connective tissue of the m. vastus lateralis in 69-year-old men and women. J. *Journal of Gerontology, 32,* pp. 33–37.

Thomas, S.G., Cunningham, D.A., Rechnitzer, P.A., Donner, A.P., & Howard, J.H. (1985). Determinants of the training response in elderly men. *Medicine & Science in Sports & Exercise, 17,* pp. 667–672.

Topics in Geriatric Rehabilitation, 1985, 1.

Tzankoff, S.P. & Norris, A.H. (1977). Effect of muscle mass decrease on age-related BMR changes. *Journal of Applied Physiology, 43,* pp. 1001–1006.

Tzankoff, S.P., Robinson, S., Pyke, F.S., & Brawn, C.A. (1972). Physiological adjustments to work in older men as affected by physical training. *Journal of Applied Physiology, 33,* pp. 346–350.

Walker, J.M. (1984). Active Mobility of the extremities in older subjects. *Physical Therapy, 64(6),* pp. 919–923.

White, M.K., Martin, R.B., Yeater, R.A., Butcher, R.L., & Radin, E.I. (1984). The effects of exercise on the bones of postmenopausal women. *International Orthopaedics, 7,* pp. 209–214.

Wilmore, J.H., Royce, J., Girandola, R., Katch, F., & Katch, V. (1970). Physiological alterations resulting from a 10-week program of jogging. *Medicine & Science in Sports, 2,* pp. 7–14.

Young, A., Stokes, M., & Crowe, M. (1984). Size and strength of the quadriceps muscles of old and young women. *European Journal of Clinical Investigation, 14,* pp. 282–287.

4 Motor Skill Learning in Older Adults

Kathleen M. Haywood, University of Missouri

It is unfortunate that the familiar saying "you can't teach an old dog new tricks" summarizes the widely held opinion of learning in older adulthood. While there is evidence that many aspects of the learning process do change from younger to older adulthood, there are also countless examples of older adults learning new motor skills and learning them well (Figure 4.1). The real issue is not whether older adults can learn new motor skills, because they most assuredly can. Rather, the issue is what aspects of the learning process change over adulthood, how they change, and how the learning environment should be structured to accommodate these changes and maximize learning. The latter is the responsibility of those who instruct and program activities for older adults (see Environmental and Instructional Considerations).

The amount of research on motor skill learning in older adulthood is limited but increasing. There has been more research on the learning of ideas and verbal materials than skills. Fortunately, some of this research can be applied to motor learning, simply because some aspects of the learning process do not differ between conceptual learning and motor learning. Particularly when direct information on motor learning is lacking, research on conceptual learning can aid our understanding of the learning process in older adulthood.

A Model

Learning is a complex and multifaceted process. When reviewing aspects of such a complex process it is helpful to have the equivalent of a road map. Motor learning theorists provide such an aid in the form of "information processing models" of human performance. That is, they

FIGURE 4.1. Redeye mistakenly believed the old saying. Reprinted with permission of King Features, New York, New York. © King Features Syndicate, Inc.

map out the manner in which they believe information from the environment is processed by performers in order to produce skilled, knowledgeable responses. The capacity to process information relates to the rate of skill learning (Marteniuk, 1976). Many versions of information processing models exist and they all have their limitations. A simple version will be used here to guide this review of the motor learning process in older adults (Figure 4.2).

The information processing model depicts functions which fall into three areas: perceptual mechanisms, central mechanisms, and effector or motor mechanisms. That is, information from the environment must be perceived, then analyzed, before one selects and executes the appropriate motor response. For this reason, topics such as visual perception and memory are part of the motor learning process. The model also depicts a fourth area of the learning process— feedback. A performer makes use of results of one performance to refine subsequent responses, that is, to learn the appropriate response with practice. Hence, one can see from just a brief review of the model that many aspects of learning must be examined to obtain a total picture of aging and skill learning.

This review of the motor learning process in older adults begins with perceptual mechanisms. The aspects of perception most involved in skilled performance are vision, kinesthesis (body awareness), and audition (hearing). A discussion of the central and effector mechanisms and feedback follows. Additional information and examples are given in "The Learning Environment and Instructional Considerations," Chapter 7.

Perception

The performers of motor skills must have certain information in order to make a response. People, objects, and events in the environment must be sensed and perceived. Sensation involves the functioning of sensory receptors, such as the eye, and the transmittal of nerve signals to the

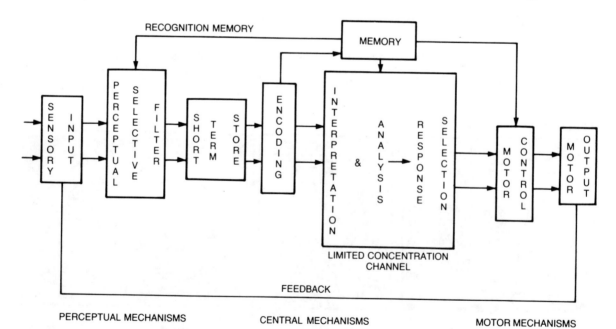

FIGURE 4.2. An Information Processing Model for Skill Performance.

brain. Perception involves the selection, processing, and organization of that neural information, and its integration across the sensory systems. A deficit in either sensation or perception could hinder performance, so age-related changes in both the sensory system and the perceptual process must be considered. Much of the information needed for motor performance comes through vision. It is the first perceptual system discussed here.

Vision

With advancing age there are changes that occur naturally in the visual system and there are conditions or diseases which become more prevalent in older adulthood. A natural change familiar to most adults is *presbyopia,* the inability to clearly focus on nearby objects. This difficulty becomes clinically significant after age 40 and worsens until age 65. Presbyopia is corrected by the prescription of reading glasses or bifocals.

Bifocals can present several difficulties for active adults. For example, a tennis player may have to exaggerate head movements to keep the ball in view through the upper lens. Objects noticed first through the upper lens then viewed through the lower lens appear to "jump!" Many adults do not realize that they can request a smaller lower lens and lower bifocal line if they participate in activities such as tennis. "No line" bifocals are available, but peripheral vision is often distorted by these lenses. Too, some adults are now purchasing monovision contact lenses; one contact for near vision, and one contact for distance vision. Binocular depth perception information suffers with these contact lenses, making them a poor choice for active adults. Activity leaders should discuss with their program participants the type of prescription they wear, particularly if they notice someone using exaggerated head positions or movements.

The incidence of poor visual acuity (sharpness of sight) rises with older age (U.S. National Health Survey, 1968). Such evidence stresses the importance of both periodic visual examination and the use of a lens prescription during sport participation. Visual acuity of 20/50 or below in the best eye after correction is enough that some states impose driving restrictions on affected people. Skill performance would be affected, too, so that wearing prescribed lenses for activities is important, even if sometimes uncomfortable. Evidence exists that the ability to see *moving* objects sharply (dynamic visual acuity) declines in older adulthood. As objects move faster, seeing them clearly is more difficult for all. Moreover, Reading (1972) found that a group in their 40s had more difficulty seeing faster moving objects than a group in their 20s. Activity leaders should be aware that older adults can have difficulty seeing fast-moving objects clearly and that those who need glasses, but do not wear them, exaggerate this difficulty.

Another natural change in the eye is *senile miosis,* a reduction in the resting diameter of the eye's pupil, resulting in diminished retinal illuminance. This means less light reaches the retina. Retinal illuminance decreases during adulthood—a 60-year-old has about one-third the illumination of a 20-year-old (Weale, 1961)—until the loss plateaus between 70 and 80 years of age. As a result of decreased retinal illuminance older adults can have difficulty working and performing in dimly lit conditions. Activity leaders should provide well lit activity settings for older adults whenever possible and avoid scheduling activities at dusk without additional lighting.

Senile miosis and a natural *yellowing* of the eye's lens also increase the visual disability caused by glare (Reading, 1968). Glare is a dazzling sensation of bright light which can reduce optimal vision. Light intensities unnoticed by younger adults can significantly affect older observers. Glare is most common around bodies of water and activity leaders in such settings should be aware of the problems glare can cause for older adults. Leaders might suggest that older adults who frequent these settings obtain a pair of polarizing sunglasses in their prescription.

Older adults find it difficult to *adapt to dark* environments after previous exposure to light. This might reflect a slower *rate* of dark adaptation (Birren & Shock, 1950; Domey, McFarland, & Chadwick, 1960; McFarland, Domey, Warren, & Ward, 1960), although smaller pupil diameter (miosis) and yellowing of the lens undoubtedly contribute to this condition. Additional time should be provided for older adults to adapt when changing lighting conditions.

Age-related changes in *contrast sensitivity* have received recent attention. Contrast sensitivity is one's ability to resolve spatial structures, varying from fine to coarse, at various levels of contrast. An example is the differentiation of faces in various conditions of contrast. Research documents a loss in contrast sensitivity by older adults at the intermediate and fine end of the continuum (Arundale, 1978; Derefeldt, Lennerstrand, & Lundh, 1979; Kline, Schieber, Abusamra, & Coyne, 1983; Sekuler, Owsley, & Hutmann, 1983). This loss is probably attributable to decreased retinal illuminance. Hence, older adults have more difficulty differentiating faces at low contrast. While the research on contrast sensitivity to date involves only stationary displays, activity leaders do well to accentuate contrasts in settings with movement for older adults (Owsley, Sekuler, & Boldt, 1981). For example, attempting to hit a white badminton bird approaching from a white background wall is even more difficult for older adults than young adults!

Peripheral vision is important in many physical activities, including driving, where movement in the periphery must be detected and the position of objects or people monitored. Shrinkage of the peripheral field of vision starts as early as 35 to 40 years of age (Burg, 1968), but is very gradual until age 60 (Wolf & Nadroski, 1971). Older adults can compensate for this loss by moving their heads more extensively than required in the younger years.

Color vision plays a limited role in activity performance, but changes in color vision can be an early symptom of some diseases. It is natural for older adults to have increased difficulty discriminating blues from blue-greens, pastel violets from yellow-greens, and pale yellows from whites (Gilbert, 1957). These difficulties are probably because of yellowing of the lens and reduced light reaching the retina (Ruddock, 1965). Activity leaders who recognize more extensive losses of color vision in an older adult might recommend a check-up by an eye care professional.

Besides these changes in visual sensation, several types of visual perception show age-related changes. One is the ability to perceive *depth,* an important aspect of activities that involve interception of balls or throwing to a target. The ability to discriminate depth declines starting at 40 to 50 years of age (Bell, Wolf, & Bernholz, 1972; Jani, 1966). Those with good visual acuity or vision corrected by prescription lenses might well retain good depth perception (Hofstetter & Bertsch, 1976).

The ability to perceive a *figure* amidst a complex *background* is more difficult in middle and older age than in the younger years (Lee & Pollack, 1978, 1980; Pollack, 1983; Stanford & Pollack, 1984). Moreover, the more complex the figure, that is, the object of attention, the more difficult the task for older adults. Most sport skills involve simple figures, usually balls, so that complexity of the figure may not be a factor. On the other hand, the background could be very complex and moving, and older adults are likely to take longer to locate the object in a complex background. Older adults benefit from a learning environment wherein the background is simplified.

Beyond natural changes in vision, some pathologic conditions become more prevalent with advancing age. Examples are cataracts, glaucoma, diabetes, and age-related maculopathy, a disease affecting the retinal area for fine, detailed (central) vision. The effect of any such pathological condition on skill performance must be considered on an individual basis.

Activity leaders can watch for signs that older adults are having difficulty with their vision. For example, a lack of coordination in hand-eye tasks can indicate possible visual problems. Table 4.1 summarizes many symptoms of visual difficulties common in older adults and provides suggestions for improving the problem. Activity leaders should encourage older adults to wear any corrective lenses prescribed for them while participating in activities (Haywood & Trick, 1983).

Instructors should provide the best learning and performance environment possible for older adults. Often, simple changes in the environment can greatly improve the quality of the experience for older adults. Table 4.2 summarizes suggestions for improving the learning environment, based on age-related changes in vision, and other perceptual systems discussed later. A discussion of the major changes in vision and visual perception with aging can give the impression of hopeless declines. Yet, the visual system functions well for most adults, especially with the aid of prescription lenses. Experience in activities also helps to compensate for slight declines in visual functioning. Accurate predictions about the environment, such as the flight or bounce of a ball, are still possible. The instructor also can use specific teaching methods that offset some of the visual difficulties common to older adults. Examples of these appear in Table 4.3.

Kinesthesis

The kinesthetic system provides information about the position of the body in space, the position of the body parts relative to each other, and the nature of objects touched. It also provides an awareness of body movement and balance. This information comes from a variety of sensory receptors located throughout the body: muscle spindles located among the muscle cells; Golgi tendon organs positioned at the muscle-tendon junctions; joint receptors located in the joint capsules or ligaments; cutaneous receptors in the skin; and the vestibular semi-circular canals, saccule, and utricle in the inner ear. Unlike our knowledge of the eye, very little is known about

TABLE 4.1
Symptoms of Visual Difficulties in Older Adults in Activity Settings

Symptom	Suggestion	Rationale
Unusual heading positioning Unusual line of gaze	Use glasses with small bifocal segment	Moving objects "jump" across lens
Poor hand-eye coordination Over- or under-reaching	Have visual acuity checked Wear prescribed glasses If using monovision contact lenses, switch to another system for activity	Good binocular depth cues not available
Squinting, discomfort	Use polarizing sunglasses	Increased effects of glare
Tunnel vision "Foggy" vision	See eye care professional	Retinal maculopathy Cataract
Objects in peripheral vision are misjudged when wearing "no line" bifocals	Switch to another corrective system for activity	No line bifocals often distort peripheral vision

TABLE 4.2
Suggestions for Structuring the Learning Environment for Older Adults

Environmental Change	Contributing Aspect of Aging
Provide good indoor lighting Avoid outdoor activities at dawn and dusk	Senile miosis
Reduce glare	Yellowing of eye's lens
Accentuate contrasts	Contrast sensitivity
Simplify backgrounds	Figure-ground perception
Eliminate slippery surfaces Increase traction Provide additional handrails Encourage use of shoes with good traction	Balance
Reduce background noise	Auditory perception
Reduce distractions	Selective attention
Adapt equipment Large tennis balls Higher volleyball net	Slowed central processing
Shorten distances, as in laying out fields and courts	Reduced force production

TABLE 4.3
Teaching Methods Helpful to Older Adults

Teaching Method or Practice	Rationale
Allow extra time before activity when changing lighting conditions	Slower dark adaptation
Use frequent reminders to attend to feel of a movement	Slight decline in kinesthetic discrimination
Allow self-guided practice after instructor's manual guidance	Increased error in judging passive movement
Face participants and stand close to them	Decline in auditory perception
Make frequent references to previous experience and instruction	Slowed associations to memories
Allow additional time between practice repetitions	Slowed speed of memory processes and response preparation
Give frequent emphasis to cues important to performance	Decline in selective attention
Allow extra time after providing feedback	Slowed speed of processing feedback
Avoid pressure to be speedy, if possible	Slowed central processing
Correct errors early	Persistance of early errors
Provide extra encouragement	Self doubt
Use discovery learning	Allows self-pacing
Use videotaped demonstrations repetitously or in slow motion	Slower assimilation of rapid actions

the way aging affects the kinesthetic receptors themselves. On the other hand, some age-related changes in the kinesthetic perceptual process are known.

Sensitivity to touch (Jalavisto, Orma, & Tarvist, 1951), vibration (Cosh, 1953), temperature, and pain (Schludermann & Zubek, 1962) decrease with advancing age. That is, the stimulation must be more intense before older adults detect it (Kenshalo, 1977). The impairment, though, seems to occur in only a portion of older adults. For example, Howell (1949) tested 200 men between 65 and 91 years of age to find that 24 percent had some type of impaired cutaneous sensitivity. Loss was more common in those over 80 years of age. This research indicates that the *frequency* of impairment in cutaneous sensitivity increases with aging, but not all older adults experience impaired function in the cutaneous system.

More complex kinesthetic perceptions involve the integration of kinesthetic information from two or more body areas. The accuracy of these perceptual integrations also declines in older adults. For example, older adults have failed to note touches to their skin when they receive touches on the face simultaneously (Bender, Fink, & Green, 1952; Bender & Green, 1952). They have more difficulty distinguishing one touch from two nearby touches on their fingers and toes, and they have more difficulty identifying by touch various geometric forms embedded in a complex form (Axelrod & Cohen, 1961). Activity leaders should be ready to remind older adults to feel for and attend to kinesthetic cues pertinent to the task at hand.

Investigators rarely study the perception of passive and active movement in older adults. The few studies conducted to date yield conflicting results. For example, Howell (1949) found no decline on tests of passive movement (being moved by something or someone else) in older adults. Yet, Laidlaw and Hamilton (1937) recorded increased errors in judging the direction of passive lower limb (but not upper limb) movement. Howell additionally found that only 4 percent of older adults could not make an accurate, active movement of their hand to their nose when blindfolded. Landahl & Birren (1959) found that older adults maintain their accuracy in judging the muscle tensions produced by holding various weights. As with younger adults, instructors should be certain that older adults use active rather than passive movements to practice for a task that is active. This is true even if the instructor first moves the performer passively (uses manual guidance) to illustrate the proper movement.

Decrements in kinesthetic perception can be variable among older adults. That is, many adults demonstrate little if any deficit, while others demonstrate deficits of variable types and degree. Activity instructors might need to assist individual adults by focusing their attention on kinesthetic information, that is, the "feel" of the movement. Guiding movements could be helpful initially, but participants must then be given adequate practice making the movement on their own, without guidance.

Balance. The ability to balance declines with advancing age. This is shown by the increased incidence of falls among older adults. In experimental studies, Sheldon (1963) first documented that older adults sway more than the young in a quiet stance. Hasselkus and Shambes (1975) noted that placing older adults in a "forward lean" position greatly affected postural sway, although the adults improved with practice.

Woollacott, Shumway-Cook, and Nashner (1982) attempted to identify the aspects of postural control which contribute to instability in older age. Their experimental work was done with a platform apparatus that throws subjects slightly off balance. They then recorded body sway and electrical activity from the leg muscles' automatic responses to this disturbance in balance. The greatest changes among older adults, compared with younger counterparts, involved vestibular control, followed by changes in postural adjustment. The latter included changes in the timing of muscle activation and greater variability in the delay before muscle response. These changes become significant, that is, lead to falls, when older adults are on an unstable support surface. On a stable surface, older adults can adapt to changing balance conditions, especially when given the opportunity to practice. The integration of sensory cues from different sources is well maintained. However, older adults are less able to respond in time—to regain their balance—on slippery, unstable surfaces.

Although more extensive research on balance in older adults would be useful, several things are clear. Older adults without pathological conditions and with adequate practice experience few balance decrements on stable surfaces. However, slippery or unstable surfaces pose a problem. Older adults apparently cannot regain their balance quickly enough to prevent a fall when they slip. The fear of falling can hamper participation in some activities. Directors of programs for older adults must be particularly watchful for slippery conditions and instructors might need to provide physical support and encouragement for those who fear falling. Adequate practice can help older adults build confidence in their ability to meet the demands of sport and dance skills.

Audition

Several decrements in the hearing sensation of older adults are known. The threshold for hearing pure tones and speech rises in older adults, although the greatest loss is for sounds higher than those used in speech (Corso, 1977; Konig, 1957; Spoor, 1967). The differential thresholds for discriminating pitch and speech also rise. That is, the ability to distinguish similar sounds worsens (Corso, 1977; Pestalozza & Shore, 1955). The incidence of loss in hearing sensitivity also rises in older adulthood. The cause of this loss might well be lifelong exposure to environmental noise, rather than physiologic degeneration. Older adults living in nonnoisy environments demonstrate a hearing loss similar to young adults in an industrialized area (Rosen, Plester, Elmofty, & Rosen, 1964; Timiras, 1972).

Little is known about age-related changes in auditory perception. Weiss (1963) studied the perception of "click" sounds among age groups, based on each individual's threshold. There was no performance difference among healthy participants of various ages. However, older adults with health problems performed more poorly, indicating that central factors might be involved in functional hearing loss.

It is obvious that changes in auditory sensation place older adults at a disadvantage in adverse listening conditions. Auditory perceptions are then more difficult. Auditory *figure-and-ground* perception involves separating one kind of sound or speech from background noise, such as listening to someone on the telephone while the television is on. Age-related changes in hearing, including increased differential thresholds for speech discrimination, can contribute to difficulty in perceiving an auditory "figure" amidst background noise. Instructors should remember that older adults might not understand them in the same settings where young people can hear well. Additional efforts to reduce background noise, to face participants, or position oneself closer to them will be helpful to the older adult.

Summary

Usually, more is known about the age-related changes in various sensory systems than in their perceptual counterparts. Those changes known to accompany aging in the typical adult are minor and often can be offset in planning the instructional setting. Examples include the provision of adequate lighting and elimination of unnecessary background noise. Hence, the sensory and perceptual processes do not necessarily handicap the older adult in the acquisition and performance of skills. Also, the incidence of many pathological conditions rises in old age. Such conditions have variable effects on skill performance. Hence, the instructor of older adults can expect more variation among older class members in sensory and perceptual deficits than among the young. Each individual with such a deficit will require a unique adaptation or provision in the instructional setting to achieve their potential.

Central Mechanisms

The information processing model pictures several functions carried out within the central nervous system. Those objects and people pertinent to the task at hand require attention while irrelevant features must be ignored. The present setting is compared to memories of previous experiences. Projections might be made on where moving objects will be. Finally, the performer decides how and when to act and the brain triggers appropriate neural impulses. Any declines in these functions could jeopardize the accuracy or speed of a motor response, and thus learning of a new skill. Following is a review of age-related changes in the central mechanisms investigated to date.

Selective Filtering and Attention

Accurate and speedy motor responses require the performer to attend only to environmental information pertinent to the task and to ignore irrelevant information. There is some evidence that the performance limitations of older adults involve attention. For example, Birren (1964) asked older adults to perform a reaction time task under two conditions. In one condition they were given a warning signal at a fixed interval before onset of the stimulus. In the other, the warning came at variable times before the stimulus. The fixed interval yielded the fastest performance, presumably because there was less opportunity to be distracted, although this effect reverses if the interval is very long (Strauss, Wagman, & Quaid, 1983).

Older adults are disproportionately distracted by irrelevant information, too. Rabbitt (1965) asked older adults to sort a deck of cards based on letters printed on the card. With irrelevant information placed on the card, the performance of the older adults suffered more than that of younger adults. The same held true when Rabbitt asked the older adults to say the ink color used to print the name of a conflicting color ("red" printed in green; Comalli, 1965; Comalli, Wapner, & Werner, 1962; Schonfield & Trueman, 1974). Considering this, instructors should simplify the context of the motor learning environment for older adults.

Studies of cognitive task performance show that dividing the attention of older adults is detrimental, especially if information is visual in nature (Broadbent & Heron, 1962; Broadbent & Gregory, 1965; Talland, 1962). For example, older adults do well at pressing the button below each of 12 display lights as they come on in random series. But, when they must press the key below the previous light, they perform at a level well below a young group. The age decrement becomes more severe as subjects must press the button two or three back from the present light (Kirchner, 1958).

Reducing irrelevant information in the learning environment benefits older adults. It is also helpful for instructors to remind older adults of the relevant environmental cues (such as, "watch for the spin on the ball").

Memory

Older adults can generally recall less information than younger adults (Craik, 1977) but not all aspects of memory decline. For example, adults maintain their memory span (the number of items that can be remembered over a short time) at least until their 60s (Welford, 1980). Memory storage space apparently is not deficient in older adults (Smith, 1980). In contrast, encoding, wherein information is coded for memory storage, is characteristically deficient in older age (Salthouse & Somberg, 1982; Park, Puglisi, & Sovacool, 1984). It is also possible that memory deficits result from slower processing of information. Older adults rehearse information (as a way to remember it) more slowly than younger adults (Salthouse, 1980) and retrieve information from memory more slowly (Craik, 1977). There is no evidence to support the popular notion that older adults remember remote events, as from childhood, better than recent events (Warrington & Sanders, 1971).

There is a need for more extensive memory research, but in the meantime, instructors can use several logical adaptations in teaching older adults. Because of the deficits in speed of processing, allow older adults more time between repetitions of a movement in order for them to place information into memory. Reminders ("remember that . . .") during repetitious practice can speed associations to information held in memory. Also, these associations should be limited in number since presenting too many tends to cause age-associated slowing (Salthouse & Somberg, 1982).

Response Choice and Preparation

After perception and assessment of the task at hand, a response must be chosen, prepared (what muscle units are to contract and when), and triggered. This aspect of information processing had been an elusive one for study, but researchers have made recent progress by using a time-accuracy trade-off procedure. Salthouse & Somberg (1982) applied this method in testing young and old adults. The participants performed a choice reaction time task (make one response to one stimulus, but another to another stimulus), but within successively decreasing then increasing time spans. Older adults required more time before their accuracy reached a level above chance, but their rate of improvement was the same as that of young adults. This suggests that aging does not affect the rate of information extraction regarding the decision to respond. Rather, aging affects the speed of response preparation, or integration of the information, or both. Allowing older adults extra time between turns of a skill is a helpful way to compensate.

It is also possible that practice or training improves older adult response selection. Clark, Lanphear, & Riddick (1987) tested older adults on a two-choice reaction time task at two levels of compatibility between the response movement and the stimulus. Half the adults practiced by playing videogames for seven weeks. They were significantly faster than the nonpracticers, especially at the low compatibility level, in a repeat testing. Hence, their response selection improved.

The investigations of reaction time in older adults are numerous. The reaction time is that time period between onset of a signal and beginning of a response movement. Most of the time period is taken up by central processes rather than peripheral ones. Simple reaction time, using one signal and one response, is known to slow with aging over the adult years (see Welford, 1977a, 1977b for a summary). The slowing exists in all sensory systems and lack of motivation cannot account for it. Central mechanisms are most likely the major aspects of this slowing, rather than peripheral ones (Welford, 1977a, 1977b).

Choice reaction time studies are also numerous. Here, an investigator presents one of several signals, each matched with a different response. The central processes required in such a task are more complex and the length of the choice reaction time increases over the simple case. Choice reaction time also slows with age. Moreover, the slowing is a little greater than that in simple reaction time. Choice reaction time tasks can become complex if they involve spatial transpositions of the response and signal or symbolic translations. When older adults perform such complex tasks, their times lengthen disproportionately compared with the young (Welford, 1977a, 1977b; Cerella, Poon, & Williams, 1980). The increased time for older adults to respond involves both lengthened perceptual processing and lengthened time to choose the response (Naylor, 1973; Simon & Pouraghabagher, 1978).

Several studies suggest that age-related slowing is far less dramatic in older adults maintaining an active lifestyle than in their sedentary peers. Spirduso (1975) found that active older men were not significantly slower than younger men in a simple reaction time task. Inactive older men, in contrast, were much slower. The active older men were slower than the younger men on a choice reaction task, but not nearly as slow as the inactive older men. Rikli and Busch (1986) obtained similar results with older women (see also Spirduso, 1980). A full explanation of the effects of activity level on reaction time must await further, longitudinal study. Yet, the findings suggest that exercise may influence the function or production of neurotransmitters within the brain (Spirduso, Gilliam, & Wilcox, 1984) or the oxygen level in the brain (Birren, Woods, & Williams, 1980; Shephard & Kavanaugh, 1978). If so, exercise could also have a positive effect on the maintenance of psychomotor tasks other than reaction time.

The case is also quite different on motor tasks which do not require the fastest response possible. Older adults challenged to match movements to a stimulus without the demand of speed, perform at a level similar to young adults. They maintain repetitive movements, such as alternately tapping two targets a short distance apart (Welford, Norris, & Shock, 1969). Older adults can accurately steer a ballpoint pen along a track at slow track speeds. It is only at faster speeds that performance deteriorates (Welford, 1958). In a longitudinal study, Haywood (in press) found that older adults improved, then maintained, performance on a motor task requiring accurate anticipation after their initial exposure to the task. Hence the greatest age-related change in response choice and preparation centers on change in the *speed* of these processes rather than their execution. Older adults will perform motor tasks at a more proficient level if not pressured to be speedy.

In continuous tasks, performers must respond continually over a span of time. Young adults are able to overlap the time required to relate responses to a signal and the time required to execute the response. Older adults seem less able to do this (Welford, 1980; Rabbitt & Rogers, 1965) because they must monitor their movements more closely than the young. This is manifest in tasks requiring the coordination of the limbs. For example, Talland (1962) asked older adults to work a manual counter in one hand and transfer beads with tweezers with the other. The time required to complete these tasks together rose significantly between participants in their 20s and those in their 60s, in contrast to the time needed to perform them separately. The extra time taken was presumably that needed to monitor the movements separately. That is, older adults had difficulty performing the two tasks as a coordinated whole.

Summary

Obviously, aging affects the speed of central processing. When motor performance is not under the pressure of time, older adults can perform quite accurately. Scholars offer several theoretical explanations of this slowing, but the favored viewpoint attributes slowing to a lower signal-to-noise ratio in the central nervous system. That is, neural signals move within the central nervous system against a background of random, neural "noise." If the signal-to-noise ratio is low, the signal (neural impulse of importance) loses clarity and errors rise. Signal levels might fall with aging because of a loss in brain cells or cardiovascular deficiencies, while noise levels tend to rise (Crossman & Szafran, 1956; Gregory, 1974). Older adults, however, can compensate for low signal-to-noise ratios by taking more time with a task to let signal strength accumulate.

Changes in central mechanisms imply that older adults do not perform motor tasks demanding quick decisions and responses as well as those tasks allowing more time or self-pacing, when compared with young adult levels. This does not mean that groups of older adults would not enjoy learning or perfecting skills involving speedy responses. Rather than dismissing those activities traditionally demanding fast responses, activity leaders might well modify those activities for older adults. For example, the larger tennis balls now available are slower and allow players more time to reach oncoming shots and prepare their stroke. A higher volleyball net dictates more arced, slower returns, and so on. Also, many older adults find self-paced tasks, such as bowling and archery, the more enjoyable ones.

Instructional plans for older adults should feature adequate time between practice turns and simplification of the setting to avoid distractions. Identification of the important features in the task and frequent reminders will also assist the older learner.

Motor Mechanisms

After perception of environmental conditions, comparison to information stored in memory, and planning of an appropriate response, the response must be executed. Aging could affect transmission of nerve impulses from the brain to the muscles, muscle contraction, and movement of the limbs. An examination of each of these topics is warranted.

Nerve conduction speed is a basic consideration in the aging of motor mechanisms. Any loss of speed in conducting nerve impulses to the muscles results in the general slowing of motor responses. As discussed earlier, the minimum reaction time to a stimulus slows with aging. Also, the maximum speed of movement is known to decline around 90 percent over the span from the 20s to the 60s (Pierson & Montoye, 1958). However, the slowing of nerve conduction with aging is only about 4 ms per meter of nerve. It thus accounts for a very small portion of the slowing in motor response (Norris, Shock, & Wagman, 1953; Birren & Botwinick, 1955). Slowing then is attributable in the largest part to central mechanisms, as discussed earlier. Wagman and Lesse (1952) did note a more significant decrease in nerve conduction speed in those 60 to 82 years of age. In very old age, then, additional slowing due to nerve conduction speed is possible and warrants continued research.

There is some evidence that slowing of motor mechanisms occurs. Spirduso (1975) also recorded movement time in her study (mentioned earlier) of age and activity level. The active older men were slightly slower than active young men, but faster than inactive young men. They were much faster than inactive older men. The similarity of these results to those for reaction time suggests that the source of slowing might be both central and peripheral (motor) processes. Rich (1988) fractionated reaction time into premotor (stimulus onset to appearance of muscle action potential) and motor (muscle action potential to overt movement) times in testing adults. She also used resistance to the response on some trials of the task. Motor time and total motor time both slowed with advancing age on the *resisted* trials. These results also suggest that slowing occurs in motor mechanisms.

A loss of muscle units, especially of fast twitch fibers used for rapid movements, and higher thresholds for neural excitation of muscle accompanies aging (Frolkis, Martynenko, & Zamostyan, 1976; Gutman & Hanzlikova, 1976; Larsson, Sjodin, & Karlsson, 1978). These changes result in a loss of 15 to 35 percent in the maximum, instantaneous force an older adult can exert (see Welford, 1982 for a summary). Hence, the performance of older adults will reflect this loss, especially in activities where maximum force production is desirable. There is also an indication from one research study that the large neurons innervating the muscles may degenerate after age 60 (McComas, Upton, & Sica, 1973).

It is likely that stiffness of the joints or reduced mobility in the joints affects motor performance. Older adults would need to account for this in planning a movement. Moreover, Welford (1982) suggests that pain from such conditions could disturb kinesthetic information and result in the loss of accuracy and speed.

Although the aging process affects these aspects of the motor mechanism, the changes are small compared with those in central mechanisms (Welford, 1977a, 1977b). Some considerations, such as joint stiffness, are variable across individuals. Others, such as motor nerve degeneration, might be influenced by the general activity level of an individual person.

Feedback

Feedback is an important aspect of motor performance. For example, motor performance can be disturbed by distortion or interruption of the feedback normally available to individuals. Feedback can be intrinsic or augmented. Intrinsic feedback comes to the central nervous system through the senses, including kinesthesis, vision, and audition. Augmented feedback, or knowledge of results, includes the information provided by a teacher. It can be informational or reinforcing, or both. Reinforcing feedback would include comments such as "good," "keep it up," or "that's the way." Both informational and reinforcing feedback are known to benefit the performance of young performers and there is little reason to doubt the same holds true for older performers. Researchers know how the manner and timing of feedback affects young performers, and it would be valuable to know if their findings carry over to older adults.

Extensions of feedback research to older adults are not common. Wiegand and Ramella (1983) varied the time frame for giving knowledge of results (KR) during the learning of a motor task by young and older adults. They found that older adults benefitted from increased post-KR intervals (15 seconds as opposed to 3 seconds). That is, the older adults needed more time between receiving KR and beginning their next trial, presumably to process and digest the information. Applying this to teaching settings, older adults should be given additional time, compared with young adults, between the comments provided by an instructor and their practice turn. If additional time is not available, attention to the feedback may divert attention from the next practice attempt (Welford, 1977c).

Learning New Skills and Compensatory Strategies: A Summary

This review of aging and various aspects of skill performance leaves the impression that older adults do not learn new skills *as efficiently as* younger adults. Research studies generally support this impression. First, older adults need more practice to reach a given level of performance (Welford, 1981). Second, older adults learn at a slower rate than young adults (Welford, 1982).

This is due in part to older adults setting a high criterion for themselves in early trials, i.e., responding accurately or not at all. This might reflect a lack of confidence, yet it could be beneficial in the long term because errors made early in learning tend to persist.

In contrast to newly learned skills, older adults maintain motor skills learned in younger years and can easily resume them after years of neglect. It should be kept in mind that older adults can learn new skills and at least one study documents a learning rate on an anticipation task similar to that of a young group on an anticipation task (Wiegand & Ramella, 1983). It is simply that the learning process tends to take longer in older adults.

A decline in the capacity to learn new skills quickly, however, might be offset by effective and efficient strategies. Welford (1982) has outlined those compensatory strategies that would apply to motor performance (see Table 4.4). First, older adults can increase their effort. There is evidence that this is a tendency among older industrial workers who work more continuously and take fewer breaks than younger counterparts. Second, older adults can anticipate and prepare in advance for events. Experience is particularly helpful in such anticipations. Third, older adults can emphasize accuracy over speed. While this trade-off does not account fully for slowing with advancing age, it is a tendency among older adults. Older adults can achieve the accuracy levels of young adults by taking additional time (Vickers, Nettelbeck, & Willson, 1972; Salthouse, 1979). Moreover, older adults can set higher standards of performance to minimize, or quickly detect and correct, errors (Craik, 1969; Rees & Botwinick, 1971; Hutman & Sekuler, 1980; Gordon & Clark, 1974; Hertzog, 1980; Marks & Stevens, 1980). Of course, being overly cautious results in greater slowing.

The use of compensatory strategies implies that performance in older age might be qualitatively different from that in younger years. Instructors must be willing to allow active adults to adapt to the setting. Among the adaptations in learning environment and instructional strategy that could be helpful to older adults are:

1. Structure the learning environment to be as simple as is practical. Provide simple backgrounds and well lit spaces. Provide good traction and reduce unnecessary noise.
2. Remind older learners to have their vision checked and to wear their prescription lenses.
3. Provide enough time between practice turns so that information can be registered into memory. Give feedback, especially informational knowledge of results, but allow enough time for it to be assimilated.
4. Allow older adults to proceed at a slower pace if they so desire.
5. Provide demonstrations, as with younger learners, but consider videotaping them for replay to older adults at a slower speed. They might not assimilate a speedy response executed by a young performer.

TABLE 4.4
Compensatory Strategies Available to Older Adults to Offset a Longer Learning Process

1. Increased effort by more continuous work with fewer breaks.
2. Anticipation of events through rich experience.
3. Advanced preparation for events through rich experience.
4. Emphasis on accuracy over speed.
5. Setting of higher standards to quickly detect and correct errors.

Note. Based on Welford, A. T. (1982). Motor skills and aging. In J. A. Mortimer, F. J. Pirozzolo, & G. J. Maletta (Eds.), *The aging motor system* (152–187). New York: Praeger.

6. Correct errors early in the learning process.

7. Provide frequent reminders of the important features in performance of the skill at hand.

8. Finally, Welford (1982) suggests the use of discovery learning for older adults. This method provides a minimal introduction to the task followed by ample opportunity for learners to discover for themselves how to perform the task. Instructors should correct errors quickly, but learners actively make the choices involved in the performance.

A final point should be made concerning confidence. It is unlikely that skills will be well learned by those of any age if they doubt their ability to learn skills. It is important for instructors of older learners to instill confidence and make older learners comfortable in the learning environment. There is every reason to do so, because older learners can attain new skills, even if at a somewhat slower pace than their younger counterparts.

References

Arundale, K. (1978). An investigation into the variation of human contrast sensitivity with age and ocular pathology. *British Journal of Ophthalmology, 62*, 213–215.

Axelrod, S., & Cohen, L.D. (1961). Senescence and embedded-figure performance in vision and touch. *Perception and Psychophysics, 12*, 283–288.

Bell, B., Wolf, E., & Bernholz, C.D. (1972). Depth perception as a function of age. *Aging and Human Development, 3*, 77–81.

Bender, M.B., Fink, M., & Green, M. (1952). Patterns in perception on simultaneous tests of the face and hand. *Archives of Neurology and Psychiatry, 66*, 355–362.

Bender, M.B., & Green, M. (1952). Alterations in perception in the aged. *Journal of Gerontology, 7*, 473.

Birren, J.E. (1964). *The psychology of aging.* Englewood Cliffs: Prentice-Hall.

Birren, J.E., & Botwinick, J. (1955). Age differences in finger, jaw, and foot reaction time to auditory stimuli. *Journal of Gerontology, 10*, 429–432.

Birren, J.E., & Shock, N.W. (1950). Age changes in rate and level of dark adaptation. *Journal of Applied Psychology, 26*, 407–411.

Birren, J.E., Woods, A.M., & Williams, M.V. (1980). Behavioral slowing with age: Causes, organization, and consequences. In L.W. Poon (Ed.), *Aging in the 1980s.* Washington, D.C.: American Psychological Association.

Broadbent, D.E., & Gregory, M. (1965). Some confirmatory results on age differences in memory for simultaneous stimulation. *British Journal of Psychology, 56*, 77–80.

Broadbent, D.E., & Heron, A. (1962). Effects of a subsidiary task on performance involving immediate memory in younger and older men. *British Journal of Psychology, 53*, 189–198.

Burg, A. (1968). Lateral visual field as related to age and sex. *Journal of Applied Psychology, 52*, 10–15.

Cerella, J., Poon, L.W., & Williams, D.M. (1980). Age and the complexity hypothesis. In L.W. Poon (Ed.), *Aging in the 1980s* (pp. 332–340). Washington, D.C.: American Psychology Association.

Clark, J.E., Lamphear, A.K., & Riddick, C.C. (1987). The effects of videogame playing on the response selection process of elderly adults. *Journal of Gerontology, 42*, 82–85.

Comalli, P.E. (1965). Cognitive functioning in a group of 80–90-year-old men. *Journal of Gerontology, 20*, 14–17.

Comalli, P.E., Wapner, S., & Werner, H. (1962). Interference effects of Stroop Color-Word Test in childhood, adulthood, and aging. *The Journal of Genetic Psychology, 100*, 47–53.

Corso, J.F. (1977). Auditory perception and communication. In J.E. Birren & K.W. Schaie (Eds.), *Handbook of the psychology of aging* (pp. 535–553). New York: Van Nostrand Reinhold.

Cosh, J.A. (1953). Studies on the nature of vibration sense. *Clinical Science, 12,* 131–151.

Craik, F.I.M. (1969). Applications of signal detection theory to studies of aging. In A.T. Welford & J.E. Birren (Eds.), *Decision making and age* (147–157). Basel: Karger.

Craik, F.I.M. (1977). Age differences in human memory. In J.E. Birren & K.W. Schaie (Eds.), *Handbook of the psychology of aging* (384–420). New York: Van Nostrand Reinhold.

Crossman, E.R.F.W., & Szafran, J. (1956). Changes with age in the speed of information intake and discrimination. *Experientia Supplementum, 4,* 128–135.

Derefeldt, G., Lennerstrand, G., & Lundh, B. (1979). Age variations in normal human contrast sensitivity. *Acta Ophthalmologica, 57,* 679–689.

Domey, R.G., McFarland, R.A., & Chadwick, E. (1960). Threshold and rate of dark adaptation as functions of age and time. *Human Factors, 2,* 109–119.

Frolkis, V.V., Martynenko, O.A., & Zamostyan, V.P. (1976). Aging of the neuromuscular apparatus. *Gerontology, 22,* 244–279.

Gilbert, J.G. (1957). Age changes in color matching. *Journal of Gerontology, 12,* 210–215.

Gordon, S.K., & Clark, W.C. (1974). Application of signal detection theory to prose recall and recognition in elderly and young adults. *Journal of Gerontology, 29,* 64–72.

Gregory, R.L. (1974). *Concepts and mechanisms of perception.* New York: Charles Scribner's Sons.

Gutmann, E., & Hanzlikova, V. (1976). Fast and slow motor units in ageing. *Gerontology, 22,* 280–300.

Hasselkus, B.R., & Shambes, G.M. (1975). Aging and postural sway in women. *Journal of Gerontology, 30,* 661–667.

Haywood, K.M. (1980). Coincidence-anticipation accuracy across the life span. *Experimental Aging Research, 6,* 451–462.

Haywood, K.M. (1982). Eye movement pattern and accuracy during perceptual-motor performance in young and old adults. *Experimental Aging Research, 8,* 153–157.

Haywood, K.M. (in press). A longitudinal analysis of anticipatory judgment in older adult motor performance. In A.C. Ostrow (Ed.), *Aging and motor behavior.* Benchmark Press.

Haywood, K.M., & Trick, L.R. (1983). Age-related visual changes and their implications for the motor skill performance of older adults. *Proceedings of the Annual Conference of the American Alliance for Health, Physical Education, Recreation and Dance.* ERIC Document Reproduction Service No. ED 230–538.

Hertzog, C. (1980). Applications of signal detection theory to the study of psychological aging: A theoretical review. In L.W. Poon (Ed.), *Aging in the 1980s* (568–591). Washington, D.C.: American Psychological Association.

Hofstetter, H.W., & Bertsch, J.D. (1976). Does stereopsis change with age? *American Journal of Optometry and Physiological Optics, 53,* 644–667.

Howell, T.H. (1949). Senile deterioration of the central nervous system: A clinical study. *British Medical Journal, 1,* 56–58.

Hutman, L.P., & Sekuler, R. (1980). Spatial vision and aging. II. Criterion effects. *Journal of Gerontology, 35,* 700–706.

Jalavisto, E., Orma, L., & Tarvast, M. (1951). Aging and relation between stimulus intensity and duration in corneal sensitivity. *Acta Physiologica Scandinavica, 23,* 224–233.

Jani, S.N. (1966). The age factor in stereopsis screening. *American Journal of Optometry, 43,* 653–657.

Kenshalo, D.R. (1977). Age changes in touch, vibration, temperature, kinesthesis and pain sensitivity. In J.E. Birren & K.W. Schaie (Eds.), *Handbook of the psychology of aging* (562–579). New York: Van Nostrand Reinhold.

Kirchner, W.K. (1958). Age differences in short-term retention of rapidly changing information. *Journal of Experimental Psychology, 55,* 352–358.

Kline, D.W., Schieber, F., Abusamra, L.C., & Coyne, A.C. (1983). Age, the eye, and visual channels: Contrast sensitivity and response speed. *Journal of Gerontology, 38,* 211–216.

Konig, E. (1957). Pitch discrimination of age. *Acta Oto-laryng, 48,* 475–489.

Laidlaw, R.W., & Hamilton, M.A. (1937). A study of thresholds in appreciation of passive movement among normal control subjects. *Bulletin Neurol Inst, 6,* 268–273.

Landahl, H.D., & Birren, J.E. (1959). Effects of age on the discrimination of lifted weights. *Journal of Gerontology, 14,* 48–55.

Larsson, L., Sjodin, B., & Karlsson, J. (1978). Histochemical and biochemical changes in human skeletal muscle with age in sedentary males, age 22–65 years. *Acta Physiologica Scandinavica, 103,* 31–39.

Lee, J.A., & Pollack, R.H. (1978). The effects of age on perceptual problem-solving strategies. *Experimental aging Research, 4,* 37–54.

Lee, J.A., & Pollack, R.H. (1980). The effects of age on perceptual field dependence. *Bulletin of the Psychonomic Society, 15,* 239–241.

Marks, L.E., & Stevens, J.C. (1980). Measuring sensation in the aged. In L.W. Poon (Ed.), *Aging in the 1980s* (592–598). Washington, D.C.: American Psychological Association.

Marteniuk, R.G. (1976). *Information processing in motor skills.* New York: Holt, Rinehart, & Winston.

McComas, A.J., Upton, A.R.M. & Sica, R.E.P. (1973). Motorneurone disease and aging. *Lancet, 7844,* 1477–1480.

McFarland, R.A., Domey, R.G., Warren, A.B., & Ward, D.C. (1960). Dark adaptation as a function of age. I. A statistical analysis. *Journal of Gerontology, 15,* 149–154.

McGrath, C., & Morrison, J.D. (1980). Age-related changes in spatial frequency perception. *Journal of Physiology, 310,* 52 p.

Naylor, G.F.K. (1973). The anatomy of reaction time and its relation to mental function in the elderly. *Proceedings of the Australian Association of Gerontology, 2,* 17–19.

Norris, A.H., Shock, N.W., & Wagman, I.H. (1953). Age changes in the maximum conduction velocity of human motor fibres in human ulner nerves. *Journal of Applied Physiology, 5,* 589–593.

Owsley, C., Sekuler, R., & Boldt, C. (1981). Aging and low-contrast vision: Face perception. *Investigative Ophthalmology and Visual Science, 21,* 362–64.

Park, D.C., Puglisi, J.R., Sovacool, M. (1984). Picture memory in older adults: Effects of contextual detail at encoding and retrieval. *Journal of Gerontology, 39,* 213–215.

Pestalozza, G., & Shore, I. (1955). Clinical evaluation of presbycusis on basis of different tests of auditory function. *Laryngoscope, 65,* 1136–1163.

Pierson, W.R., & Montoye, H.J. (1958). Movement time, reaction time, and age. *Journal of Gerontology, 32,* 436–440.

Pollack, R.H. (1983). Perceptuo-sognitive performance in the aged. In S. Wapner & B. Kaplan (Eds.), *Toward a holistic developmental psychology.* New York: Erlbaum.

Rabbitt, P. (1965). An age decrement in the ability to ignore irrelevant information. *Journal of Gerontology, 20,* 233–238.

Rabbitt, P., & Rogers, M. (1965). Age and choice between responses in a self-paced repetitive task. *Ergonomics, 8,* 435–444.

Reading, V. (1968). Disability glare and age. *Vision Research, 8,* 207–214.

Reading, V. (1972). Visual resolution as measured by dynamic and static tests. *Pfluergers Archiv European Journal of Physiology, 333,* 17–26.

Rees, J.N., & Botwinick, J. (1971). Detection and decision factors in auditory behavior of the elderly. *Journal of Gerontology, 26,* 133–136.

Rich, N. (1988). The effects of age on unresisted and resisted fractionated reaction time. In J.E. Clark & J.H. Humphrey (Eds.), *Advances in Motor Development Research* (Vol. 2) (71–82). New York: AMS Press.

Rikli, R., & Busch, S. (1986). Motor performance of women as a function of age and physical activity level. *Journal of Gerontology, 41,* 645–649.

Rosen, S., Plester, D., Elmofty, E., & Rosen, H.V. (1964). High speed audiometry in presbycussis: A comparative study of the Mabaans in the Sudan with urban populations. *Archives of Oto-laryng, 79,* 18–32.

Ruddock, K.H. (1965). The effect of age upon color vision. II. Changes with age in light transmission of the ocular media. *Vision Research, 5,* 47–58.

Salthouse, T.A. (1979). Adult age and the speed-accuracy trade-off. *Ergonomics, 22,* 811–821.

Salthouse, T.A. (1980). Age and memory: Strategies for localizing the loss. In L.W. Pool, J.L. Foxard, L.S. Cermak, D. Arenberg, & L.W. Thompson (Eds.), *New directions in memory and aging.* Hillsdale, NJ: Lawrence Erlbaum Associates.

Salthouse, T.A., & Somberg, B.L. (1982a). Isolating the age deficit in speeded performance. *Journal of Gerontology, 37,* 59–63.

Salthouse, T.A., & Somberg, B.L. (1982b). Time-accuracy relationships in young and old adults. *Journal of Gerontology, 37,* 349–353.

Schludermann, E., & Zubek, J.P. (1962). Effect of age on pain sensitivity. *Perceptual and Motor Skills, 14,* 295–301.

Schonfield, D., & Trueman, V. (1974). Variations on the Stroop theme. *Gerontologist, 14,* 59.

Sekuler, R., Owsley, C., & Hutman, L. (1983). Assessing spatial vision of older people. *American Journal of Optometry and Physiological Optics, 59,* 961–968.

Sheldon, J.H. (1963). The effect of age on the control of sway. *Gerontologia Clinica, 5,* 129–138.

Shephard, R.J., & Kavanagh, T. (1978). The effects of training on the aging process. *The Physician and Sportsmedicine, 6,* 33–40.

Simon, J.R., & Pouraghabagher, A.R. (1978). The effect of aging on the stages of processing in a choice reaction time task. *Journal of Gerontology, 33,* 553–561.

Skalka, H.W. (1980). Effect of age on Arden grating acuity. *British Journal of Ophthalmology, 64,* 21–23.

Smith, A.D. (1980). Age differences in encoding, storage, and retrieval. In L.W. Poon, J.L. Fozard, C.S. Cermack, D. Arenberg, L.W. Thompson (Eds.), *New Direction in memory and aging.* Hillsdale, NJ: Lawrence Erlbaum Associates.

Spirduso, W.W. (1975). Reaction and movement time as a function of age and physical activity level. *Journal of Gerontology, 30,* 435–440.

Spirduso, W.W. (1980). Physical fitness and psychomotor speed: A review. *Journal of Gerontology, 35,* 850–865.

Spirduso, W.W., Gilliam, P., & Wilcox, R.E. (1984). Speed of movement initiation performance predicts differences in [3H] spiroperiodol receptor bings in normal rats. *Psychopharmacology, 83,* 205–209.

Spoor, A. (1967). Prebycusis values in relation to noise-induced hearing loss. *International Audiology, 6,* 48–57.

Strauss, M.E., Wagman, A.M.I., & Quaid, K.A. (1983). Preparatory interval influences on reaction-time of elderly adults. *Journal of Gerontology, 38,* 55–57.

Stanford, T., & Pollack, R.H. (1984). Configuration color vision tests: The interaction between aging and the complexity of figure-ground segregation. *Journal of Gerontology, 39,* 568–571.

Talland, G.A. (1962). The effect of age on speed of simple manual skill. *Journal of Genetic Psychology, 100,* 69–76.

Timiras, P.S. (1972). *Developmental physiology and aging.* New York: Macmillan Company.

United States National Health Survey. (1968). Monocular-binocular visual acuity of adults. (Public Health Service Publication No. 100-Series 11-No. 30). Washington, D.C.: U.S. Department of Health, Education and Welfare.

Vickers, D., Nettelbeck, T., & Willson, R.J. (1972). Perceptual indices of performance: The measurement of "inspection time" and "noise" in the visual system. *Perception, 1,* 263–295.

Wagman, I.H., & Lesse, H. (1952). Maximum conduction velocities of motor fibers of ulnar nerve in human subjects of various ages and sizes. *Journal of Neurophysiology, 15,* 235–244.

Warrington, E.K., & Sanders, H.E. (1971). The fate of old memories. *Quarterly Journal of Experimental Psychology, 23,* 432–442.

Weale, R.A. (1961). Retinal illumination and age. *Transaction of the Illuminating Engineering Society, 26,* 95–100.

Weiss, A.D. (1963). Auditory perception in aging. In J.E. Birren, R.N. Butler, S.W. Greenouse, L. Sokoloff, & M.R. Yarrow (Eds.), *Human aging: A biological and behavior study.* Public Health Service Publication No. 986. Washington, D.C.: U.S. Government Printing Office.

Welford, A.T. (1958). *Aging and human skill.* Oxford University Press for the Nuffield Foundation. Reprinted 1973 by Greenwood Press, Westport, Conn.

Welford, A.T. (1977a). Causes of slowing of performance with age. *Interdisciplinary Topics in Gerontology, 11,* 43–51.

Welford, A.T. (1977b). Motor performance. In J.E. Birren & K.W. Schaie (Eds.), *Handbook of the psychology of aging* (450–496). New York: Van Nostrand Reinhold.

Welford, A.T. (1977c). Serial reaction times, continuity of task, single-channel effects, and age. In S. Dornic (Ed.), *Attention and Performance VI* (79–97). Hillsdale, NJ: Erlbaum.

Welford, A.T. (1980). The single-channel hypothesis. In A.T. Welford (Ed.), *Reaction times* (215–252). London: Academic Press.

Welford, A.T. (1981). Learning curves for sensory-motor performance. In R.C. Sugarman (Ed.), *Proceedings of the Human Factors Society* (566–570). Buffalo: Calspan Corporation.

Welford, A.T. (1982). Motor skills and aging. In J.A. Mortimer, F.J. Pirozzolo, & G.J. Maletta (Eds.), *The aging motor system* (152–187). New York: Praeger.

Welford, A.T., Norris, A.H., & Shock, N.W. (1969). Speed and accuracy of movement and their changes with age. *Acta Psychologia, 30,* 3–15.

Wiegand, R.L., & Ramella, R. (1983). The effect of practice and temporal location of knowledge of results on the motor performance of older adults. *Journal of Gerontology, 38,* 701–706.

Wolfe, E., & Nadroski, A.S. (1971). Extent of the visual field-changes with age and oxygen tension. *Archives of Ophthalmology, 86,* 637–642.

Woollacott, M.H., Shumway-Cook, A., & Nashner, L. (1982). Postural reflexes and aging. In J.A. Mortimer, F.J. Pirozzolo, & G.J. Maletta (Eds.), *The aging motor system* (98–119). New York: Praeger.

Suggested Readings

Poon, L.W., Fozard, J.L., Cermack, C.S., Arenberg, D., & Thompson, L.W. (Eds.). (1980). *New directions in memory and aging.* Hillsdale, NJ: Lawrence Erlbaum Associates.

Welford, A.T. (1977). Motor performance. In J.E. Birren & K.W. Schaie (Eds.), *Handbook of the psychology of aging* (450–496). New York: Van Nostrand Reinhold.

Welford, A.T. (1982). Motor skills and aging. In J.A. Mortimer, F.J. Pirozzolo, & G.J. Maletta (Eds.), *The aging motor system* (152–187). New York: Praeger.

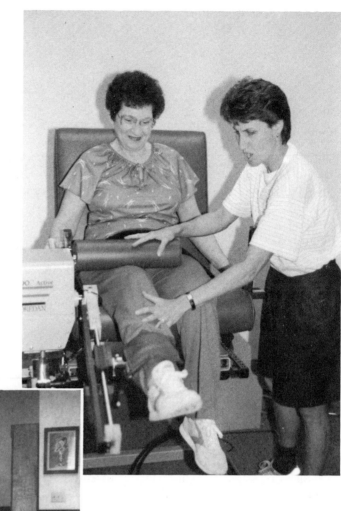

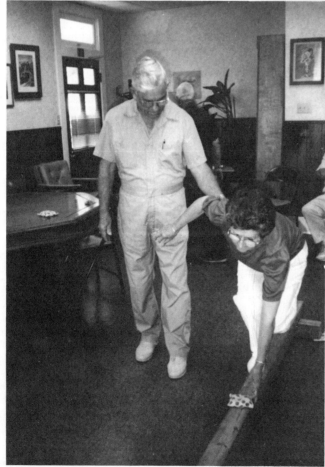

5 Biomechanics and Related Sciences for the Older Adult

Marlene Adrian, University of Illinois
Kay Flatten, Springfield College
Ruth Lindsey, California State University—Long Beach

Overview

Biomechanics is an integral part of the information base for the design of exercise programs for all ages, because most exercise programs require movement, and movement is the domain of biomechanics. The biomechanical analysis of movement includes the observation of speed, range of motion, sequence of movement of body parts, muscles producing the movements, and estimation of mechanical stresses to the body. The utilization of a basic knowledge of biomechanics in exercise program design will increase the potential for maximum benefits, and concomitantly reduce the risk of injury to the older person.

Exercise programs should enhance the quality of life. From a biomechanics perspective, such an enhancement means that, as an individual ages, he or she retains the ability to independently perform the activities of daily living, to work, and to participate in leisure activities of choice, including sports. Thus, an analysis of the age-related changes that occur in body tissues and systems, including how an older person moves, should be part of the information base when one constructs exercise programs and selects teaching procedures and assessment tools. The purpose of this chapter is to briefly review, from a biomechanics perspective, changes in (1) the body tissue and systems and their ability to create and tolerate forces during safe movement, (2) the ability of the older person to produce and regulate movement patterns, and (3) an analysis of selected movements with a focus on safety considerations.

The material includes information and descriptions that are, in some cases, similar to what appears in other chapters, but the overall content in this chapter differs because of the biomechanical implications.

Tissue and System Changes

Bones

The changes that take place in bone, from a biomechanical point of view, reduce the ability of the bone to withstand stresses. These stresses may be caused by impacts to the bone from external objects, from the body falling or colliding with external objects, or from forces exerted upon the bone by muscles and tendons. Loss in bone strength and bone elasticity due to osteoporosis and other causes may occur as early as age 35 and is much more common in white women than in men or women of other races. As has been mentioned in the description of osteoporosis in the chapter on physiology, the bones most susceptible to fractures are the radius, the neck of the femur, and the vertebrae.

If osteoporosis exists, bone porosity increases and the loss in density causes the bone to be more susceptible to fractures. Older bones, most likely because of the high prevalence of osteoporosis in the bones, break in single or few places, with each fracture line traveling a long distance. Younger bones will superficially splinter into many stress lines of short distance, not resulting in a broken bone. In general, the internal resistance to stress of the old bone is much less than that of the young bone.

The major forces acting upon bones are from gravity and muscle tension. When muscles produce movement, they concommitantly produce one or more of the following stresses in the bones: tension, compression, and bending. Such stresses normally activate the formation of new bone cells to strengthen bone or to maintain bone strength, but when bones have been weakened due to osteoporosis, stresses can traumatize the bone and cause fractures.

Osteoporosis, however, is not the only culprit. Unexercised bone, the aging process, diet, and other factors also influence bone strength. Sedentary old persons, or active old persons, who have restricted their previous movements to slow–moderate speeds using only the body segments that are involved or who handle only light loads, such as 2–5 lb. packages or tools, frequently have weakened bones. Activities should be selected for exercise programs which consider speed of movement and resistance loads. Speed and loads may be progressively increased, but progression may need to be in terms of weeks or months. The risk of fractures may be reduced considerably if exercise programs are conducted in an aquatic environment, but conversely the benefits to bone density associated with the movements on land may be reduced or eliminated. When movements put bone at risk due to gravity in a land exercise program, the buoyancy of water may safely allow the movement and muscular and flexibility benefits to be realized.

Joints

The parts of the joint of primary concern biomechanically are the cartilage, synovial fluid, ligaments, and tendons. All except the fluid are connective tissue and with aging show degradation or alteration to their fibrous proteins, elastin and collagen. The changes result in increased rigidity or stiffness in the joint and reduced response to stresses. The age-related degenerative changes in cartilage are similar to osteoarthritis in younger persons, but may or may not be osteoarthritic. The condition appears more frequently in weight-bearing joints such as the knee, hip, and vertebral column.

Gravitational forces tend to compress the joints and may accelerate the wearing of the cartilage. For example, airborne activities such as jogging and jumping result in repetitive landings with high-impact forces. The ability of an older person to reduce these forces through skilled landing techniques should be considered by the exercise leaders with respect to appropriate usage of airborne activities in an exercise program. An aquatic program would be the most desirable type program for some people.

Because adequate range of motion (ROM or flexibility) at a joint is a protective measure against injury, ROM exercises should be an integral part of an exercise program. The ability to withstand forces and to react quickly to avoid a force is related to the ROM of the joints. Furthermore, trauma to a joint usually occurs only at one position in the ROM of the body parts forming the joint. Thus, early recognition of trauma can be facilitated if total ROM is a regular part of an exercise program. Prevention of problems in the joint also may occur if ROM activities are utilized.

Muscles

Many histochemical and histological changes occur in human muscles during aging. The biochemical significance of these changes is in decreases in muscular strength and endurance which reduces the ability to perform movements efficiently, effectively, and safely. The aging of muscles is a result of a complex number of factors including hormonal, disuse, disease, and changes in the cardiovascular system, and fortunately they do not appear in all muscles at the same time. For example, the soleus muscle appears to show aging changes first, and the diaphragm may not show any aging changes prior to death.

Relevant changes reported in muscle structure (Larsson 1978) include a decrease in size and number of type 2 fibers (fast twitch) with age. If this is the case, the speed and strength of muscle contractions would be reduced and muscular endurance would increase. In a study reported by Aniansson et al. (1980), physically active 70 year olds did not show the aging changes reported by Larsson, but showed equal loss in both type 1 and type 2 muscle fibers. These investigators concluded that the amount of physical activity, the health status, and the age of the subjects influence the muscle structure and function.

Based upon the facts described in the chapter on physiology and the changes listed in this section, it is important that the exercise leader construct an exercise program that utilizes all the muscles of the body and all their muscle fibers. Thus, speed of movement should be varied and progressive loading of muscles should be used. Muscles required for activities of daily living should particularly be strengthened. The extensors of the arm, foot and legs are often weak among older persons and the flexor muscles of the fingers, hands, arms, and foot are used in many activities of daily living and need to be maintained, if not strengthened. Observation and assessment of each individual is necessary to appropriately individualize a total "muscle fitness" program.

Lungs and Cardiovascular System

In the case of respiratory and circulatory systems, biomechanics is primarily an investigation of fluid mechanics, that is, the velocity of fluid flow and pressure upon tissues of the airways and blood vessels. During inhalation and exhalation, volume in the lungs obviously changes and the pressure normally changes between positive and negative. In the older person, pressure changes may be reduced since the tissues would not be performing the act automatically. As much as 30 percent of the elastic recoil which aids in expiration may be lost in the older person.

In addition, losses in elasticity and compliance of intercostal muscles (those between the ribs) and cartilage and the smooth muscles of the airways will result in resistance to lung expansion. Thus the vital capacity and expiratory reserve volume could decrease. These composite biochemical attributes may occur as a result of tuberculosis, pneumonia, emphysema, cancer, pulmonary embolism, and disuse.

As with the airways, the blood vessels may show loss in elasticity and an increase in distension and stiffness, causing resistance to blood flow. Blood pressure often rises with age. This phenomenon however, may be a result of hypertension, atherosclerosis or a sedentary lifestyle, as well as aging. The mechanical functioning of the heart is affected, resulting in a lesser stroke volume, less efficiency, and higher heart rates for a given task.

Breathing exercises and aerobic exercises are suggested as activities which will improve the mechanical characteristics of the cardiovascular/respiratory systems which have been decreased because of disuse. If the cause of reduced functioning is disease, these activities should also be performed, but with medical prescription.

Brain and Nervous System

Failures in this system may cause failures of the musculoskeletal system. The major changes with age which interfere with normal neurological functioning are the loss of dendrites in the brain and accumulation of senile plaques. From a motor perspective, these changes are related to a slowing of, or inability to, function. To the biomechanics and motor learning specialists, the evidence of less adaptability and slower reaction and movement times of aged sedentary persons has serious implications. With respect to reaction and movement responses, aged active persons are more similar to young active persons than to older inactive persons.

The exercise leaders must include an adaptability factor within the exercise program. The common imitation-type aerobic dance program and aerobic jogging, cycling, and swimming programs must not constitute the major or sole exercise program for the older person. Exercises which encourage the older person to think and to cope with new movements and new situations should be devised. Use of objects that can be manipulated, activities which require balancing and kinesthetic perceptions, and changes in tempos within an activity will be beneficial for maintaining the brain and nervous system. Creating one's own aerobics' choreography also may be a viable approach to maintaining or enhancing the nervous system.

Anatomical Changes

The combined effect of all the changes described earlier in this chapter is a general change in the appearance (anatomy) of the body of the older person. These changes are usually perceived as structural, postural changes. Those affecting the spine, shoulders, and chest will be described below.

Changes in the Spine

The adage, the older one grows, the shorter one becomes, appears to be true. Starting at age 40 years, a decrease in height is noticeable. By the time a person is 80 years of age, the loss in height may be as much as 1½ inches. Most of this loss in stature occurs in the spine, usually caused by degeneration of the intervertebral disks. These disks comprise approximately one-fourth of the length of the 20-year old spinal column. With age, the disks tend to dehydrate and degenerate, causing the spacing between vertebrae to decrease. There is no longer a cushion between the bodies of the vertebrae to prevent them from rubbing against each other. Bone spurs can result, which in turn can press on soft tissue or narrow the openings through which nerves and arteries pass.

The vertebrae in the lumbar (lower back) and cervical (neck) region are more apt to show degenerative changes than the vertebrae in the thoracic (upper back) region. The loss in bone mass from the bodies of the vertebrae causes the bodies to change in shape and size and become "squashed" or "wedged" in appearance, contributing further to the loss in height. A woman with osteoporosis of the spine may lose as much as 5–6 inches in height because of the increase in curvature due to the "squashing" and "wedging" of the vertebrae.

Another reason for loss in height among older persons is poor posture. The normal adult spine is slightly concave in the cervical region, convex in the upper back, and concave in the lumbar region. Poor posture accentuates one or more of these curves by "giving in" to gravity over the years. This may, in large part, be due to loss of strength of the antigravity muscles that support the spine—the spinal extensor muscles in the upper back and neck and the abdominal muscles in the lumbar region. Over a period of years, the combination of weak muscles and the squashing and wedging of the degenerated disks and vertebrae tend to produce the dowager's hump or humped back (kyphosis) and forward head (poke neck) postures. In the extreme case of the osteoporotic spine, there is a tendency for the head to sink into the shoulders and the ribs to sink down onto the pelvis. The waistline then disappears and the abdomen protrudes.

Changes in Shoulder and Chest

The older adult has narrower shoulders than he/she did as a youth. Partly because of weakened muscles between the shoulder blades and partly because of the kyphosis which tends to occur in the upper back, the tips of the shoulders tend to ride forward around the rib cage in a position called "round shoulders." Most older adults experience the consequences of this when they try to buy clothing and find "it is always too long in the shoulders."

Hand-in-hand with the changes in the spine and shoulders is a loss in chest depth. As the upper back becomes more convex, the chest (rib cage) becomes flatter and more shallow as it sinks. A loss in the flexibility of the rib cage contributes to this condition.

Thus, an integral part of every exercise program should be positive improvement/maintenance component of posture. The ability to stand, sit, walk, and execute other movements with correct posture will influence the efficiency, effectiveness, and the safety of performance. There must be an emphasis upon "standing tall," extended upward with the trunk and top of the head, and "tucking in the abdomen and the buttocks" during all exercise programs. Biomechanically correct postures should be taught prior to the start of each exercise. These postures also include dynamic postures during walking, not merely static posture of the trunk during arm and leg exercises.

It is important that the exercise leader observe movement performance of each older person in order to determine specific needs and contraindications.

Production and Regulation of Movements

Depending upon the degree of anatomical change in the movement apparatus (bones, muscles, joints, brain, nerves), the older person may experience differing amounts of difficulty when performing movements. Older persons without signs of degenerative changes in the movement apparatus move faster, transfer their body weight more easily, have greater range of motion, move with a more erect trunk posture, and have better coordination as evidenced by greater continuity of sequencing of the phases of movement patterns than do persons with signs of degeneration (Adrian, 1983). Persons with excess body weight, with respect to muscle mass, have greater difficulty in moving their body compared to persons with recommended percents of body fat, especially when moving from a low to a high position, such as rising from sitting on the floor.

Since many older persons utilize a limited number of movement patterns in their daily lives, they are apt to have limited use of their bodies. For example, movements to the side, overhead, and behind the body are seldom performed, therefore the respective joints, muscles, and neurological pathways tend to deteriorate.

The exercise leader must assess the ability of each older person in an exercise class to perform the exercises to be taught. One cannot necessarily expect the exercise to be performed correctly the first time it is practiced.

Analysis of Selected Movements

Activities of Daily Living

Range of motion (ROM) is the arc of active motion in a joint, usually reported in degrees with respect to normal limits. Ranges of motion essential to lifting and moving the body include dorsiflexion (flexing foot upward at the ankle) and plantarflexion (flexing foot downward at the ankle), and flexion and extension at the knee and hip. Motions of daily living such as lifting and reaching for objects and dressing need ROM at shoulder and elbow joints, flexion of body parts, and extension at the shoulder. The two essential questions for older persons are whether ranges of motion decrease significantly at healthy joints with advancing age, and how much ROM is required to accomplish the most important activities of daily living (ADLs). The loss of degrees of motion is of concern if the remaining mobility is insufficient for required ADLs.

Walking Patterns of Older Persons

One of the major determinants of walking skill is the speed at which a person can walk. Since velocity is equal to the product of stride length and cadence, we would expect to find differences in these parameters at varying walking speeds. Stride length is the linear distance in the plane of progression between successive points of foot-to-floor contact of the same foot, and step length is the distance between contact points of opposite feet. The rhythm of walking is found in the cadence or the number of steps per minute.

As walking speed decreases, so does the stride length and cadence, yet the rhythm stays even. There is an increase in both stance time and swing time. A greater toeing out occurs at slower speeds, however, all other ranges of motion decrease in amplitude as the walk slows. There is also a greater stride width at slower speeds. With only a few exceptions, these are the exact same changes found in the mechanics of walking as one ages. A comparison of the mechanical changes occurring with changes in walking speed and age can be found in research (Murray, 1967; Murray et al., 1969; Schwanda, 1978; Adrian, 1982).

Some of the age differences include a more pronounced forward tilt of the head, a displacement of the arm action to include more extension in the backward swing and less flexing in the forward swing, a smaller amount of extension at the elbow as the arm swings back, a decreased stride length, and a decreased angle between the sole of the foot and the floor at heel strike.

Other significant changes occurring with age include an increase in the height of toe clearance as the foot is swung through, and an increase in the width of the stride. The authors believe that the latter two factors are due to an increased effort to remain balanced and stable and to not stub the toe. Care must be taken to attribute changes in the motions of walking to appropriate causes such as disease, and the slower speed associated with aging.

Rising from a seated position

Whereas walking is seen to be mechanically efficient and requiring only a small propulsive force to maintain, rising to a stand from a seated position is much more strenuous. This is because the body is stationary when seated and must progress upward, against gravity, as well as forward in a brief time period. The center of mass of the body rises approximately 30 cm when standing from a seated position depending upon a person's height. This vertical work occurs over a relatively short time period ($\approx$ 2 sec.) and there is a fair amount of power required. One important consideration is the effect of body weight. More strength is required to lift a heavy body than a light body. Observers of older persons rising from a chair have noted that many have modified their motions to compensate for decreased leg strength. Probably the first modification to occur is with the use of the arms to assist in rising. Seedhom and Terayama (1976) found that an involvement of the arms decreased the requirement to use the quadriceps and hamstring muscles. It is evident that using the arms to get out of a chair causes a considerable reduction in knee forces during this activity because the peak of the quadriceps force occurs at a much nearer position to full extension. A second modification observed more commonly in heavy older people is the "catapult" technique. In this technique the person uses the mass of the upper body to develop momentum, and transfers that momentum to the lower body. The action is started with a rocking of the trunk back and forth in the sagittal plane and then abruptly blocking or stopping the motion at the end of a forward motion. The momentum developed in the trunk is transferred to the hips, and the person is able to rise.

Rise from the floor.

Rising from the floor to a standing position is the most taxing activity of daily living movement. The mechanical work required involves lifting the center of mass as much as one meter vertically. People from western cultures do not frequently use the floor for sitting or sleeping. The result of years of living in chairs, beds, or upright is a feeling of uncertainty about getting down on the floor and getting back to a stand. It is a chicken and egg phenomenon. Older people are not quite sure if they have quit getting down on the floor because they can't get back up, or if they can't get back up because they quit trying. Whatever the cause and effect, it is certainly a physical movement for which exercise leaders can teach proper technique and work to strengthen appropriate musculature.

If rising to a stand from the floor is a problem, a person can learn appropriate techniques which require minimal strength while maximizing mechanical forces. For example, the person would be asked to do the following: First, roll onto one side and tuck the legs up by flexing at the knees and hips as much as possible. The body now is curled as in the fetal position. Place the hand which is free, palm down in the armpit of the shoulder you are resting upon. Next, push down on that hand until the other arm can be pulled into position so that both hands are pressing down right under their respective shoulder joints. Keeping a tight tuck, lift your hips up over your knees until you are on all fours. Crawl to a couch or chair, continue until the top half of your body is on the chair seat with the front edge of the seat near your belly-button. Now bring one foot up under the hip for support. On a count of three, push down on the chair seat with the arms and push down on the floor with the tucked leg. Once you have pulled the second leg up to stand on and you are leaning over the chair seat, pause for a moment to let the heart adjust to the change in body position. Finally turn and sit in the chair (see Figures 5.1–5.5).

The important mechanical points to be aware of in this procedure are: 1) fright leads to increased muscle tension and random struggling movements which merely serve to fatigue the muscles, 2) achieving the hands and knee position before attempting to stand breaks the rise of the center of gravity into two stages, 3) crawling all the way over the seat of the chair before attempting to stand moves the pushing forces from the arms closer to the body's center of mass, 4) taking time to position the foot close to the chair and under the hip also moves the pushing force from that leg closer to the body's center of mass.

Teaching this technique and practicing it in senior exercise classes is useful. It prepares for future falls, gives feelings of self-confidence, and provides the means to include floor exercises in a work-out. Additionally, it is reassuring to try such demanding movements when others are around to assist if needed.

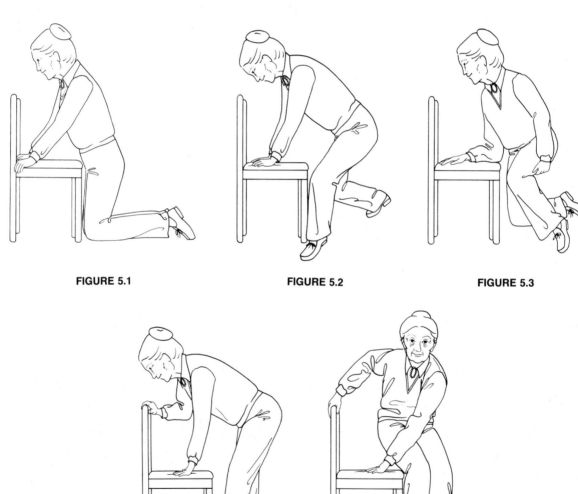

FIGURE 5.1   FIGURE 5.2   FIGURE 5.3

FIGURE 5.4   FIGURE 5.5

Ramps and Stairs

Are ramps as easy to negotiate as stairs if the older person is not in a wheelchair? Ramps were designed originally with the wheelchair in mind! Researchers have shown that the acceleration of going down the ramp may be more difficult for older persons than descending stairs. The person can stop and rest at each stair tread. During ramp descent, muscular strength must be used to prevent "running down the ramp out of control." All skills of daily living must be evaluated and observation of movement skills of the older person must be continually made to assure independent and safe performance. Similar biomechanical analysis of the activity in tasks of daily living, work, and leisure (including sports) should be conducted so that appropriate training, conditioning, and skill development programs may be formulated.

Exercise

All important to the analysis of exercises are the posture for initiating the exercise, the precise movement directions and ranges, and the high stress areas to the body. For example, all leaders should know what muscle groups will function during a given exercise (see Figure 5.6, The Mule Kick, and Figure 5.7, Take a Little Drink, for examples).

Dangerous Exercise

There are some exercises which are hazardous to perform at any age because they place mechanical stress on the body which can be damaging to a variety of tissue. Improper exercise can overstretch tendons, muscles, and ligaments and cause tearing or even a separation of their

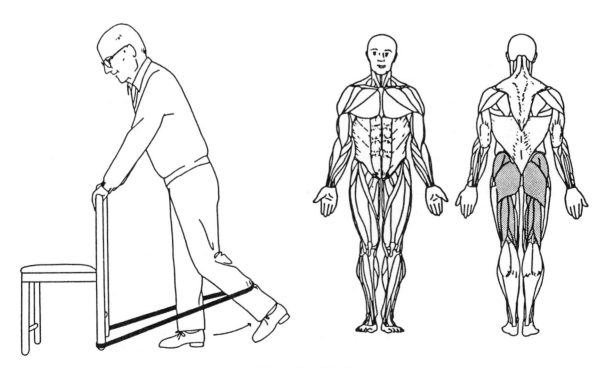

FIGURE 5.6. The Mule Kick.

attachments from the bone. Poor exercise can tear, detach, and grind down cartilage and disks, it can irritate bursae, and it can overstretch or pinch nerves, blood vessels and synovial membranes. Even bone is not immune to damage from improper exercise. It can be fractured from too much compression or tension and spurs may develop on the bone.

You cannot rely on popular magazines, television, books by movie celebrities, or the local "health club" to provide correct information about exercise. Those most qualified to prescribe, recommend, or teach exercise are professionals with university degrees plus certification or registration in Corrective Therapy, Physical Therapy, or Physical Education. In the absence of an expert, you need to follow the suggestions provided throughout this book.

Bibliography

Adrian, Marlene and Cooper, John (1989). *Biomechanics of Human Movement.* (Developmental Biomechanics Chapter: Toole, Tonya and Lynda Randall), Indianapolis: Benchmark Press.

Adrian, Marlene J. (1982). *Maintaining Movement Capabilities in Advanced Years.* Presented at AAHPERD National Convention, Houston, Texas.

Bajd, T. and Kralij; A. (1982). Standing-up of a Healthy Subject and a Paraplegic Patient. *Journal of Biomechanics 15, No. 1*, 1–10.

Corbin, C. and Lindsey, R. (1985). *Concepts of Fitness* (5th Edition), Dubuque, Iowa: Wm. C. Brown Company Publishers.

Ellis, M.I., Seedhom, B.B., Amis, A.A., Dowson, D., and Wright, V. (1979). Forces in the Knee Joint While Rising from Normal and Motorized Chairs. *Industrial Mechanical Engineering, 8, No. 1*, 33–40.

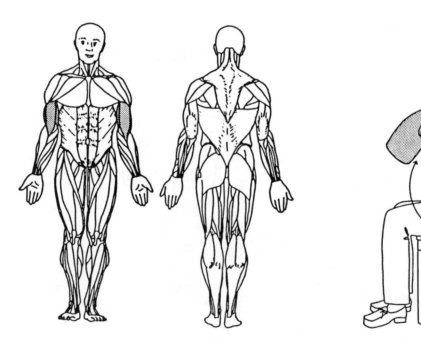

FIGURE 5.7. Take a little drink.

Flatten, E. Kay. (1983). Physical Fitness and Self-sufficiency in Persons Over 60 Years. Activities and the "Well Elderly". Phyllis M. Foster (Ed.), New York: Haworth Press, 699–78.

Flatten, E. Kay and Rice, Priscilla. (1982, September). Plantar Flexion Strength, Range of Motion and Energy Expenditure in Older Adults. *Proceedings of the Locomotion II*, Canadian Society of Biomechanics Conference.

Flatten, E. Kay, Wilhite, B. and Lryes-Watson, E. Reach: Recreation and Exercise Activities Conducted at Home. Springer Publishing Co., in print.

Grieve, D.W. (1968, March). Gait Patterns and the Speed and Walking. *Biomedical Engineering*, 119–122.

Johnston, Richard C. and Smidt, Gary L. (1970, September–October). Hip Motion Measurements for Selected Activities of Daily Living. *Clinical Orthopedics and Related Research*, 72, 205–215.

Kelly, D.L., Dainis, A. and Wood, G.K. (19—). Mechanics and Muscular Dynamics of Rising from a Seated Position. *Biomechanics V-B, International Series on Biomechanics*, 1B, 127–131.

Larsson, Lars. (1978). Morphological and Functional Characteristics of the Aging Skeletal Muscle in Man: A Cross-Sectional Study. *Acta Physiologica Scandinavica, Supplementum 457*, Stockholm, Sweden: Department of Physiology, Karolinska Institutet.

Laubenthal, Keyron N., Smidt, G.L. and Kettelkamlp, D.B. (1972). A Quantitative Analysis of Knee Motion During Activities of Daily Living. *Physical Therapy*, 52, No. 1, 34–42.

Murray, M.P. (1967). Gait as a Total Pattern of Movement. *American Journal of Physical Medicine*, 46, No. 1, 290–333.

Murray, M.P., Kroy, R.C. and Clarkson, B.H. (1969). Walking Patterns in Healthy Old Men. *Journal of Gerontology*, 24, 169–178.

Piscopo, John. (1985). *Fitness and Aging*. New York: Wiley and Sons.

Schwanda, Nancy. (1978). A Biomechanical Study of the Walking Gait of Active and Inactive Middle-Aged and Elderly Men, D.P.E. (unpublished dissertation), Springfield College.

Seedhom, B.B. and Terayama, K. (1976, August). Knee Forces during the Activity of Getting Out of a Chair With and Without the Aid of Arms. *Biomedical Engineering* 278–282.

Smith, Everett L. and Serfass, R.C. (Editors). (1981). *Exercise and Aging: The Scientific Basis*. New Jersey: Enslow Publishers.

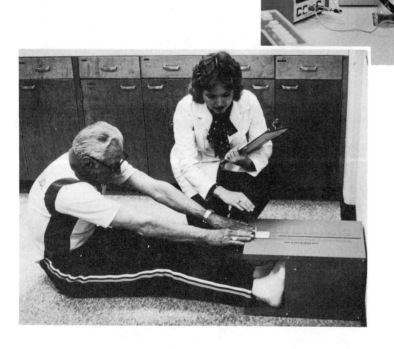

6 Assessment of Physical Function Among Older Adults

Wayne H. Osness, University of Kansas

Introduction

The strong relationship between the physical condition of the older adult and their health status has been well established. Although both of these conditions have many factors, the general relationship is very apparent. It has also been well established that the lifestyle of the individual relates strongly to physical condition and that a change in lifestyle will elicit a change in that condition. This relationship is even stronger in older populations than in younger populations because of the great variability in physical condition, lifestyle, and health status among older people.

Because of this individual variability and the relationship between these parameters, intervention strategies to alter lifestyle have become very popular and are shown to be quite effective. A given intervention strategy may elicit a specific change, while another may elicit a more generalized change in physical condition. However, both could relate to the health of the individual in a specific way. For example, an appropriate aerobic program will significantly alter the blood pressure of individuals who are in the high normal range but not in the low normal range. For those in the high normal range, the change will subsequently improve the efficiency of the cardiovascular system which is positive to the health status of the individual. Only during the last decade has research evidence been available to establish this cause and effect of given intervention strategies. However, because of the large number of variables involved, additional research is needed to quantify this change and more accurately relate it to the health status of a given individual. Primary to this process is the evaluation and further development of measurement procedures to insure the reliability and validity of the data collected as part of this ongoing research.

Initially, it is critical to know the condition of the individual prior to starting an intervention program. This is necessary to increase the margin of safety for the participants as well as to establish an appropriate base line for comparisons or the evaluation of change. The condition of the individual must be divided into two separate categories, the medical condition and the physical condition. The medical condition should be evaluated on a regular interval by qualified physicians. If a medical problem exists, a physician should supervise the physical evaluation and an exercise test technologist should supervise the accuracy of the test procedure and the resulting information.

This chapter will address the assessment of the physical condition associated with aging and assume that appropriate medical assessments have been conducted at appropriate intervals. If this is not the case, it is unwise to continue the physical assessment process.

The Selection of Parameters

Because one cannot measure health as a single quantity, and because it is difficult to measure physical condition, one must first select appropriate parameters that provide a comprehensive evaluation of physical condition or a specific component of it. In some cases this selection is very direct and in others it becomes somewhat abstract. There are no guidelines for this selection and an appropriate selection necessitates a very deep understanding of the physiological process and the biological function of each of the systems in the body. It is not enough to understand the procedures involved in either the intervention strategies or the testing procedures; it is critical to understand how these procedures relate to biological function and the effect that a given parameter will have on the body as it responds to the challenges of its environment.

A specific problem in evaluating the physical condition of older populations is that most measures have been developed for younger populations, and the reliability and validity were established using those younger populations. One cannot assume that because a given parameter is reliable and valid for younger populations that it is also reliable and valid for older populations. Also, a given physical performance parameter may be much more appropriate for an older population as opposed to a younger population. An example would be the measurement of neuromuscular steadiness which is not necessarily important for the average younger populations, but is very critical for the average older population. When selecting a test procedure it is extremely important that reliability and validity measures are either available or established prior to using the results of this evaluation for follow-up work.

The Evaluation Process

In evaluating test results it is also important to compare the numbers collected to a set of norms that are age and sex specific to older populations. Because of the great variability in performance among older populations, it is important to reduce the comparative age range for effective use of the data. An age range of three to five years among middle-aged populations may be appropriate, whereas an age range beyond 12 months may be quite inappropriate for older populations. It is equally important that the exact protocols used for the testing procedure to establish the norms are also used as one compares a given set of data from an individual to the larger population.

The assessment process for older populations is complicated by several additional factors that are not nearly as critical for the assessment of younger populations. First, the population has several identifiable subpopulations. These are particularly apparent after the age of 70 years. The most obvious is the ambulatory versus the nonambulatory populations. The available assessment techniques are limited in the nonambulatory group, yet critical to the development of an intervention strategy leading to the possible rehabilitation of those individuals. It may be that the most meaningful parameters cannot be measured in a nonambulatory condition. Even among the ambulatory there is a great deal of variation among those over 70 years. If movement of the total body or parts of the body are necessary to complete an evaluation, the data generated may relate to a restricted movement as opposed to the desired physical function indicated by the test involved.

Second, a very high percentage of persons over 60 years of age are on some type of prescribed or nonprescribed medication. At present, the only alternative the clinician has is to determine whether the medication is the type or quantity that will affect the result of the assessment process.

If it is not contraindicated, the test may proceed. If it is, the test should not be done because there is no predictable method of determining how that medication will affect the results of the test. This problem is inherent in virtually every physical performance measure currently in use. The problem is exaggerated by changes in dosages of the medication as well as the timing involved between dosages.

Third, the psychological factors associated with maximal performance among older populations is greater as compared to younger populations. It is very possible that one may be testing the psychological desire the individual has to do well on the test. This changes significantly from one psychological state to another as well as from one individual to another. The measurement of physical function is based on the assumption that a given protocol will provide maximal opportunity for a given subject to give a maximal response to a given procedure. If this is not the case, the assessment process is meaningless.

Fourth, it is often difficult to determine the true limiting factor associated with a given assessment procedure. Although the conditions for a given test are controlled to assure that the parameter being evaluated is in fact the limiting factor, other physical factors are more likely to affect this process among older populations. An example is that of the measurement of grip strength. Most older individuals have some type of joint problem and all have different pain thresholds. It may be that in the measurement of grip strength one is simply measuring the ability to withstand pain or the extent to which the joints in the hand are affected by the pressure. It could be argued that all these factors are, indeed, related directly to the grip strength of the individual. However, if that is the case, the clinician must understand these factors and consider them as the data are evaluated and used to compare the data of a given individual to a normative base.

It must be remembered that all of these factors are involved in the assessment of the physical condition of the young as well as the old. The difference is the extent to which these factors affect a set of data or data collected from a given individual. When dealing with older populations the clinician must exercise a greater degree of caution and control as the data are collected and the results reported.

Procedures Prior to Testing

Prior to the testing process, the individual should be advised concerning appropriate preparation for the evaluation. Although the dietary state is not critical for most of the tests commonly used, it is a good idea for the participant not to eat within an hour or two prior to the testing session, and the individual should not have engaged in moderate or heavy physical activity for several hours prior to testing. If blood testing is part of the evaluation process, an additional set of preliminary procedures may be called for which are specific for the type of blood test.

If the individual enters the testing process with excess apprehension, noninterest, depression, or the like, the test should be deferred until these conditions are reduced. These are subjective evaluations made by the clinicians at the time when the testing session is conducted. Some researchers have indicated the need to address the time of day or even the time of year as one compares data among individuals or a given individual within a given time frame.

A reasonably extensive personal history is also a necessary preliminary to the testing session. A formal medical examination including blood and urine analysis may be considered; however, for nonexhaustive test protocols, self-reported history may be sufficient. The presence or absence of medical personnel may also affect the necessity to obtain precise information relative to the individual's medical status. The American College of Sports Medicine has established guidelines (Guidelines, 1980) for obtaining preliminary information that can be used prior to exercise assessments.

Historical data collected prior to the testing process should include (1) a family history of heart attacks, high blood pressure, strokes, diabetes, blood lipids, heart surgery, premature death, and other conditions related to specific testing involved. (2) Past personal history relating to rheumatic fever, heart murmurs, high blood pressure, general cardiac conditions, abnormal blood chemistry, cardiac or pulmonary surgery, chest discomfort, heart palpitations, diabetes, gout, vascular diseases, surgery, muscular diseases, unusual fatigue, or other medical problems that have been treated during the last five years. (3) Medications that are being taken which would include the type of medication, the dosage of the medication, timing of the dosage, and the length of time this medication has been used. Common medications can simply be listed and checked if the response of the individual is affirmative. (4) A physical activity history that includes occupational activity, recreational activity, the frequency of the activity, the duration of the activity, the intensity of the activity, and the type of physical activity involved.

Prior to conducting the assessment process, the activity and medical history should be reviewed by a qualified clinician who then makes the decision concerning whether the assessment should be done at all, the possible effects on the accuracy of the resulting test data, and the possible danger associated with the testing process considering this individual's background.

In most cases, the battery of tests can be modified to eliminate those protocols affected as opposed to a total postponement or rejection.

Procedures During the Testing Session

The information taken from the individual history should be used to minimize discomfort and increase testing accuracy. It is important that each individual understand exactly what is to be done, the procedure to be used, the basic rationale for the test, and its significance. The length of time for this procedure can vary as the clinician observes the physical and psychological condition of the patient. The clinician must decide if the individual is in the best possible state to provide a maximal performance on the test to ensure meaningful data. In some cases the history might indicate the necessity for a closer monitoring of blood pressure during an exercise test or a more careful approach to an evaluation that involves maximal flexibility or joint action. The fatigue factor is also critical when a battery of tests is used. In addition to these generalized precautions, specific precautions for each of the testing situations should be considered as they relate to maximum performance and individual safety. The American College of Sports Medicine guidelines provide the clinician with a functional set of criteria that will aid in deciding whether to terminate or proceed with the test.

Procedures Following the Testing Session

Whenever exercise or physical movement is involved in a testing situation, the older individual should be carefully observed for at least three to five minutes after the conclusion of the test. This time may be extended if the clinician observes any abnormality in behavior. This time can be used to explain to the individual how the data will be treated and how the information will be given back and used in the followup procedures. It is important for the individual to respond in some way to the clinician for a more effective evaluation of possible after-effects of the testing process.

The results of the testing process can be explained to the individual immediately after the evaluation if the process is computerized with immediate output. In most cases, it is necessary for the individual to return for a second visit after the clinician has had an opportunity to adequately assess the data, compare it to normative values, and prepare a response. Computer packages are now available that will present the data in graphic form which is easily understood by the consumer as well as the clinician. It is advisable that the data be stored for future reference and comparisons. The fact that the older individual can expect a decline in most physical functions over time creates a need to assess this change from time to time and the effect that interventions in lifestyle have on this predicted change. As the individual advances in age it is more critical to compare the individual to a more finite age range as well as to his or her sex cohorts. In this sense, the individual is being compared to the larger population as it progresses through the entire age range. This provides the opportunity for the assessment of a physical age which is more critical to health and well-being than chronological age. For older populations, it is somewhat apparent that chronological age is a "meaningless myth." It is the functional age that is truly most important to the quality of life. However, the contents of this chapter should very clearly indicate the need for a quality assessment process to better determine a true functional age.

Field versus Clinical Assessments

Although a clinical testing situation is preferred, it is not always possible because of limitations in equipment, numbers of individuals involved, or the availability of qualified personnel. In some cases, field testing or screening is appropriate. The difference not only resides in the procedures involved, but also in the way the data is treated and the conclusions that can be drawn from the data as it relates to a given individual.

The testing situation will also affect the selection of parameters to be used in the total assessment process. Some parameters are simply not appropriate in a field test situation. In some cases the number of parameters may be so limited and the accuracy so low that the assessment process is meaningless. The clinician can be assisted in the determination of that possibility by reviewing the validity of a given field test as compared to a laboratory or clinical test measuring the same physical performance. Each parameter and each protocol has its own level of validity as well as reliability. In some cases the validity must simply be assumed based on a careful evaluation of the biological process involved.

Another factor associated with this decision is the intended use of the data. Data that may be useful for individual feedback may not be sufficient to evaluate subtle differences in the performance elicited by a given intervention strategy.

The lack of reported data may necessitate the need for a pilot study using a given population of older individuals, the specific assessment of the procedures desired, and the data evaluated prior to a more extensive assessment program. Generally, no data at all is better than data that does not meet reliability and validity standards.

Parameters to be Evaluated

Most assessment procedures begin with evaluation of height and weight which is followed by resting heart rates and blood pressures. The protocols are quite consistent and uniform as one observes current practices. Consistency and a steady state condition for heart rate and blood pressure are a necessity.

Height, Weight, and Body Composition

Although height and weight can give a general indication of body composition among older populations, these measures are not nearly as meaningful as with younger populations. Hydrostatic weighing or isotopic dilution techniques are necessary for older populations, if accuracy is needed. At the present time, the validity of anthropometric measurements among older populations is questionable even though some of the formulas have age correction factors. These factors are not nearly as effective when the age of the population goes beyond 60 years. Although anthropometric formulas are often used, one must demonstrate caution as the data are analyzed. To improve this accuracy, often multiple formulas are used with averages calculated. At the present time, the clinician must be prepared to analyze the data collected using a given procedure on a given population of older individuals and simply assess the ability of that procedure to meet the specifications for accuracy considering the proposed use of the data.

Flexibility

Flexibility can be assessed using a variety of body sites or one or two indicators of total body flexibility. The typical indicator is that of trunk and leg flexibility because of the ease of collecting the data and the ability of this measure to predict total body flexibility. Recently, studies have reported greater reliability in the measurement of specific site flexibility and the techniques appear to be improved over those used a decade ago. This is indeed fortunate because it appears that, among older populations, the ability to alter body flexibility among those who are below the norm is very possible. It is somewhat surprising that a greater amount of research has not been reported relating to the reliability and validity of the flexibility measurement as well as the effects of intervention strategies.

Neuromuscular Function

Neuromuscular function is assessed using hand-eye coordination, neuromuscular steadiness, reaction time, and response time. With the exception of reaction time, where sensory input is minimized, both the efferent and afferent systems are evaluated. Although these procedures center on the evaluation of the neuromuscular system, there is a visual component as well. It is very important that the older individual does not limit the performance level by visual insufficiency. The learning factor is also one that must be considered as protocols are designed for the assessment of these parameters. The fatigue factor also may affect the performance level with considerable individual differences. In a sense, these are acting in opposition to one another. As the number of trials increases, the performance level may increase by learning. The fatigue factor also increases with increased number of trials and is detrimental to performance. There is a point where the performance level, as affected by these two factors, is maximal and a point at which the performance should be uniformly assessed. The clinician may select the peak performance in a given number of trials, an average of a given number of trials, or the average of a given number of trials taken from a larger number of trials. A pilot study to determine the best procedure is indicated.

Pulmonary Function

Pulmonary function for older populations is vital capacity and forced expiration volume per second. These procedures are rather routine and can be obtained from most any pulmonary function manual. However, care must be taken to use either the body temperature pressure standard (BTPS) or the standard temperature pressure dry (STPD) values consistently within a given testing program, when comparing data from one study to another or using published normative values. These parameters are particularly critical for older populations in that decreased performance is predictable with age and with decreased activity.

Strength

Strength can either be measured using specific body segments or specific indicators of general body strength. For example, grip strength is often used to indicate upper body strength and leg strength is often used to indicate lower body strength. More specific measurements are generally used in clinical settings because of the equipment available. Although static strength is commonly used, clinical assessment usually includes isokinetic evaluations of strength through a range of motion. This provides a more valid indicator of total body strength as well as possible weak segments and imbalances. Strength is very specific and usually a limitation to performance. As the lack of strength limits a given performance and the intensity of the performance, the possibility of an overload is reduced and the result is a spiraling downward of the total strength of that segment of the body. Therefore, it is critical to concentrate on each segment within a given movement to evaluate possible limitations. Specific interventions can then provide a continued opportunity for overload and subsequent tissue development. Accurate assessment is necessary through the entire range of motion to accomplish this task.

Aerobic Capacity

Aerobic capacity is probably the most critical parameter relating to the physical performance of the older person and yet the most difficult to accurately assess. It is critical because it is probably the best indicator of endurance capacity and the ability to produce energy in the cells during a given time interval. Protocols that take an older individual to maximal exercise intensity and directly measuring oxygen intake are simply not advisable except in specific situations. Using a percentage of maximal heart rate or a given target heart rate at submaximal levels and then predicting the aerobic capacity is more appropriate providing the individual does not have a structural limitation or is not taking a medication that will affect heart rate during the conduct of the test. In either case, the end point of the test is masked and the data affected. The use of submaximal testing with heart rates at steady state around 120 beats per minute appears to be reasonable if the individual is apparently healthy without medications. Although the same restrictions apply as indicated for the more intense exercise test, the effect is minimized by the lower heart rate requirements. However, appropriate screening is necessary. Experience has indicated that these tests can only be used for a relatively small segment of the larger population of those over 60 years of age.

Aerobic capacity can also be assessed with field tests which measure distance traveled in a given period of time or the time taken to cover a certain distance. These field tests vary considerably and have generated a great deal of discussion of their validity and reliability. Considerable research is needed to develop assessment procedures that will provide meaningful data within a framework that is appropriate for older populations. Caution must be used relative to the medical and physical condition of the individual being assessed as well as the relative value of the data collected. Although this aerobic capacity is most critical to an appropriate evaluation of the physical condition of the older individual, one must exercise extreme caution when including current protocols in the total assessment process at this point in time.

Protocols That May Be Selected For a Physical Performance Profile

Although a great deal of variability exists in test protocols used for given performance parameters, sample protocols have been included for the most common parameters that can be used as a starting point for the development of a profile. These protocols are not necessarily better than others commonly used, but they have been selected because they are relatively comprehensive and generally accepted by exercise physiologists.

Included with each parameter is an example of apparatus that can be used for the measurement process, the procedure to be used by the clinician, the instructions to the subject, and the step by step process for conducting the test. In most cases a statement of reliability and/or validity is also included. It is assumed that an appropriate computerized system will be used to evaluate the data and present it in a meaningful way. It must be noted that these protocols are not necessarily appropriate for all individuals among the older population. Both clinical and field tests are included to provide for a variety of testing situations.

The descriptions are purposely detailed and described using terminology developed through the testing of a large number of older individuals in both clinical and field conditions. The reliability values can only be used if the protocols are duplicated precisely as they are written.

Clinical Tests

These test parameters are particularly suited for a clinical situation where equipment is available and trained professionals are present. Clinical tests include those for:

- Height
- Weight
- Resting heart rate
- Resting blood pressure
- Vital capacity and forced expiratory volume
- Hand-steadiness protocol
- Reaction time
- Choice response time
- Hand-eye coordination

- Grip strength
- Trunk flexibility
- Leg strength
- Anthropometric percent body fat for men
- Anthropometric percent body fat for women
- Predicted aerobic capacity (Astrand-Ryhming Bicycle Ergometer Protocol), and
- Predicted aerobic capacity (90% Balke Treadmill Test Protocol).

Field Tests

These field tests have been developed by a committee selected by the Council on Aging and Adult Development which is a unit within the Association for Research, Administration, Professional Councils and Societies within the American Alliance for Health, Physical Education, Recreation, and Dance. They have been designed to be used in situations where a clinic is not available and the persons conducting the tests do not have specific training. The test parameters have accepted reliability and validity as compared to clinical testing of the same parameter. The equipment needed can be made with minimal expense and the risk to the subject is minimal.

THIS IS NOT A TEST ITEM OF THE FUNCTIONAL FITNESS TEST, BUT PART OF THE DEMOGRAPHIC DATA

Parameter:	BODY WEIGHT
Test Item:	Weight
Equipment:	Calibrated scale with increments of one pound or smaller
Procedure:	1. Set the scale on a firm, flat, horizontal surface.
	2. Check that the scale is accurate by using known loads prior to testing.
	3. Ask the person to remove shoes and overgarments, such as coat, jacket, and sweater.
	4. Ask the person to step onto the scale and stand without moving.
	5. With subject standing on scale as directed, read the scales to nearest pound.
Scoring:	Record weight in pounds.
Trials:	one trial
Special Considerations:	none

THIS IS NOT A TEST ITEM OF THE FUNCTIONAL FITNESS TEST, BUT A PART OF THE DEMOGRAPHIC DATA

Parameter: STANDING HEIGHT MEASUREMENT

Test Item: Height

Equipment: Tape measure or other graduated scale of length; masking tape; wall

Procedure:
1. Vertically attach a tape measure to a wall that has no molding strip or other protuberances.
2. Ask the person to remove shoes, and to turn and place the heels together. Ask the person to stand erect with head upright and eyes looking straight ahead.
3. With the person standing as directed, place a flat object, such as a 2″×4″×6″ long wood block, ruler or clipboard, horizontally on the top of the crown of the head with one end against the wall. Read to the nearest half inch the intersection point of the flat object and the tape measure. If it is difficult to see, ask the subject to stoop slightly and step to one side.

Scoring: Record height in feet and inches to nearest half inch.

Trials: One trial

Special Considerations: None

Parameter: FLEXIBILITY

Test Item: Trunk/Leg Flexibility.

Equipment: A yardstick, chalk, and masking tape.

Procedure: 1. *Equipment Set-Up:* Draw a line approximately 20 inches long on the floor, or you may use masking tape for this line. Tape the yardstick to the floor perpendicular to the line, with the 25-inch mark directly over the line. If masking tape is used for the line, the 25-inch mark should be right at the edge of the tape. Next, draw two marks on the line, each six inches away from the center of the yardstick (see Figure 6.1).

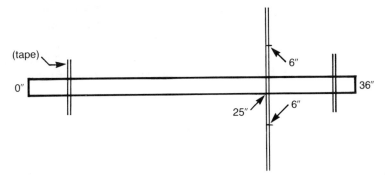

FIGURE 6.1. Equipment set-up for the Trunk/Leg Flexibility Test.

2. *Directions:* The subject should remove the shoes for this test and sit on the floor with legs extended, feet 12 inches apart, toes pointing straight up, and heels right up against the line (at the 25-inch mark, and each heel centered at the 6-inch marks on the line). The yardstick should be between the legs, with the zero point toward the subject. The hands are placed one directly on top of the other. The subject may then slowly reach forward sliding the hands along the yardstick as far as possible, and must hold the final position for at least two seconds. The technician administering the test should place one hand on top of one knee (only) to insure that the subject's knees are not raised during the test.

Scoring:

Record the final number of inches reached to the nearest one-half inch.

Trials:

Two practice trials followed by two test trials are given. Only the scores for the two test trials are recorded.

Approximate Range of Scores:

10 to 30 inches.

Special Considerations:

Be sure that the subjects are properly warmed-up prior to this test. Specific exercises related to this task should be conducted prior to the test. Help all subjects into the sitting position and subsequently when getting up from the floor. The forward reach should be a gradual movement along the top of the yardstick, the tip of the middle fingers must remain even during the entire reaching action, and the final position must be held for at least two seconds. Be sure that the toes are straight up and that the legs are kept as straight as possible. If feet start turning outward or the knees start to come up during the reaching action, ask the subject to maintain the correct position.

Parameter:	AGILITY/DYNAMIC BALANCE
Test Item:	Agility/Dynamic Balance
Equipment:	Chair with arms (average seat height 16″) Masking or duct tape Measuring tape Two cones Stopwatch

Procedure:

1. *Set Up:* The initial placement of the chair should be marked with the legs taped to the floor, if possible, because the chair tends to move during the test. Measuring from the spot on the floor (x) in front of the chair where the feet will be placed, the cones are set up with their farthest edge located six feet to the side and five feet behind the initial measuring spot (x). One cone is set up at either side behind the chair (see Figure 6.2). The area should be well lit, the floor even and nonslippery.

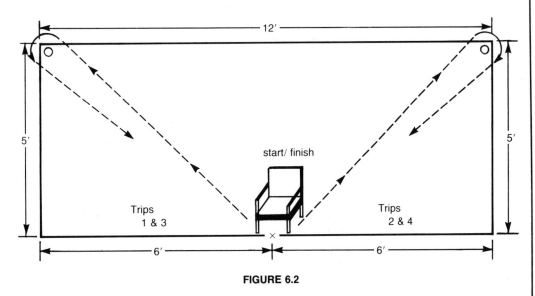

FIGURE 6.2

2. *Test Administration:* The person begins fully seated in the chair with their heels on the ground. On the signal "Ready, Go," the person gets up from the chair, moves to *their* right going to the inside and around the back of the cone to their right (counterclockwise), returns directly to the chair and sits down. Without hesitating the person gets up immediately, moves to *their*

left again going to the inside and around the back of the cone to their left (clockwise), returns directly to the chair and sits down completing one circuit. The person gets up immediately and repeats a second circuit exactly as the first. One trial consists of 2 complete circuits (going around the cones 4 times (right, left, right, left)).

During the test, after circling the cones, the person must sit down fully in the chair. This means having the person lift their feet ½ inch from the floor before getting up. The person must use their hands to help get in and out of the chair. The person should go as fast as they feel comfortable without losing their balance or falling.

3. *Instructions to the participant:* Explain the test procedure, then walk the person through the course to make sure they circle the cones correctly and lift their feet each time they sit down.

After sufficient practice the person should be given the following instructions: "Walk as fast as comfortable without feeling you will lose your balance or fall. One trial consists of circling the cones four times. The first time go to your right then to your left, right, and left. Go around the cone from the inside to the outside, come back and sit down after circling each cone. Sit down fully and lift your feet off the floor each time. Use your hands to help you get in and out of the chair without falling. If you feel dizzy, light headed, or any pain stop immediately and tell me."

4. *Administrative Cues:* Give directions, supervise practice, and start each trial with "Ready, Go." Start the stopwatch when the person begins to move, stop the watch when the person sits down the fourth time.

During the test give verbal directions (ex: right, left, around, sit down, etc.) so the person does not have to stop or hesitate because they are confused. Make sure the person lifts their feet each time they sit down.

If the person moves the chair, the technician should readjust it to the original position during the trial.

Trials: A practice "walk through" will be administered until the person demonstrates that they understand the test. Three trials are administered with 30 seconds rest provided after each trial.

Scoring: Record the time for each trial to the nearest 0.1 seconds.

Approximate Range of Scores: Most people will score between 15 and 35 seconds.

Parameter:	COORDINATION

Test Item: "Soda Pop" Coordination Test.

Equipment: Three unopened (full) cans of soda pop, a stopwatch, ¾″ masking tape, a table, and a chair.

Procedure:

1. *Equipment Set-Up:* Using the ¾″ masking tape, place a 30″ strip of tape on the table, about five inches from the edge of the table. Draw six marks exactly 5 inches away from each other along the line of tape, starting at 2½ inches from either edge of the tape. Now place six strips of tape, each three inches long, centered exactly on top of each of the six marks previously drawn. For the purposes of this test, each little "square" formed by the crossing of the long strip of tape and the three-inch strip of tape is assigned a number starting with 1 for the first square on the right to 6 for the last square on the left (see Figures 6.3 and 6.5).

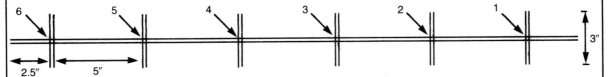

FIGURE 6.3. Masking tape placement for the "Soda Pop" Coordination Test.

2. *Directions:* To administer the test, have the subject sit comfortably in front of the table, the body centered with the diagram on the table. The preferred hand is used for this test. If the right hand is used, place the three cans of pop on the table in the following manner: can one is centered on square 1 (farthest to the right), can two on square 3, and can three on square 5. To start the test, the right hand, with the thumb up, is placed on can one and the elbow joint should be at about 100–120 degrees. When the tester gives the signal, the stopwatch is started and the subject proceeds to turn the cans of pop upside down, placing can one over square 2, followed by can two over square 4, and then can three over square 6; immediately the subject returns all three cans, starting with can one, then can two, and can three—turning them right side up—to their original placement. On this "return trip," the cans are grasped

with the hand in a thumb down position. This entire procedure is done twice, without stopping, and counted as one trial. In other words, two "trips" down and up are required to complete one trial. The watch is stopped when the last can of pop is returned to its original position, following the second trip back. The preferred hand (in this case the right hand) is used throughout the entire task (a graphic illustration of this test is provided in Figure 6.4). The object of the test is to perform the task as fast as possible, making sure that the cans are always placed over the squares. If a can misses a square at any time during the test, the trial must be repeated from the start. A miss indicates that a can did not completely cover the entire square formed by the crossing of the two strips of tape (see Figure 6.5).

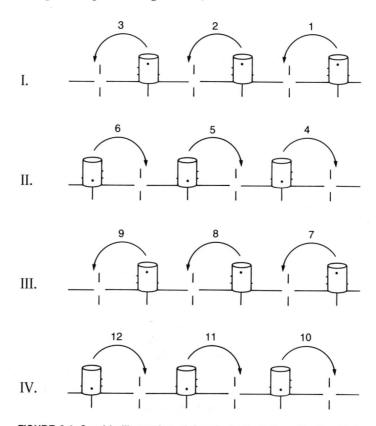

FIGURE 6.4. Graphic illustration of the "Soda Pop" Coordination Test.

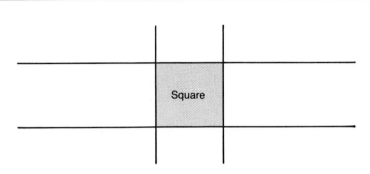

FIGURE 6.5. Shaded area illustrates the square that must be completely covered when turning the cans during the "Soda Pop" Coordination Test.

If a participant chooses to use the left hand, the same procedures are used, except that the cans are placed starting from the left, with can one over square 6, can two over square 4, and can three over square 2. The procedure is initiated by turning can one upside down onto square 5, can two onto square 3, and so on.

Scoring: Record the time of each test trial to the nearest tenth of a second.

Trials: Two practice trials followed by two test trials are given. Only the scores for the two test trials are recorded.

Approximate Range: 8 to 25 seconds

Special Considerations: During the entire procedure the cans must completely cover the squares formed by the crossing of the two tapes. If the person has a mistrial (misses a square), repeat the test until two successful trials are accomplished.

Parameter:	STRENGTH/ENDURANCE
Test Item:	Strength/Endurance Test
Equipment:	Two-quart plastic milk bottle with handle One-gallon plastic milk bottle with handle Sand, water or other similar material Stop watch Normal chair without arms
Procedure:	1. *Set-Up:* The two-quart empty milk bottle should be filled with sand, water or other material to four pounds of total weight and the cover tightened. The one-gallon empty milk bottle should be filled in the same way to eight pounds and the cover tightened. A straight back chair with no arms is placed in an area with no obstructions. 2. *Test Administration:* The subject is asked to sit in the chair with back straight and against the back of the chair as much as possible. The eyes should be looking straight ahead and feet flat on the floor in a comfortable position. The nondominant hand should be resting in the lap with the dominant arm hanging to the side. The arm should be straight and relaxed. The weighted milk bottle is placed in the dominant hand that is extended toward the floor. The subject is asked to grasp the handle and hold in the extended position. The four pound weight (quart container) should be used for women and the eight pound (one gallon container) should be used for men. The running stop watch should be placed in the nondominant hand resting in the lap and facing the dominant side of the body. The clinician testing the subject should stand on the side of the dominant arm and place one hand on the dominant bicep and the other helping to support the weighted milk bottle. The hand helping to support the milk bottle is then removed and the subject asked to contract the bicep through the full range of motion until the lower arm touches the hand of the clinician on the bicep. This represents one total repetition. If the subject cannot bring the weight through the full range of motion, the test is terminated with a score of zero. If the practice repetition is complete, the weight is placed on the floor for approximately one minute and again placed in the hand supported by the clinician. The clinician then instructs the subject to make as many repetitions as possible in 30 seconds. The lower arm must touch the clinician's hand (on the bicep) for a complete repetition.

While watching the timepiece, the clinician instructs the subject to begin (unassisted) and counts the number of repetitions the subject can do in the 30-second period. The clinician starts and stops the time interval at a convenient time on the stop watch.

Scoring: Record the maximal number of complete repetitions in the 30 second interval.

Range of Scores: 0 to 40

Special Considerations:

1. If the subject cannot grasp the handle of the weight to hold it in place this test should not be done.
2. Subjects should be instructed to breathe normally during the test.
3. The weight should not be bounced off the floor. If this is the case, elevate the chair.
4. Subjects should be instructed to stop the test if the subject experiences pain in the tested arm. The clinician must determine if the pain is due to a structural condition or the lack of strength. If the former, the test will be invalid and no score recorded.

Parameter:	ENDURANCE
Test Item:	Half Mile Walk (or 880 Yard Walk)
Equipment:	Stopwatch Measuring tape Cones
Procedure:	1. *Set-Up:* The test involves a continuous walk of 880 yards. The person will walk around a measured lap until they have walked a total of 880 yards. Using a measuring tape or similar device, measure an oval or rectangle of 67 yards or longer. Make the inside edges of the lap (oval or rectangle) with the cones. The lap should be designed with sufficient space to turn, if conducted in a hallway a minimum length of 50 yards and width of 5 feet is recommended. The area should be well lit, the surface nonslippery and level. All obstacles should be removed from the path. People not taking the test should not be allowed to walk onto the course during the test.
	2. *Test Administration:* Instruct the person to walk the course (x number of laps) as fast as they feel comfortable; they may not run. They should walk at their own pace independent of the other participants. It is important they pace themselves so they are able to finish the distance and do not experience discomfort. If a person is dizzy, lightheaded, nauseous, or experiences any pain they should stop the test immediately and let you know. On the signal "Ready, Go," the person begins at a designated spot and walks the necessary laps until they reach 880 yards.
	3. *Administrative Cues:* Screen individuals for cardiovascular or orthopedic contraindications. Give directions, start the test with "Ready, Go," and start the stopwatch. Either the test administrator or assistant counts each person's number of laps and records the time at the completion of 880 yards.
Scoring:	Record the time to the nearest second.
Approximate Range of Scores:	7.5 to 12 minutes.

Special Considerations:

A. Under the following circumstances the test administrator should either discourage or not allow the participant to perform this test without first consulting their physician about:

1. Significant orthopedic problems that may be aggravated by prolonged continuous walking (>8−10 minutes).

2. History of cardiac problems (i.e., recent heart attack, frequent arrhythmia, valvular defects) that can be negatively influenced by exertion.

3. Lightheadedness upon activity or a history of uncontrolled hypertension (high blood pressure).

B. The walk test should be administered last in the battery of tests. The warmup session is left to the discretion of the test administrator.

C. Individuals should practice walking on several days prior to the test to determine their appropriate walking pace.

Summary

This chapter has attempted to provide information relating to the factors critical to the assessment of physical performance among aged populations. Both clinical and field testing situations have been considered. The conditions surrounding the assessment situation will dictate the type of testing to be done and how the data collected will be used. The chapter has been designed to provide the reader with a state of the art overview of the status of physical assessment as indicated by reported research in the field and an understanding of the physiological mechanisms involved. It is obvious that a great deal of work needs to be done to effectively assess the physical capacities of older people and to relate this assessment to the effective intervention strategies as well as personal health. It is also obvious that the quality of the assessment process will determine the ability to look quantitatively at the effect of specific intervention strategies on given populations, both short and long term. One must understand that the accuracy of these procedures depends on appropriate equipment calibration as well as consistent testing conditions. The reader is referred to guidelines established by the American College of Sports Medicine for subject selection and the qualifications of clinical personnel. The reader is also referred to the bibliography for more detailed information and documentation of the preceding content.

Bibliography

Christensen, C. and Ruhling, R. (1983, Dec.). Physiological and perceptual responses of women to equivalent outputs on the bicycle ergometer and treadmill. *Journal of Sports Medicine and Physical Fitness, 23(4):* 436–444.

Guidelines for Guided Exercise Testing and Exercise Prescription (1980). *American College of Sports Medicine*, 2nd Edition. Philadelphia, PA: Lea and Febiger.

Housh, T., Thorland, W., and Johnson, G. (1983, Sept.). An evaluation of intertester variability in anthropometry and body composition assessment. *Journal of Sports Medicine, 23(3):* 311–314.

Indications and Contraindications for Exercise Testing. *Journal of the American Medical Association, 246(9):* 1015–1018, Aug. 28, 1981.

Miller, D. and Demmentt, R. (1985, Jan.). Fitness evaluations for recreational athletes. *The Physician and Sports Medicine, 13(1):* 67–72.

Osness, W.H. (1981). Biological aspects of the aging process. *The Dynamics of Aging*, Ch. 3. Boulder, CO: Westview Press.

Osness, W.H. (1978). Aging now and in the future: a physiological perspective. *Journal of Social Welfare.* Spring: 15–21.

Pollock, M., Wilmore, J., and Fox, S. (1984). *Exercise in Health and Disease Evaluation and Prescription for Prevention and Rehabilitation*. Philadelphia, Pa.: W.B. Saunders Company.

Potiron-Josse, M. (1983, Dec.). Comparison of three protocols of determination of direct VO max amongst 12 sportsmen. *Journal of Sports Medicine, 23(4):* 424–435.

Powers, S., Baker, B., Deason, R., and Mangum, M. (1984, June). A trend analysis of steady state oxygen consumption during arm crank ergometry. *Journal of Sports Medicine, 24(2):* 131–134.

Smith, E. (1980). Bone mass and strength decline with age. *Exercise and Aging: The Scientific Basis.* Hillside, NJ: Enslow Publishers.

Wetzler, H. and Cruess, D. (1984, Jan.). Aerobic capacity of selected young air force officers and officer candidates. *The Physician and Sports Medicine, 12(1):* 131–134.

Williams, J., Cottress, K., Powers, S., and McKnight, T. (1983, Mar.). Arm egometry: a review of published protocols and the introduction of a new weight adjusted protocol. *Journal of Sports Medicine, 23( )*: 107–112.

Wilson, G., and Skienka, M. (1983, June). A system for measuring energy cost during highly dynamic activities. *Journal of Sports Medicine, 23(2)*: 155–156.

Young, T. (1984). Prediction of functional maximal oxygen intake for persons aged 60–76 years from the Astrand-Ryhming nomogram. Unpublished Masters Thesis, University of Kansas.

Zinkgraf, S., Squires, W., and Maneval, M. (1983, June). On measuring heart rate during exercise. *Journal of Sports Medicine, 223(2)*: 210–212.

PART II:

PROGRAMMING CONSIDERATIONS

7 The Learning Environment and Instructional Considerations

Helen M. Heitmann, Professor Emeritus, University of Illinois—Chicago

Based on data generated by the exercise physiologists and motor behaviorists, the role of exercise and physical recreational activities has been affirmed in maintaining and/or rehabilitating physical functioning for the elderly. As has been detailed in earlier chapters, chronological age does not always reflect biological or functional age. Many of the decrements associated with aging have been shown to be more a result of inactivity than of the aging process itself. Trained older adults have demonstrated muscular strength, flexibility, cardiorespiratory functioning, and reaction/movement times comparable to untrained younger adults. If inactivity has been part of the older adult's lifestyle, the decrements in all facets of physiological and neurological functioning will be greater than those of the longitudinally active older adult.

It is apparent then that great variability in physiological functioning exists among the older adults. Even though the U.S. Surgeon General has identified an Objective stating that "by 1990, 50 percent of adults 65 years and older should be engaging in appropriate physical activity" (U.S. Department of Health and Human Services, 1980) the older adults may be reluctant to participate in physical activity programs because of culture, lifestyle or simply because they believe their reduced capacities cannot be restored.

Knowing that programs properly conducted and geared to individual needs can assist in attaining functional health, it becomes imperative that the program be inspected for its conformity to sound instructional and practice procedures. Each of the decrements noted in older adults have implications for the instructional or recreational program. (See chapters 4 and 13.)

Concerns in the instructional or recreational program should be parallel to those inherent for any age group, but should focus specifically on accommodating perceptual, physiological, psychological, and sociological decrements or needs which may be present in the participants. To lure the older adults into programs only to have them feel out of place or to have nonproductive sessions will serve no beneficial purpose.

"You can't teach an old dog new tricks." If that is so maybe it is because they have already tried the tricks and discarded them as useless, or maybe we need to learn new tricks in order to teach the older adult. Topics to be included in this chapter are implications of aging conditions on motivation, perceptual capabilities, learning styles, and practice conditions, and the instructional accommodations and instructor qualifications necessary to establish a productive learning and participation climate.

Motivation

The biggest deterrent to older adult participation in physical activity programs probably is motivation. Most people are products of their times. Current older adults have not had broad physical recreation participation as part of their lifestyle.

Surveys to determine the extent to which older adults participate in vigorous physical activities reveal a low incident of participation. This seems to be universally true (Cunningham, Montoye, Metzler & Keller, 1968; Harris, 1979; Heikkinen & Kayhty, 1977; Hobart, 1975; Kenyon, 1966, McPherson, 1978; President's Council on Physical Fitness and Sport, 1974; Sidney & Shephard, 1976; Wohl & Szwarc, 1981).

Reasons for lack of participation include "nothing can be done to correct the deficits" (Kriete, 1976), "too old, not enough time, insufficient health" (President's Council on Physical Fitness and Sport, 1974; Harris, 1979), or "not part of the culture" (McPherson, 1978; Wohl & Szwarc, 1981). Recognizing these concerns, the activity program directors must seek to make appropriate information available to potential participants to dispel the myths under which the older adult may be laboring. Once the participant enters the program, care must be taken to provide an environment which will keep the participant interested and willing to continue.

Continued motivation will depend upon the participants' perceived capability to engage in the activities with safety, enjoyment, and beneficial returns from the encounter. Atkinson & McClellan (1968) identify four components essential for continued motivation. These include the person perceiving that he/she has the ability, a motive, an incentive, and an expectancy that he/she will be successful.

To attend to these factors the activity director must determine each participant's ability and motives, establish appropriate incentives, and assure that success will be forthcoming. The goals for success should not be so high that the tasks are perceived as too difficult nor should they be so low that challenge is not present.

Ability

Ability will vary with each person. As chronological age does not always reflect biological or functional age, and the decrements associated with aging have been shown to be more a result of inactivity than the aging process itself, considerable variability will exist from person to person. In addition to differences between people, considerable variability is shown to exist among the various perceptual, physiological, or neurological attributes within the person (Mowatt, Evans & Adrian, 1984). Ability differences can be seen in cardiovascular and respiratory functioning, strength, flexibility, perceptual acuity, and brain and central nervous system efficiency. Each of these differences will have implications on interactive functioning. They will affect balance, agility, eye-hand coordination, reaction and movement time, comprehension, and the ability to perform gross and fine motor, and locomotor tasks. (See Chapter 4.) In addition to basic decrements in these fundamental areas, disease, organic or functional, is common and can further inhibit ability. For example: 86 percent of the elderly suffer from chronic illnesses of arthritis, heart disease, and high blood pressure (Flynn & Fash, 1981), all of which influence one's ability to exercise.

Therefore, to address ability differences, programs of physical activity should accommodate the hierarchy of needs identified by Maslow. The first level relates to basic physiological needs.

People who are infirmed or have minimal opportunities for adequate nutrition will have suboptional endurance and strength and will have little interest in seeking higher desires. The second need is for safety and security. Participation may be deterred by poor strength, balance, or coordination. For people in these categories provisions must be made to improve nutrition, strength, balance, and coordination before higher expectations for ability can be assumed.

Motives

Studies have revealed a variety of reasons why persons participate in physical activity programs. Surveys have shown that elderly men and women differ from young adults in their motives for participation (Massie & Shephard, 1971, Sidney & Shephard, 1976; Telama, Vuolle, & Laasko, 1981; Mobily & de Amorin Sa, 1982). The elderly subjects sought physical activity more for aesthetic, health and fitness, and social reasons than did young subjects. Differences can also be noted by gender for elderly subjects.

Heitmann (1986) surveyed 227 older adults participating in physical activity programs in midwestern U.S. senior citizen sites. The results revealed differences in motives between genders and among age groups. Male respondents age 60–69 (M = 67) and 70 + (M = 72) did not differ significantly from each other and ranked in order their reasons for participation as health, achievement, coping, social, appearance, and aesthetics. Female respondents age 60–69 (M = 65) and 70 + (M = 75) also did not differ from each other in their ranking, however they differed from their male cohorts by ranking their reasons for participating as health, social, coping, appearance, achievement, and aesthetics. Although both genders placed health reasons first, it is apparent that secondary motives varied. The females differed in their rankings from females age 40–50 who ranked their motives as health, appearance, achievement, coping, aesthetics, and social.

If it is the intention to attract older adults to activity programs and sustain their interest, it becomes imperative that the activity instructor understand that there may be differences between and among ages and genders. Even though certain commonalities may be present in cohort groups, individual differences could also be present. An attempt to determine individual motives is most important to the success of the program.

Incentives

Incentives or desired consequences of the actions may also vary. These incentives may be intrinsic or extrinsic. That is, the incentive may come from internal feelings of desire, accomplishment, ego satisfaction, or seeking external rewards of winning ribbons or trophies, championships, prizes, or public acclaim. In some instances both types may be present to varying degrees.

Interviewing older adults as to what their incentives are to enter or continue in a program, it can be found that they range from simple to complex incentives. One woman said she did it because at the end of the month, trips to the theaters were planned; another did it because she wanted to be able to get down on the floor and play with her grandchildren. A man indicated that he wanted to be with his wife and they could go to the classes together. Another man said he wanted to use the class as a warm up before his racketball tournament and took pride that he was in the top four players. Others looked forward to the contests at the end of the program where they could get ribbons and their names on the bulletin board. Some responded that they desired to feel better and stay healthy. All in all each person can have his/her own incentive and the incentives may not be unlike those found in younger people. However, the incentives may be more ingrained in the elderly than in younger people.

Expectancy of Success

Expectancy of success is dependent upon many factors. Initially it may inhibit participation because the potential participant may not have had prior success in physical activity skills or had the opportunity to participate in middle adult years. Without longitudinal participation they may believe they are too old to succeed. Welford and Birrens (1965) have substantiated slower reaction and movement time for older adults than younger people, which means that older adults require more time to perform sensorimotor tasks than younger people. People can perceive this decline and may be reluctant to put themselves in a potentially nonsuccessful situation. It has been found that given the choice of "risk" and "no risk," older persons would take a "no risk" option more frequently than younger persons. This desire for no risk may be due to their lessening ability to physically cope with a potentially changing environment (Botwinick, 1969).

Furthermore they may not like to be confronted with objective evidence of their reduced capabilities. This stress of failure may adversely affect their ego.

On the other hand, skillful older persons who may be attracted to the program may find the program geared to the unskilled and as such it may not be of interest to them. Atkinson and McClelland (1968) indicate that success-oriented persons favor a 50/50 chance of success. But tasks which might represent a 50/50 chance of success for one person may not represent it for another.

Another consideration is that participants may not all agree at which activities they should be successful. Some may desire attaining healthful conditions, others may seek successful social experience, while some may prefer achievement in competition. So while they may have success in achievement, if their goal or motive for attending was for social interaction which was not forthcoming they may not feel successful in the endeavor.

Therefore, when planning the activity sessions it becomes necessary to determine not only the capability of the participants, so the task difficulty level can be set to conform to their success ability, but also to determine in which area it is most important to them to attain success.

Instructional Accommodations of Age Related Conditions

The considerations involved in motivation rely on the ability of the activity director to establish an environment which will accommodate possible perceptual, physiological, psychological, and sociological conditions which may be present. Although each participant may have unique needs, some generalization can be made in establishing a climate which will be conducive to assuring successful participation. These considerations include perceptual capabilities, participant's learning style and comprehension levels, physiological and neurological needs, practice conditions, and the instructional accommodations necessary to establish a productive learning and participation climate.

Perceptual Considerations

The participant, in order to be successful, must be able to react to stimuli with accuracy. Research has shown that certain decrements in perceptual systems may be present.

Visual Considerations. Visual decrements include: (a) reduced visual acuity due to presbyopia which is the inability to focus on near objects, (b) senile miosis, a reduction in the diameter of the pupil at rest, (c) susceptibility to glare, (d) contrast sensitivity which makes adaptation to darkness slower, (e) reduced depth perception, (f) lessened color discrimination, and (g) diseases of cataracts and glaucoma (Weale, 1965; Botwinick, 1978; Haywood & Trick, 1983). Each of these decrements, should it be present, necessitates certain adaptations in the environment, activity and equipment selection, and safety. Since vision is important in game activities, it is necessary that visual accommodations be made. (See Chapter 4.)

Activities should be conducted in a brightly luminated room with contrasting background colors to the equipment being used. Glare producing surfaces should be reduced or eliminated if possible.

Activity selection. Individuals who have had cataracts removed, and who have not had a lens transplant, should avoid activities which require side vision since peripheral vision will be limited. If the participant must wear bifocal glasses during an activity, it should be noted that the field of vision is affected between the upper and bifocal lenses. Activities which create a need to switch between lenses should be avoided. For individuals affected by glare, they will have difficulty with activities where they must distinguish the object against the lights. Fast moving objects may be difficult to perceive if depth perception has been impaired. For seniors with cloudy lenses, certain colors become less distinguishable. Blues and greens are more difficult to discern than yellows and reds (Weale, 1965). Selecting equipment or establishing targets in yellow, orange, or red may make the object easier to see.

Safety considerations should include selecting soft equipment which is to be caught. Should the visual system not perceive the object, and if the person is hit with it, less serious damage would occur to glasses or the body. The participant should be encouraged to secure eye glasses with a band around the head and/or wear protective lenses such as are worn in racketball.

Instructional activities should include deliberate practice with the equipment, beginning with individual manipulation of the objects at the person's own pace to determine what can and cannot be done. It is not definitely known if depth perception or other functional disorders can be restored through exercise, but practice with tracking tasks may bring about certain successful accommodations.

Auditory Considerations. Successful group activities often depend upon oral communication. Impairments in auditory discrimination can be frustrating to the participants and also can be dangerous if the participant cannot be alert to auditory cues.

Often the higher frequencies are harder to distinguish for the older adult. Background noise may interfere with distinguishing the spoken word. If the participant must wear hearing aids, sounds can be distorted.

Environmental considerations should include proper acoustical treatment to walls, floors, and ceilings so sounds do not echo or reverberate unnecessarily. The instructor should speak distinctly, slowly, and in lower tone frequencies. The organization of the group in relationship to the instructor should be such that all participants and particularly those with hearing impairments can see the instructor's face. This can help the participant to possibly lip read or at least to see that the instructor is speaking. If the instructor raises an arm it can be a signal that instructions are being given.

The reducing of background noise such as fans, other groups talking, music playing while instructions are being given, or other activity noise will help to make it easier to pay attention to the directions. Background noise is particularly disturbing to those wearing hearing aids. Sudden loud sounds such as blowing a whistle near someone with a hearing aid can be uncomfortable as well as injurious to the person. If the hearing aid must be worn during activity, care should be taken to avoid blows to the ear or requiring quick head movements which may cause the aid to dislodge.

If the instructor uses discernable gestures the participant can often interpret what is meant. Those with hearing disorders should be placed close to the instructor.

Activity selection should avoid those activities where rapid responses to commands are required. The person may not hear or understand the command and, therefore, not react sufficiently fast for satisfaction or safety. Also if the command is misinterpreted the hearing impaired may feel foolish when they respond incorrectly. The volume of the music should be comfortable and not so loud that additional commands cannot be distinguished.

Kinesthetic and Tactile Considerations. Due to the lessening of joint and proprioceptor acuity, awareness of the position of the limbs may be reduced. This can interfere with the older adult's ability to perform with accuracy or in some instances with safety.

Tactile sensitivity may also be reduced (Johansson, & Vallbo, 1979; Thornbury & Mistretta, 1981). Tactile discrimination is often necessary when throwing or catching balls or other objects. Smooth surfaces are difficult to feel.

Environmental considerations to accommodate kinesthetic decrements would be to have long mirrors available where visual guidance could assist with the proper positioning of the limbs. The equipment should be adapted to heighten hand tactile stimulation. For instance, tape can be affixed to bats, rackets or stick handles, and balls with pebbly surfaces could be selected.

Activity selection should include specific exercises to heighten kinesthetic awareness by helping the participant to feel the correct position of the limbs. For instance, with participants working with partners, call out certain positions alternating sides or moving the limbs in unison. The participants could also watch their movements in a mirror to visually assist in attaining correct patterns. Manual assistance activities should also be given by the instructor or a partner. This can help in calling attention to the desired movements and also accommodates their desire for physical contact.

Learning Style, Comprehension Abilities, and Information Processing

As with younger people, the elderly have a certain affinity for learning through various perceptual modes. Some may need visual or auditory stimulation, others need kinesthetic stimulation. Some may prefer learning by immediately trying the activity utilizing a trial and error approach while others may prefer reflecting on the activity before attempting the task.

Denney (1980) found the elderly less efficient on problem-solving tasks than younger persons. However, on more difficult problems, the elderly used a more effective strategy than on standard problems or on those with more easily classified stimuli.

The ability of unfit persons, and especially older unfit adults, to perceive relationships, reason, and deal with abstractions is less than for those who are highly fit (Powell & Pohndorf, 1971; Elsayed, Ismail & Young, 1980). This attribute is called fluid intelligence. This condition was improved for the lesser fit after aerobic exercises were performed.

Welford and Birren (1965) determined that older adults have slower reaction and movement times than do younger people. However, Spirduso (1980) concluded after reviewing correlation studies that a relationship exists between physical fitness and psychomotor speed. She suggests perhaps increased circulation in the brain and stimulation of the central nervous system slowed deterioration of the speed of reaction and movement time.

However, if the older adult has not indulged in fitness and neuromuscular training, the central nervous system may not be sufficiently efficient to process stimuli fast enough for effective response. Another compounding factor includes "noise" in the central nervous system which produces interference and reduces the number of cells to transmit the sensory information to appropriate mechanisms which initiate motor responses. Short term memory losses are attributed to a decline in retrieval capabilities rather than the acquisition of new knowledge (Birren, 1965). Welford (1977) speculates that a slowing of information processing affects psychomotor speed.

The effect of practice and the conditions of practice have not had sufficient research to warrant definitive conclusions. However, it appears that practice, properly paced and monitored, over a longer period of time than that needed for younger people has a positive influence on fitness and skill acquisition. Most of the studies have examined reactime and movement time under a variety of practice procedures (Surburg, 1976; Weigand & Ramella, 1981; Mowatt, Evans & Adrian, 1984). Conclusions center on the fact that longitudinal involvement in physical activity rather than age alone was a primary influence in performance (Welford, 1973; Mowatt, Evans & Adrian, 1983). Mowatt et al. suggest that practice resulting in familiarity with the task contributes to more successful performance.

Barr (1981) investigated the effects of a massed versus distributed practice schedule on the acquisition of a novel striking skill. She concluded that distributed practice was more beneficial and seemed a more natural way for older adults to practice. This schedule was also less fatiguing and boring for them.

Rapidly paced learning appears to be harder for older adults to assimilate than for younger adults. They prefer to set their own pace (Welford & Birren, 1965; Monge & Hultsch, 1971). This may be due to slowed processing mechanisms or to a desire to avoid risk.

Environmental Considerations

The instructor should provide a variety of modes and practice experiences for the participants to learn new tasks or to rehearse previously learned tasks which may have been lost due to disuse. Activities which require strategies should be structured to accommodate possible slowness in strategy selection. Activities requiring processing quickness or coordination should be preceded by circulation increasing exercises to assure adequate circulation to the brain and central nervous system.

Peripheral commands, extraneous activities and attentional demands, and conditions which contribute to high arousal may increase "noise" in the central nervous system and should be minimized. Cues should be given often and simple directions offered. Complex tasks and those which increase anxiety should be avoided.

Recognizing that differences will occur between the fit and unfit, the length of practice, type of feedback, and success criteria must be established according to the participants' needs and capability. Fatigue, interest, and motivation will affect continued participation.

Individual pacing of the learning or activity should be allowed rather than group-paced cadence or suggesting that all must keep up with the group. Frustration can occur for those who are slower in movements or processing information as well as for those who desire a faster pace.

Activity Selection

Simple games, exercises, and rhythmic activities should be selected for those whose physical condition and previous experience is lacking. Gradual complexity can be added as improvements are shown in reaction/movement times and coping with more complex demands.

Instructional Program Evaluation

As with any enterprise the product must be subjected to evaluation. It is important to know the extent to which the process is contributing to success. In order to assess any post program data, preliminary baseline data must be available. At the onset of the program the instructor should evaluate the physical capabilities of the participants (see Chapter 3, the section on functional evaluation), their motives for attending, and their expectancies of the program.

Keeping a profile sheet on various physical and neuromuscular capabilities can, over a period of time, reveal improvements which will encourage continued effort. At various times throughout the program the participants should be allowed to express, anonymously, their feelings about the extent to which they feel comfortable, are accomplishing their goals, the degree to which they look forward to attending, and so forth. Their responses can give direction to planning future sessions which will continue to be effective or to correct any problems which may be identified.

Attendance records can be kept which will indicate the degree of continuing interest on the part of the participants. These records can, over time, show the degree of program participant growth or decline.

Instructor Qualifications

The most important ingredient in a successful program is the instructor. When questioning participants in many successful senior citizen physical activity programs about why they attended , their first response is usually that they come because of the instructor. Often they are enthusiastic about the instructor's cheerful personality, how the instructor cares for them as individuals, and has patience while carefully explaining the exercise, the value of the exercise, and the cautions which they should heed. Observing successful programs, it can be noted that the participants laugh a lot in contrast to less successful ones where silence is more the norm. The instructor who can inspire comraderie, fun, and free communication has little trouble with motivation.

In addition to these qualities, the instructor should be fully knowledgeable of the physical conditions which may be present in the participants and know how to accommodate them. The instructor should know how to motivate the older adult and how to assist in physical fitness and skill acquisition.

The instructor of the exercise and recreation programs for young people is usually older than the participants and has some feeling for what it is like to be young. However, in senior citizen programs, the instructor is usually younger than the older adults, and has not had first hand experience with the conditions or attitudes the older person may have.

It is helpful to have some experience and awareness of what it is like to have joint stiffness, reduced vision or hearing, and the like. These conditions can be simulated by viewing trigger films showing the world through reduced vision and faded colors. Glasses can be worn with a light coating of soluble grease to simulate vision disorders. Try on a hearing aid to experience the transmitted sound. Wear ear muffs or ear plugs to reduce the volume of someone speaking. To simulate reduced tactile feeling surgical gloves can be worn while manipulating objects. The binding of joints to reduce flexibility can give an appreciation of these handicaps. These types of simulations can sensitize the instructor to some of the handicaps experienced in aging.

Other differences between the instructor and the participants may be culture, mores, and economic and political concerns. The cultural differences could stem from the older adult having lived through different times in history and not being attuned to current entertainment modes or music. Mores have also changed considerably through their lives, and ethnic differences may be more ingrained due to their experiencing less mobility and infusion of counter cultures in their neighborhoods than today's younger adults. With few avenues to increase their economic status concern may be present for keeping their resources for basic needs.

It is important that the instructor explore these conditions with their particular population. Imposing activities even innocently upon the participants may make them feel uncomfortable and will yield no beneficial results. It is only relatively recently that women wore shorts or slacks, and gym shoes were only for kids in their day. Some may have expended considerable physical energy in housework or on the job and may view strenuous exercise as more of the same. But they may view ethnic dancing and games as recreational and be more receptive to doing these things. On the other hand the group may be very modern in their views, economically affluent and able to afford and desire more costly clothing and fees for the program.

Of great concern at the present time is that there is no required certification for instructors. The majority of programs are being conducted by volunteers or other people with little or no understanding of the scientific basis upon which the exercises or recreational activities are founded (Heitmann, 1984). As a profession concerned about quality programs, criteria should be forwarded to program administrators.

All instructors should have an understanding of exercise physiology, kinesiology, motor learning, and the effects that aging and disuse have on these systems. They should also be aware of the psychological and sociological conditions which may be present in senescence. They should be able to develop sound programs to improve cardiovascular-respiratory functioning based on appropriate testing and developmental activities; understand muscular activity, exercise techniques, and body mechanics; be able to conduct diagnostic testing and therapeutic exercise activities to increase range of motion; conduct skill acquisition sessions to improve neuromuscular functioning; and be able to establish appropriate instruction and practice sessions compatible with personal needs and learning requirements to assure the participants' comfort and improved status.

The AAHPERD has adopted the following guidelines for assuring safety in exercise programs:

Guidelines for Exercise Programs
for Older Persons (Age 50 and Older)

There can be risk in sudden, unregulated, and injudicious use of exercise. However, the risk can be minimized through proper preliminary screening and individualized prescribing of exercise programs. It is important for older persons entering an exercise program to have a medical evaluation by a physician knowledgeable about physical exercise and its implications.

For programs involving vigorous exercises (i.e. exercises that exceed the level of intensity encountered in normal daily activities such as walking and climbing stairs), the medical evaluation should ensure that the individual can participate in vigorous exercise without any undue risk to the cardiovascular and other bodily systems. Normally, a test that ascertains an individual's cardiorespiratory adjustment to the stress of exercise is an advisable part of the examination. Minimally, it would ascertain if the cardiovascular system, by such appropriate indicators as heart rate and blood pressure, can adequately adjust to vigorous exercise.

For exercise programs involving low intensity exercises (i.e. exercises that do not exceed the level of intensity encountered in normal daily activities), participants should have their personal physician's approval.

Regardless of whether or not a program of exercises is vigorous or of low intensity, the following guidelines to ensure the safety of the participants are offered:

(1) In that each person's response to the stress of exercise is specific to that individual, it is important that each person's response to exercise be monitored periodically for signs of undue stress (unduly high heart rate, nausea, dyspnea, pallor, pain). Participants should be taught to monitor their own heart rate and to recognize these indicators of stress. Unusual responses should be reported to the exercise leader immediately. Exercise leaders, also, should be vigilant of these warning signs.

(2) Every exercise program must have a well-defined emergency plan for exercise leaders to follow in the event of cardiac arrest or other accidents.

(3) Exercise programs must have adequate supervision. Exercise leaders should be trained in Cardio-Pulmonary-Resuscitation (C-P-R) Techniques. At the very minimum, CPR trained personnel should be present during every exercise session or in close proximity to the exercise program.

Since exercise/recreation programs may be new to the participant it is important that the instructor take nothing for granted and expend considerable energy in selecting appropriate activities to meet the varied needs of each older adult. A caring environment based on scientific principles can go a long way to help older adults enjoy the process of the instruction as well as the product of improved physical functioning. They deserve the best.

References

Atkinson, J., & McClellan, D. (1968). Motivation and behavior. In G.H. Litwin & R. Stringer (Eds.), *Motivation and organizational climate.* Cambridge, MA: Harvard University, Division of Research, Graduate School of Business Administration.

Barr, T. (1981). A distributed vs massed practice schedule on the acquisition of a novel motor skill by senior citizens. Unpublished research report, University of Illinois at Chicago.

Birren, J.E. (1965). Age changes in speed of behavior: Its central nature and physiological correlates. In A.T. Welford & J.E. Birren (Eds.), *Behavior, aging, and the nervous system.* Springfield, IL: Charles C. Thomas.

Botwinick, J. (1969). Disinclination to venture response versus cautiousness in responding: Age differences. *Journal of Genetic Psychology, 115,* 55–62.

Cunningham, D.A., Montoye, H.J., Metzner, H.L., & Keller, J.B. (1969). Active leisure time activities as related to age among males in a total population. *Journal of Gerontology, 23*, 551–6.

Denney, N. (1980). Task demands and problem-solving strategies in middle-aged and older adults. *Journal of Gerontology, 35*, 559–564.

Elsayed, M., Ismail, A.H., & Young, R.J. (1980). Intellectual differences of adult men related to age and physical fitness before and after an exercise program. *Journal of Gerontology, 35*, 383–387.

Flynn, M., & Fash, V. (1981). *Illinois White House conference on aging: Background papers.* Springfield, IL: Illinois Department on Aging.

Harris, L., & Associates. (1979). *The Perrier study: Fitness in America.* New York: Great Waters of France, Inc.

Haywood, K.M., & Trick, L.R. (1983). Age-related visual changes and their implications for the motor skill performance of older adults. Paper presented at the Annual Conference of the American Alliance for Health, Physical Education, Recreation, and Dance.

Heikkinen, E., & Kayhty, B. (1977). Gerontological aspects of physical activity—Motivation of older people in physical training. In R. Harris & L. Frankel (Eds.), *Guide to fitness after 50* (pp 191–205). New York: Plenum Press.

Heitmann, H.M. (1984) Status of Older Adult Physical Activity Programs in Illinois, *Physical Educator.* March: 35–39.

Heitmann, H.M. (1986) Motives of older adults for participating in physical activity programs. In B.D. McPherson (Ed.), *Sport and Aging.* Champaign, IL: Human Kinetics Publishers, Inc., 199–204.

Hobert, C.W. (1975). Active sport participation among the young, the middle-aged and the elderly. *International Review of Sport Sociology, 10* (3–4) 27–40.

Johansson, R.S. & Vallbo, A.B. (1979). Tactile sensitivity in the human hand: Relative and absolute densities of four types of mechanoreceptive units in glabrous skin. *Journal of Physiology, 286*, 283–300.

Kenyon, G.S. (1966). The significance of physical activity as a function of age, sex, education and socio-economic status of northern United States adults. *International Review of Sport Sociology, 1*, 41–54.

Kriete, M.M. (1976). *The effects of a static exercise program upon specific joint mobilities in healthy female senior citizens.* Unpublished masters' thesis. Springfield College.

Massie, J.F. & Shephard, R.J. (1971). Physiological and psychological effects of training. *Medicine and Science in Sport, 3*, 110–117.

McPherson, B.D. (1978). Aging and involvement in physical activity: A sociological perspective. In F. Landry & W. Orban (Eds.), *Physical activity and human well being* (111–125). Miami, FL: Symposia Specialists, Inc.

Mobily, K., & deAmorin Sa, H. (1982 Fall.) Attitudes of the elderly toward physical activity: A cross-cultural comparison. *Iowa Association of Health, Physical Education, Recreation and Dance Journal*, Fall, 16–18.

Monge, R., & Hultsch, D. (1971). Paired-associate learning as a function of adult age and the length of anticipation and inspection intervals. *Journal of Gerontology, 26*, 157–162.

Mowatt, M., Evans, G.G., & Adrian, M. (1984). Assessment of perceptual-motor abilities of healthy rural elderly men and women. *The Physical Educator, 41*, (3), 114–120.

Powell, R.R. & Pohndorf, R.H. (1971). Comparison of adult exercisers and non-exercisers on fluid intelligence and selected physiological variables. *Research Quarterly, 42*, 70–77.

Presidents' Council on Physical Fitness and Sport. (1974). National adult physical fitness survey. *Physical Fitness Digest* (Series 4, No. 2). Washington, D.C.: Author.

Sidney, K.H., & Shephard, R.J. (1976). Attitudes toward health and physical activity in the elderly: Effects of a physical training programme. *Medicine and Science in Sports, 8*, 246–252.

Spirduso, W. (1980). Physical fitness, aging, and psychomotor speed: A review. *Journal of Gerontology, 35*, 850–865.

Surburg, P.R. (1976). Aging and the effect of physical-mental practice upon acquisition and retention of a motor skill. *Journal of Gerontology, 31,* 64–67.

Telama, R., Vuolle, P., & Laakso, L. (1981). Health and physical fitness as motives for physical activity among Finnish urban adults. *International Journal of Physical Education, 38* (1), 11–16.

Thornbury, J., & Mistretta, C. (1981). Tactile sensitivity as a function of age. *Journal of Gerontology, 36,* 34–39.

U.S. Department of Health and Human Services, Public Health Service. (1980). *Promoting health/preventing disease: Objectives for the nation.* Washington, D.C.: U.S. Government Printing Office.

Weale, R.A. (1965). On the eye. In A.T. Welford & J.E. Birren (Eds.), *Behavior, aging and the nervous system.* Springfield, IL: C.T. Thomas.

Welford, A.T. (1973). *Aging and human skill.* Westport, CT: Greenwood Press.

Welford, A.T., (1977). Motor performance. In J.E. Birren & K.W. Schaie (Eds.), *Handbook of the psychology of aging.* New York: Van Nostrand Reinhold.

Welford, A.T., & Birren, J.A. (1965) *Behavior, aging, and the nervous system.* Springfield IL: Charles C. Thomas.

Wiegand, R.L., & Ramella, R. (1983) The effect of practice and temporal location of knowledge of results on the motor performance of older adults. *Journal of Gerontology, 38,* (6), 701–706.

Wohl, A., & Szwarc, H. (1981). The humanistic content and values of sport for elderly people. *International Review of Sport Sociology, 16* (4), 5–11.

8 Principles of Physical Activity Programming for the Older Adult

Bruce A. Clark, University of Missouri

Introduction

The term physical fitness is frequently used as a "one size fits all" concept. That concept is inaccurate. Physical fitness is multifaceted, means different things to different people, and is composed of separate, specific entities. Most contemporary definitions of physical fitness include health-related components of cardiorespiratory endurance, muscular strength and endurance, flexibility, body composition, cardiovascular disease risk reduction, and emotional stability, all of which are important to overall health and well-being. In addition there are performance-related variables such as speed, power, agility, coordination, and specific skills—factors that are important to a sport skill performance.

Physical Gerontology and The Purpose of Exercise

This author coined the term "physical gerontology" to describe physical activity programming undertaken by older adults. Documented research the world over (deVries, 1976; Shephard, 1978; Smith & Serfass, 1981) has demonstrated the benefits of exercise to people of all ages who undertake a program of regular progressive, sensible, physical exercise individually prescribed to meet each person's fitness requirements. But to reap those benefits, participants must use a carefully developed exercise prescription to ensure safety and desired change. In the parlance of the practitioner, "use it or lose it."

Individualizing Physical Activity Prescription

Effectively applying physical activity principles to varied groups and individuals requires individualization. Exercise principles are specified for adults (ACSM, 1978), older adults (deVries, 1976), and special risk populations (Pollock, Wilmore, & Fox, 1984). The contemporary exercise prescription principles used for younger people may be readily adapted for use by older adults by considering factors such as age, sex, fitness level, and health. Activity program providers and leaders must understand those factors and principles to effectively prescribe exercise.

Beginning Considerations

Safety and Liability. Safety is important to both participants and leaders because it helps to generate the confidence so necessary to program satisfaction and adherence. Reasonable safety practices must be an integral part of the entire program from initial screening through participation and followup.

Physical Pre-Testing and Participant Information. Most authorities agree that some form of medical/physical fitness evaluation should be taken by individuals prior to beginning or altering a physical exercise program, especially if they are older or sedentary. The purpose of a preliminary evaluation is to determine the individual's medical and fitness status, note problem areas, and provide a baseline for future medical judgment. It also provides information about the individual's physical fitness that can be used in designing and evaluating the exercise program, and may enhance motivation by making the participant aware of both strengths and weaknesses.

A number of factors to consider in evaluating participants can be found in sources like *Guidelines for Graded Exercise Testing and Exercise Prescription*, by the American College of Sports Medicine, which is a good source to use when planning this stage of the program. Three areas of the medical evaluation, are noted: (1) comprehensive medical history, (2) physical examination, and (3) laboratory evaluation (ACSM, 1980).

The medical history includes the participant's personal and surgical medical history, family, work, and habit background, along with present health habits. Any past or present problems and symptoms that might affect exercise programming also are noted. The physical examination should be inclusive, with special consideration given to the signs and symptoms of cardiorespiratory disease and other contraindications to exercise testing. Another source is the Council on Aging and Adult Development, a council in the American Alliance for Health, Physical Education, Recreation, and Dance. The Council has developed a simple medical evaluation form. The laboratory evaluation may be quite encompassing including a 12-lead resting ECG, comprehensive blood work, and chest X-ray, although they are frequently less so. For example, the Functional Fitness Test described in Chapter 3 is much more practical for most programs.

Additional Physical Activity Program Information. Other information may be obtained to improve program effectiveness. For example, in order to ensure that the participant is physically able to undertake exercise, the sponsoring agency or institution may require a physician approval form. The form may include an explanation of the intensity, frequency, duration, and activity modality, and may solicit specific information regarding the participant's health that the program leaders should take into account. The form can also be used to summarize other important programmatic considerations such as safety precautions, emergency factors, and personal qualifications, and serves not only as a professional courtesy but also may function as a meaningful public relations tool.

A properly written participant release form, required of each participant prior to physical testing or exercise, will serve to inform her/him of important program tenets and provide a record of such. Participant information provided on another form will be invaluable in an emergency when additional information may be required.

Building information, policies, and procedures can be provided regularly to participants in a variety of ways. For example, this information may be posted in a prominent place or announced during class.

Most authorities agree that the fitness of the prospective exerciser should be evaluated before a program is begun. Often both health-and performance-related variables are evaluated using tests that range from relatively fast, easily administered field tests, to very extensive laboratory tests. These are considered in another section of this text. Program planners must decide what objectives are to be addressed; for example, do you want muscular strength, flexibility, cardiovascular endurance, muscle tone, etc.

Program Design Considerations

Specificity and Individuality. The concepts of "specificity" and "individuality " are important in prescribing physical exercise. Specificity, in this context, refers to training the body's physiological systems so that they will adapt as precisely and completely as possible to the exercise imposed. In other words, training benefits are specific first to the kind of exercise undertaken and how it is performed, and second, to the individual to whom they are applied. Body structure and function changes resulting from physical training are specific to the body systems involved and the way they are used. Therefore, specific activities must be designed and implemented in a way that affects each individual change that you attempt to alter.

Individuality means that the participant's personal characteristics must be considered in the exercise prescription. Factors such as personal health and fitness needs, interests, physique, and capabilities must be considered when formulating an individual's program. The principles of specificity and individuality are invaluable when applying contemporary training methods because of their efficiency of effort and how they relate to safety, motivation, and program adherence.

The key factor here is that fitness is *not* a "one-size fits all" concept. Physical fitness programs must be designed to meet the fitness needs of each specific individual and must be implemented in a way that allows the individual to adapt positively to the program.

The Body Barometer. This author coined the term "body barometer" to ensure that the individual's comfort and safety are major considerations in an exercise prescription. Most people are well "in touch" with their bodies and understand them better than anyone, including their personal physicians. With reasonable exercise guidance from leaders, older adults can judge the intensity, frequency, duration, and modality that will effectively and safely influence their progress. The participant's self-awareness, coupled with regular health appraisal, can help them to design and implement efficient physical activity programs. The body barometer concept should be stressed, because it allows participants to have some control over their program, thus limiting injury and magnifying fitness and wellness benefits.

Overload and Progression. The principles of overload and progression may be safely implemented with older adults. The overload principle states that functional improvements occur when the body systems are challenged; this occurs only when the work load is greater than that to which the individual is accustomed (deVries, 1980). This principle is applicable to both body systems and fitness components. In general, the average elderly adult's physical capacity is lower than that of active older or younger individuals, and less exercise stimulus is required to provide an overload.

Progression is a systematic approach in which work loads are gradually increased to provide the body with an appropriate overload (deVries, 1980). Progression will usually be quite gradual in the older adult because adaptation requires more time than in younger people. This factor should be considered both with respect to the individual activity period, as well as the long-term training program. Methods of providing overload are illustrated in the discussion of exercise intensity.

If an interruption occurs in the training program, participants must realize that some decrement in fitness may occur, necessitating program resumption at a level somewhat less strenuous than the point that had been reached prior to the layoff. Also, participants should set realistic exercise and fitness goals consistent with their capabilities.

Warm-up and Cool-down. The older individual's physical capabilities should be reflected in the warm-up and cool-down periods, because these phases are especially important components of an exerciser's total workout (deVries, 1976). Structural changes in muscles, bones, and joints, as well as slower functional adaptation of cardiorespiratory, thermoregulatory, and other systems (Shephard, 1978; Smith, 1984) suggest the use of prudence in the warm-up and cool-down phases of exercise prescription. Arthritic involvement may increase the importance of a proper warm-up regimen for some. The warm-up allows the exerciser's functional systems to gradually adjust to the exercise stress imposed (Barnard, Gardner, Diasco, MacAlprin, & Kattus, 1973; Wilmore, 1982).

The cool-down period is as important as the warm-up for safe exercise. It is light activity following strenuous output, and allows the body to gradually return to the pre-exercise level. The movement helps to keep blood from pooling in the extremities and maintains the return of blood to the heart. Proper instruction and implementation of warm-up and cool-down periods, coupled with the use of the body barometer concept, will help to ensure safe activity participation.

Intensity, Frequency, and Duration. Frequency, duration, and intensity are considered by some to be the most important factors in ensuring participant safety, injury prevention, motivation, program adherence, and prescription effectiveness. They have been extensively documented in the literature with respect to younger individuals. Adaptation of these factors is suggested for older adults (ACSM, 1978; deVries, 1971, 1976; Morse & Smith, 1981; Shepherd, 1978; Smith & Gilligan, 1983). Training intensity is most commonly estimated in one of three ways: (1) metabolic cost (Kcal/min.) in METS,* (2) exercise heart rate in beats per minutes, and (3) perceived exertion (Pollock, *et al.*, 1984).

Improved cardiovascular-respiratory function is related to the percentage of heart-rate range of the work load. The minimal training threshold for older men is 40 percent of their heart-rate range (deVries, 1971), with a range of up to 70 percent of the maximum MET level required to maintain efficiency of the cardiovascular system (Smith and Gilligan, 1983). Normal older adults can improve cardiovascular-respiratory function with postexercise heart rates in the mid to upper 90 beats/minute range, while those who are well conditioned need to maintain exercise heart rates in the 100–120 range. Specific individual rates can be determined using various formulae, including the heart rate reserve method described by the American College of Sports Medicine (ACSM, 1980), and other "target heart rate" techniques noted by Cooper (1982) and Smith (1984).

Maximum heart rate can be predicted by subtracting the individual's age from 220, however this method is somewhat unreliable (Astrand and Rodeahl, 1977; Shepherd, 1978), because of the variation between actual and estimated levels that occurs at any age. Smith and Gilligan (1983) have demonstrated a correlation of .95 between an individual's heart rate and energy cost on a work capacity test. They modified a chair step test (Smith & Gilligan, 1983) that estimates energy cost, and may be used in circumstances where modified and minimal work output is necessary. Table 8.1 summarizes reasonable methods of determining exercise intensity.

Perceived exertion, as conceived by Borg (Borg, 1978), has proven to be a reasonably effective way to estimate exercise intensity. This method uses a 15-point scale from 6 to 20 using descriptions to estimate exertional stress from "very, very light" (7), to "very, very hard" (19). By adding a zero to each number, the estimated heart rate correlates quite well with the actual rate. (Pollock, *et al.*, 1984) This method should not be used at the exclusion of the heart rate or MET level methods, but as an adjunct to them as another "body barometer" resource. Factors

---

*A MET is equal to using 3.5m of oxygen per kilogram of body weight per minute.

TABLE 8.I.
Methods of Determining Exercise Intensity

A. American College of Sports Medicine Method (ACSM, 1980)	B. Cooper Method (Cooper, 1982)	C. Smith Method (Smith, 1984)
MHR = Maximum Heart Rate (beats per minute); actual or estimated using 220 minus age − RHR = Resting Heart Rate (beats per minute); actual × CI = Conditioning Intensity (the % selected, usually ranging from 40% to 85%) + RHR = Resting Heart Rate (beats per minute); actual RESULT = Minimum Training Heart Rate	1. PMHR (Predicted Maximum Heart Rate) (beats per minute) Male = 205 − ½ your age Female = 220 − your age 2. Take conditioning intensity desired (in percent of PMHR)	Formula: EXMET = % HR/100 × MAXMET where: EXMET = Exercise met level % HR = Percentage heart rate at which the individual participates % HR = (EXHR − RESTHR)/(MAXHR − RESTHR) × 100 MAXMET = Maximum met level
Example: 160 = 220 − 60 (220 − age of participant in years) −60 = Resting Heart Rate 100 ×.60 = 60% = Conditioning Intensity 60 +60 = Resting Heart Rate 120 = Result; Minimum Training Heart Rate (beats per minute)	*Example:* 1. PMHR Male 60 years old = 205 − 30 = 175 (beats per minute) Female 60 years old = 220 − 60 = 160 (beats per minute) 2. 60% conditioning intensity is desired. Male = 175 × .60 = 105 = Result; minimum training heart rate (beats per minute) Female = 160 × .60 = 96 = Result; minimum training heart rate (beats per minute)	*Example:* Individual had a maximum met level of 5 mets on a treadmill test, at an exercise level of 70% heart rate, the exercise level would be: EXMET = % HR/100 × MAXMET EXMET = 70/100 × 5 mets = 3.5 mets

such as individual variability and drug regimen should also be considered in evaluating exercise intensity.

With some variation exercise duration and frequency factors for older adults are similar to those recommended for young people (deVries, 1976; Morse & Smith, 1981). A duration of 20–60 minutes is commonly recommended for general programs. Exercise stress is lessened if older adults increase the duration and decrease the intensity of their program. Generally, a frequency of three days per week is recommended, however, if a participant's activity level and functional status are low, as few as two days per week might produce significant improvement. At the other end of the continuum, the tendency of the elderly to lower intensity and shorter duration might be reasonable if the frequency of workouts is greater than three per week (Morse & Smith; 1981). Another argument for limited intensity, frequency, and duration is that the older adult lacks the structural and functional capability to withstand high stress levels associated with more intense activity, and requires a longer recovery period. Smith and Gilligan (1983) illustrate an effective method for estimating exercise duration using MET level noted in Table I.

Individual Comfort and Safety Factors

Clothing and Footwear. Wearing clothing and shoes appropriate for the exercise activity is especially important for older adults. Therefore, some general guidelines should be followed.

Comfort and support are important considerations. Loose fitting clothing that gives freedom of movement, such as shirt or blouse and shorts or slacks, should be worn for most activities. Sweat suits may also be worn, but the better quality styles are expensive, and unless they are made specifically for weather protection, offer little benefit over normal clothing. Athletic supporters for men, and bras for women, elastic socks and tights, are preferred by some but others find them restrictive and uncomfortable. Specialty activities such as racketball or hiking require eye protection and boots, respectively, for safe participation.

Dressing properly for weather and environmental conditions provides the participant both a safety and comfort edge (Paul, 1983). When exercising outdoors in cold weather, precautions must be taken to insulate the body from the elements. Exposing the head, ears, fingers, and toes should be limited because body heat will be lost (Kaufman, 1983). For short periods of time this need not be a significant problem; however, it is heat expensive over long periods (Kaufman, 1982). Knit hats and scarfs will reduce heat loss. Some garments allow perspiration to evaporate while maintaining warmth and protection from rain and/or snow. Earmuffs, porous caps, and headbands provide moderate protection for less severe weather.

Keeping the torso insulated eases the burden of maintaining extremity heat. Layering clothes is recommended, with removal of garments as required as heat generated from increased body metabolism builds. Layering helps to insulate the body by trapping air between the clothing layers. Clothing that allows perspiration to escape without moisture entering is preferred. Wool close to the skin helps to retain heat without trapping moisture. Warm weather apparel is important also. Minimal clothing that allows the skin to breathe, yet protects against harmful ultraviolet rays, should be worn. Light colors that reflect rather than absorb heat are preferable.

Because of exercise unfamiliarity and conditions such as arthritis, older adults may not be able to withstand the rigors of increased exertion. Therefore, the type and fit of shoes are important. For most activities a good quality athletic structure shoe is adequate, but some activities require specialty shoes. For example, because of forces exerted upon the foot and the rest of the body, jogging and running require shoes that can absorb that stress (Bates, 1982; Cavanaugh, 1980; Clark, 1982). Shoes should have good shock absorbing qualities, as well as a supportive heel, arch support, adequate toe area, and supportive mid-soles. A number of good quality name brand specialty shoes are presently on the market. Unfortunately lower quality look-alikes are also available but often do not possess the necessary qualities for safe and effective performance. It is a good idea to purchase shoes from a reputable specialty dealer who can answer questions and fit the foot properly. Here again, individual attention is important.

Good quality socks that fit and provide warmth, blister protection, and shock and perspiration absorption are recommended. Wool and cotton, as well as various material blends, are commonly used. Preference, environmental factors, and type of activity will dictate the choice. Some prefer socks with a heel rather than tube socks because the form fitting type ensure a better fit, preventing foot movement inside the shoe, and reducing friction-induced blisters or tenderness.

Environmental Conditions. During the part of the year when weather conditions may be extremely hot or cold, most people are forced to exercise indoors in a controlled environment. Some however, prefer the outdoors or engage in activities that can only reasonably be done outside. For these people, some specific knowledge regarding safety when the body is exposed to temperature extremes is necessary.

Physical exercise often elevates the body temperature to over 100 degrees F. In order for the body to adjust to the increased heat, cooling must occur. The most effective method is evaporation in the presence of moving air and low humidity. Even quite warm temperatures can be tolerated reasonably well under those favorable conditions. High temperatures place greater stress on the active body and, in combination with high humidity, produce unfavorable conditions that limit evaporation. Perspiration occurring under favorable conditions is often imperceptible because evaporation is so rapid, whereas under unfavorable conditions the sweat drips off the body and provides little cooling effect. Both participants and leaders must be cognizant of temperature, humidity, and wind velocity effects in prescribing exercise.

Rubberized suits, saunas, steam rooms, and hot showers must be used cautiously because they do not allow body cooling. They can increase stress to dangerous levels and are not recommended. People who exercise regularly in the heat or become sufficiently heated that they sweat profusely, must take care to avoid dehydration by replacing the fluid loss with plenty of water. It may be necessary to take some water *while* exercising to maintain a safe hydration level. Most elderly people were raised at a time when it was believed that drinking water while exercising was bad for you. That misconception may need to be corrected. In most cases electrolyte losses are replaced with normal diet. To avoid health problems, those who wish to take additional salt or commercial electrolyte replacements should consult their physicians.

Exercising in the cold is not usually as problematic as exercising in the heat because precautions can be taken, such as wearing proper clothing and limiting exposure. Care must be taken, however, to avoid dangerous conditions like hypothermia and frost bite. Also, breathing in very cold air can cause considerable discomfort and could be dangerous. By following the suggestions noted in the clothing and footwear section, suitable clothing can be chosen for the existing conditions.

Another environmental variable is that of altitude. The higher the elevation above sea level, the more difficult it is for the body to use oxygen. Exercise intensity must be reduced if a person exercises at higher altitudes than that to which they are accustomed. A period of several days acclimatization is necessary for safety and exercising at higher altitudes may be contraindicated for some people.

Program Activities

A wide range of activities may be undertaken by older adults. These include activities done by younger people with necessary adaptation to suit the individual's preference and capability. The activity categories include conditioning programs, sports, and dance, and most can be done individually or in groups. The participant and activity leader must determine the specific fitness components they wish to emphasize when choosing the exercise program. Two key points should be emphasized: First, "one size does not fit all," so the program must be designed to develop specific fitness component needs that suit the individual. Second, fitness cannot be stored, so exercising regularly is important.

Older adults generally should concentrate on improving the health-related fitness components. Performance-related fitness activities may also be included for those who wish some variety or want to take part in sports. Table 8.2 summarizes some of the benefits of selected activities.

TABLE 8.2.
The Benefits of Various Physical Activity Programs
Activity Program Benefits*

Activity	Stamina	Muscular Strength	Muscular Endurance	Weight Control	Flexibility	Skill Improvement	Indiv.	Group	Both	Comments**
Aerobic Dance	XX	X	XX	XX	X	X			X	Very popular; widely available
Bicycling	XX	X	XX	XX	—	X			X	
Boating (rowing and canoeing)	XX	X	XX	XX	—	—			X	Stationary rowing machines can provide similar benefits
Bowling	—	—	—	—	—	X			X	A major participation activity in the U.S.
Dancing	X	—	X	X	—	X		X		Varied opportunities exist for participation
Fitness Trail or Par Course	XX	X	XX	XX	X	—			X	Requires more space and precautions
Golf (walking)	X	—	X	X	X	X			X	
Handball/Racketball	X	—	X	X	X	X		X		
Hiking	X	—	X	X	—	X			X	
Interval Training	XX	X	X	XX	—	—			X	
Rhythmical Endurance	XX	X	XX	XX	—	—			X	
Skating (ice & roller)	XX	—	X	XX	—	X			X	Seasonal aspect may add variety
Skiing: cross country	XX	X	XX	XX	—	—			X	Seasonal
Skiing: downhill	X	X	X	X	—	X			X	Seasonal; somewhat costly
Swimming	XX	X	XX	XX	X	X	X			Facility availability is a concern
Swim exercise	XX	X	XX	XX	X	—			X	
Tennis	X	—	X	X	—	X			X	
Walking/Jogging	XX	—	XX	XX	—	—			X	Readily available
Weight training	—	XX	X	—	X	—	X			Equipment is needed
Yoga Relaxation	—	—	—	—	X	—			X	Often a good addition to other programs

XX = Very good   *The extent of benefit will relate to the intensity, frequency, and duration of the activity undertaken.
X = Moderate   **The Fun factor is possible in all the activities and is dependent upon the individuals attitude and approach.
— = Limited

(Corbin, C.B., Dowell, L.J., Lindsey, R., & Tolson, H., 1983; News, 1981).

Remember that most fitness components are related and, therefore, may be enhanced using a variety of activities. Factors such as cost, location, social support, and convenience of scheduling will affect participant adherence. It is important for participants to recognize the factors that help them to remain active. Knowledge and enjoyment will encourage participants to continue those activities that they feel are physically and emotionally beneficial.

The American College of Sports Medicine (ACSM, 1978) recommends rhythmical, large muscle, continuous, aerobic activities for healthy adults. Activities such as jogging, walking, swimming, skating, bicycling, cross-country skiing, rope skipping, and aerobic dancing are suggested. Overweight, arthritic, or sedentary individuals should choose nonweight bearing aerobic activities or ones that do not involve exercising the same joints every time they exercise. Structural and functional recovery from physical exertion is slower in the aged than in younger people. Therefore, a combination of varying of daily activity modalities and longer time periods between exercise sessions is recommended. Other specific programs and considerations are available in the literature (Bennett, 1984; Butts & Anderson, 1981; Cooper, 1982; Corbin, et al., 1983; Daniels, 1982; Exercise, 1977; Pollock, et al., 1984; Pollock, Wilmore, & Fox, 1978). An exercise program check list (see Table 8.3) may help the adult choose a safe, effective program.

Physical Activity Program Implementation

General Administration

Planning and organization are keys to effective activity program development and implementation. Proper planning requires the establishment of objectives and procedures for total program development.

Program objectives must take participant and program factors into account. Specific participant objectives will include physical fitness enhancement, safety, motivation, and behavioral modification. Program implementation objectives might include community interaction, finances, and publicity. It is necessary to develop objectives that are realistic and measurable. Setting obtainable and timely goals will help promote a feeling of accomplishment that will result in improved motivation and morale. Individualized objectives will aid personnel in providing effective classes, as well as helping to produce a coordinated, total program.

Advertising, public relations, and publicity should be consistent with the program philosophy. For example, with programs that are service oriented, small enrollments and low-key programming requiring minimal public interaction may be preferred. Publicity will likely take the form of internal communication and individualized rewards. With larger programs, publicity may include more sophisticated techniques such as media "blitzes" and promotions. In both cases budgetary and promotion variables must balance.

Scheduling, finances, recordkeeping, and other administrative functions will vary widely and are dependent upon the specific needs of each program. For example, some programs may be financed solely through individual participant fees while others may be partially funded through governmental or private agencies. These factors will relate directly to other administrative tasks like applying for grants, compiling status reports, and conducting fund raisers. Whatever the extent of recordkeeping required, it is important to maintain complete program and participant records in a safe, accessible place.

TABLE 8.3.
Exercise Program Check List

About myself

Have I completed a comprehensive physical examination including:
_____ Health history and lifestyles evaluation
_____ Notation of injuries or medications that may affect my participation
_____ Cardiovascular disease risk profile
_____ Exercise stress test—if appropriate

Have I appraised my physical fitness needs and interests?
_____ Stamina (cardiovascular endurance)
_____ Muscular strength and endurance
_____ Body composition
_____ Flexibility
_____ Specific skills

What have I done to get ready for my personal exercise program?
_____ Completed lead-up conditioning activities
_____ Obtained comfortable, supportive clothing for the environmental conditions I might encounter
_____ Obtained quality, comfortable, well-fitting shoes

What kind of exercise program do I want?
_____ Individual exercise or sport
_____ Group activity
Specific type of activity
_____ conditioning
_____ dance
_____ sports

About the program

Has the facility got?
_____ A variety of activities from which to select
_____ Moderate class size
_____ Reasonable class costs
_____ Adequate and clean dressing and shower areas
_____ Well lit, ventilated, and temperature regulated
_____ Sensible safety and emergency plans

Are the instructors?
_____ Trained and credentialed in their teaching area
_____ Willing and able to answer my exercise questions
_____ Trained and certified in safety procedures

Does the instruction?
_____ Meet at least 2–3 times per week
_____ Start and progress at a reasonable rate
_____ Allow for individual differences
_____ Provide for fitness evaluation
_____ Provide ongoing supervision

Evaluation is a tool that can be used effectively for motivational purposes. Participants and program personnel who can see the "fruits of their labor," will be more enthusiastic about continuing and improving. Reasonable policies and procedures for scheduling, recordkeeping, and other necessary program factors should be established and followed.

Personnel

As with other aspects of the physical activity program, the personnel necessary for effective programming will vary widely. The program director will provide leadership. The director's competencies should include an understanding of program components as well as effective interpersonal and administrative skills. Support staff will include secretaries, custodians, and others relating directly or indirectly to program functioning. Staff and instructor morale, an important factor, may be dependent upon difficult decisions, especially in light of budgetary and employment constraints.

Fitness leaders and instructors are the backbone of the physical activity program because of their direct contact with participants. They should be personable and enthusiastic, and effectively apply exercise theory in their instruction. They must be capable of understanding their student's needs and willing to assist them with exercise and personal matters, or to refer them to the appropriate resource. They must recognize and make adjustments for the special needs of the elderly. Instructors can benefit from the various workshops, courses, and seminars available to improve their functions.

Program consultants and advisors may work individually or on committees, and either way might serve on an ongoing or periodic basis. The day-to-day matters are best handled by standing committees or regular personnel (for example, the Medical Advisory Committee and Public Relations Department). Other committees may be convened as needed. Often a variety of advisory functions may be consolidated into one individual or a single group.

It behooves the program director to provide the best qualified personnel for each function within the program, given fiscal and other constraints. Often the services of qualified individuals and groups may be obtained through collaborative efforts with other agencies. Sometimes retired professionals or parttime personnel are quite effective at a modest cost. They may be willing to exchange their expertise for services that your facility can provide. It is important that all personnel feel important and valuable to the program.

Facilities and Equipment

The facilities and equipment necessary to conduct physical activity programming for older individuals relate to factors such as program magnitude, potential for flexible scheduling, and staffing. For example, a number of different activities can be conducted consecutively in a modest gymnasium or activity room by only one instructor, or concurrently by several.

Activities such as aquatics, weight training, racket sports, orienteering, and others require specialized facilities, however activities like dance, aerobics, and calisthenics may all be undertaken in the same facility. Collaboration with other program providers in the area may result in exchange or inexpensive or free use of facilities.

Specific facility characteristics such as cleanliness, accessibility, lighting, may require special attention when used by older adults (Smith, 1984). For example, hallways, dressing areas, and exercise rooms must be well lit to compensate for the visual decrements of aging. (See Chapter 4). Similarly, area acoustics should be good and may require that special attention be paid to pronunciation and speech speed in order to avoid distortion by the hearing impaired. Voice amplification may not improve understanding. Attention must be paid also to things such as highly polished floors, pool and shower areas to avoid slipping that is amplified by the older adults decreased reaction and movement time. Exercise areas used for dance, jogging, or other "bouncy" activities are best made of resilient, non-skid surfaces in order to reduce compression forces that are poorly accommodated by older adults.

As noted earlier, environmental considerations are important for outdoor exercisers. Clothing and shoes must be appropriate to the activity and prevailing conditions. Further, courts and other activity surfaces must be kept in good condition, with loose equipment kept in good repair and clear of the activity area in order to avoid unnecessary accidents.

Safety, Screening, Injury Prevention, and Emergency Planning

Physical activity may be safely undertaken by older adults with varying fitness and health status with little fear of untoward consequences (Shephard, 1981). Nevertheless, safety and emergency policies should be followed.

An important feature of activity programming is regular blood pressure and heart-rate screening, with the data retained for information and comparative purposes. Resting blood pressure should be taken by qualified personnel following a reasonable rest period with heart rate recorded at the same time. Exercise and/or post exercise heart rates should be taken several times during the exercise period. Participants should be taught to monitor their own pulse regularly, with instructors randomly checking their accuracy. Relatively inexpensive apparatus may be purchased for determining heart rates, however, validity and reliability varies.

As noted previously, participant safety requires that the program director and activity leaders understand and implement basic exercise and physiological principles in order to deter potential activity related problems (Kuroda, 1982). Also, they should have current cardiopulmonary resuscitation (CPR) certification, understand emergency procedures, and rehearse them periodically. Personnel with further training, such as American College of Sports Medicine (ACSM) certification and paramedical training benefit the leader and the program.

Program policies should be understood and followed by the program personnel and participants. For example, entering participants might be required to provide evidence of medical and personal clearance along with a personal release, history, and demographic data. Emergency plans, phone numbers, contacts to make, and the like, should be known and posted where appropriate. Area emergency personnel might also be contacted periodically and appraised of the program—location, number and characteristics of participants, and other special information. Hand held sirens and walkie talkies might be used for activities conducted long distances from the center (Smith, 1984). Personnel should be aware of potential problem areas specific to given activities, and teach them to the participants. Both personnel and participants should be realistically aware of potential problems and their solution. You cannot be overprepared.

Providing effective and enjoyable physical activity programs for older adults can be extremely rewarding for both participants and providers alike. It is physically and emotionally rejuvenating!

References

American College of Sports Medicine. (1980). *Guidelines for graded exercise testing and exercise prescription* (2nd ed.). Philadelphia: Lea & Febiger.

American College of Sports Medicine. (1978). The recommended quantity and quality of exercise for developing and maintaining fitness in healthy adults. *Sports Medicine Bulletin, 13*(3), vii–x.

Astrand, P.O. and Rodahl, M. (1977). *Textbook of work physiology* (2nd ed.). New York: McGraw-Hill Book Co.

Barnard, R.J., Gardner, G.W., Diasco, N.V., MacAlpin, R.N. & Kattus. (1973). Cardiovascular responses to sudden strenuous exercise-heart rate, blood pressure, and ECG. *Journal of Applied Physiology, 34*, 833–834.

Bates, W.T. (1982, March). Selecting a running shoe. *The Physician and Sports Medicine, 10,*(3), 154–155.

Bennett, J.P. (1984, June 6–7). Exercise for well or community living older adults. Paper presented at the annual Older Adult Fitness Workshop, Fairfax, Virginia.

Borg, G. (1978). Subjective effort in relation to physical performance and working capacity. In H.L. Pick, Jr. (ed.), *Psychology: From Research to practice.* New York: Plenum Publishing Corp.

Butts, F., & Anderson, G. (1981). Exercise programs for citizens sixty and over—Why not? *ERIC,* No. SP 018-483.

Cavanaugh, P.R., (1980). *The running shoe book.* Mountain View, California: Anderson World, Inc.

Clark, B. (1982). The most often asked questions on running shoes—and the answers. *Runners World, 16,* 48–49.

Cooper, K.H. (1982). *The aerobics program for total well-being.* Toronto: Bantam Books.

Corbin, C.B., Dowell, L.J., Lindsey, R., & Tolson, H. (1983). *Concepts in physical education* (4th ed.), Dubuque, Iowa: Wm. C. Brown Company Publishers.

Daniels, C. (1982). *Research and practical physical activity programs for the aged.* Pre-convention and workshop papers presented at the annual meeting of the American Alliance for Health, Physical Education, Recreation and Dance, Houston, Texas.

deVries, H.A. (1971). Exercise intensity threshold for improvement of cardiovascular-respiratory function in older men. *Geriatrics, 26,* 94–101.

deVries, H.A., (1976, Summer). Fitness afte fifty. *Journal of Physical Education,* 147–151.

deVries, H.A. (1980). *Physiology of exercise for physical education and athletics* (3rd ed.). Dubuque, Iowa: Wm. C. Brown Publishers.

Exercise and aging. (1977, April). *Physical Fitness Research Digest,* Series 7(2), 1–27.

Kaufman, W.C. (1982, February). Cold-weather clothing for comfort or heat conservation. *The Physician and Sports Medicine, 10*(2), 71–75.

Kaufman, W.C. (1983, February). The hand and foot in the cold. *The Physician and Sports Medicine,* 11(2), 156–168.

Kuroda, Y. (1982). Sports medical problems on physical activity in middle and old age. *The Journal of Sports Medicine and Physical Fitness, 22*(1), 1–16.

Morse, E., & Smith L. (1981). Physical activity programming for the aged. 109–120. In: Smith, E.L. & Serfass, R.C. (eds.) *Exercise and aging—the scientific basis.* Hillside, N.J.: Enslow Publishers.

Paul, S.H. (1983, January–February). Winter clothing. *Running and fitness, 15,* 24–26.

Pollock, M.L., Wilmore, J.H. & Fox, S.M. (1984). *Exercise in health and disease.* Philadelphia: W.B. Saunders Company.

Pollock, M.L., Wilmore, J.H., & Fox, S.M. (1978). *Health and fitness through physical activity.* New York: John Wiley and Sons.

Shephard, R.J. (1978). *Physical activity and aging.* Great Britain: Groom Helm Ltd., Publishers.

Smith, E.L., & Gilligan, C. (1983, August). Physical activity prescription for the older adult. *The Physician and Sports Medicine, 11,* 91–101.

Smith, E.L. & Serfass, R.C. (Eds.) (1981). Preface, In: *Exercise and aging—the scientific basis.* Hillside, N.J.: Enslow Publishers.

Smith, E.L. (1984). Special considerations in developing exercise programs for the older adult. In: Matarazzo, J.D., Weiss, S.M., Herd, J.A., Miller, N.E., Weiss, S.M. (Eds.) *Behavioral health—a handbook of health enhancement and disease prevention.* New York: John Wiley and Sons.

Wilmore, J.H. (1982). *Training for sport activity: The physiological basis of the conditioning process* (2nd ed.). Boston: Allyn and Bacon.

9 Handicapping Conditions and Older Adults

Julian H. Stein, George Mason University

Specialists in adapted physical education, therapeutic recreation, and special education emphasize *similarities* between persons with handicapping conditions and the able-bodied population. Many specialists believe that there are greater differences among individuals within any traditional categorical handicapping condition than between groups of those with different handicapping conditions and those categorized as the able-bodied population. In many ways these generalizations are more valid during the senior years than throughout earlier years.

However, these are not the hard and fast generalizations that they appear to be at first glance. Because there is much heterogeneity within and among persons with handicapping conditions, and there is great heterogeneity among senior citizens, relationships between senior citizens and those with handicapping conditions are extremely complex.

In programming for senior citizens, considerations must be given individuals with all the usual categorical handicapping conditions—blind and partially sighted; deaf and hard of hearing; mildly, moderately, and severely/profoundly mentally retarded; cerebral palsied; spinal cord injured; amputees; emotionally disturbed and behaviorally disoriented; those with various health related problems such as asthma, diabetes, and seizure disorders; cardiac and respiratory deficiencies; stroke and other brain-related disorders; Alzheimer's disease; and multiple conditions found in various combinations. One must consider whether handicapping conditions were congenital and individuals have dealt with inconveniences and accommodations for a lifetime, or if they were recently acquired and have been dealt with for a much shorter period of time. Individuals confronted with handicapping conditions in different ways for various lengths of time must each also deal with effects and realities of aging.

An entirely new group of senior citizens with handicapping conditions emerges and must be considered. This group consists of individuals who acquire categorical handicapping conditions through age related processes—diseases, accidents, or the aging process itself. Other factors also contribute to reduced functions due to real or pseudo handicapping conditions. Regardless of causes, such conditions affect individuals and must be considered when planning and implementing programs for them. Representative of such contributing factors are drugs and misuses of medicines, accidents, reduced vision and hearing, malnutrition, infections, depression, metabolic problems, dehydration, heart problems, and brain dysfunctions (Rhodes, 1986).

The routes by which each individual has acquired and been labeled as handicapped creates associated psychological, emotional, and social climates. Approaches for dealing with such individuals should reflect an awareness of these different climates. Personnel working with individuals possessing handicapping conditions should not generalize regarding an individual's limitations; focus on ability, not disability; stress "can do," not "can't"; accentuate the positive, not the negative. Noncategorical approaches, increasingly advocated for children and adolescents, are applicable for older individuals with handicapping conditions, regardless of type, severity, length of time possessed, or mode by which attained.

S-P-R Model

The S-P-R model is presented to assist the reader in avoiding categorical tendencies and to provide practical applications. The model is based upon the fundamental tenet that a motor act is preceded by input from a stimulus that is processed by the brain (information processing). This model is called S-P-R—(S)timulus/ (P)rocessing/ (R)esponse. Handicapping conditions, regardless of ages of individuals, should be looked upon in terms of how each affects an individual's ability to learn and perform skills. As with young persons possessing handicapping conditions, similar conditions of older individuals should be looked upon from physical activity, recreation, and sport perspectives—not medical characteristics. Concern for the large majority of persons with handicapping conditions, regardless of ages or needs, should be in ways the *S-P-R* process is affected by each individual's condition. Obviously medical contraindications to types and intensities of activities must be given priority when programming for individuals with such conditions. But this represents a minority of senior citizens.

- *(S)timulus* problems arise when individuals are blind, partially sighted, deaf, hard-of-hearing, tactile defensive, kinesthetic deficient, or proprieoceptive defective—any and all of which can be products of the aging process. Individuals possessing such conditions must be approached in ways that emphasize *in tact* sensory mechanisms. When, for example, auditory and tactile inputs are used with blind or partially sighted individuals, the total *S-P-R* process functions appropriately and the individual is able to execute skills and perform tasks effectively. For individuals with deficient sensory mechanisms, full use of other sensory devices must be made. In some cases assistance can be obtained from glasses, contact lenses, or hearing aids. For some individuals instructional approaches can incorporate manual manipulation (guiding individuals through movements physically or by structuring the environment appropriately, and tactile approaches to capitalize fully on proprieoceptive feedback provided through messages sent from sensory endings in muscles back to the brain.

- *(P)rocessing* problems arise when the brain has difficulty matching a stimulus to previous experience. To elicit an appropriate response for a given stimulus it is necessary for the brain to process input appropriately in various ways—match, discriminate, sequence, perceive, decode, use memory, *ad infinitum*. Inability to process stimuli effectively is characteristic of many mentally retarded and learning disabled persons; it is also found in some senior citizens as mental processes slow and may even deteriorate. Various techniques and approaches can be used to help such individuals learn skills and participate in related activities. Representative of such instructional approaches are:

    . . .introduce skills and movement patterns at lower and more basic levels;

    . . .break skills and movement patterns into small, more manageable portions that facilitate processing of related input;

    . . .reinforce appropriate execution of skills and movement patterns so individuals feel personal success and satisfaction;

    . . .provide varied opportunities for individuals to repeat skills and movement patterns to improve proficiency and increase situations in which they can be applied;

    . . .use behavior management techniques and approaches applicable to the individual participant;

    . . .consider shaping, chainning, reverse chainning, and related approaches as appropriate for the individual; and

. . .use positive feedback to reinforce specific strengths and accomplishments by individual participants.

These techniques have resulted in progress by learning disabled and mentally retarded individuals of all functional levels and ages, including many senior citizens. The reader may recognize this approach as it has long been used by effective teachers, leaders, and coaches, regardless of activity or level of individual function.

- *(R)esponse* problems arise when individuals have various physical impairments such as spinal cord injuries, amputations, polio, muscular dystrophy, cerebral palsy, and multiple sclerosis; reduced physical and motor functions in senior citizens can cause similar response problems. These conditions require that teachers, leaders, and coaches recognize the appropriateness of different ways for individuals to execute skills and movement patterns. For example, one should not expect double leg amputees and paraplegics to execute swimming skills in the same ways. While emphasis continues to be on individuality in executing skills and motor patterns, in no situation is it more necessary than when dealing with persons whose conditions bring about response differences. For these individuals stimuli are received from intact body parts and sensory receptors and processed appropriately by the brain. Physical impairments make it necessary to recognize how each condition affects ways in which physical skills and motor patterns are performed. We must avoid the trap of rigid adherence to the ways such skills and patterns are performed.

The effect that age has on execution of physical skills and motor patterns must also be considered in the *R* phase of the *S-P-R* process; for example, when young, complex sport skills are executed in a series of smoothly coordinated movements. In moving for a ground ball in softball, a young infielder goes laterally, bends to field the ball, and gets in position to throw, all in one motion. With age this becomes a series of separate and individual movements—go laterally to the ball, then bend to field the ball, and then get in position to throw!
This process manifests itself in various ways for different activities. The change is common with aging particularly among people who have been very sedentary for a long period.

When dealing with individuals possessing multiple handicapping conditions, appropriate instructional techniques and approaches must be selected that address whatever phases of the *S-P-R* process that are involved. For some individuals with emotional conditions, initial use of physical activities may be for therapeutic purposes. Once such conditions are under control, application of the *S-P-R* process is no different than earlier discussed.

For All the Same Reasons

Emphasis on participation for senior citizens with handicapping conditions is for all the same reasons as other senior citizens take part in all kinds of activities—for FUN, pleasure, enjoyment, social contacts, and personal satisfactions.

Activity—*movement*—can be more important to the aging disabled individual than to the aging nondisabled individual. An individual with a disability—regardless of type or severity—can find it more difficult to get around in environments that, despite accessibility laws, are often not friendly to those with disabilities. More energy and better physical condition are needed to negotiate unfriendly, possibly even hostile, and inaccessible facilities when one possesses a disability. Individual muscles and muscle groups must be used in new and different ways if an individual uses a wheelchair, walker, crutches, or brace. When these factors are coupled with tendencies for individuals to lose muscular strength, muscular endurance, and flexibility with aging, activity becomes a necessity for these individuals to remain mobile and maintain their ability to move around in the environment. Movement becomes an important foundation for maintaining a high quality of life and personal wellness.

Many individuals with disabilities have more uncommitted time than their able-bodied contemporaries. This pattern is accentuated with the onset of one's senior years. Therefore, there is more opportunity and need for these individuals to participate in a variety of physical, sport, and recreational activities. In addition to continued participation in activities that have been favorites throughout one's younger years, this can be a time to cultivate new interests and skills. One is never too old to learn and take part in new and exciting activities. In fact, some senior citizens, with or without handicapping conditions, express the thought that they are more willing to try new things with their new freedoms and increased amounts of uncommitted time. With some of these individuals, however, *haste must be made slowly*, and for others special attention must be given to motivation.

Although basic principles for maintaining appropriate levels of physical fitness must be considered in programs for senior citizens with disabilities, caution and good sense must be exercised in implementing such activities. While frequency, intensity, and duration of activities are important programmatic considerations, activity programs may not have to be held as often, may be less intense, and for shorter duration than for younger participants. Progression and overload are other factors that must be considered in planning and implementing these programs. All individuals, regardless of age or disability, can progress to higher levels of activity through appropriately planned and implemented programs. These principles apply whether an individual is walking or running, wheeling or using a walker, participating alone or with a guide (helper). Level and perspective must be maintained. The key is regular and ongoing participation. Studies and reports today tend to emphasize differences between activity levels to gain and maintain wellness and health as opposed to physical fitness.

Regular and planned activities help seniors with disabilities feel better, enjoy life more, maintain a higher quality life, and possess higher levels of wellness than is probable without such activities. These can be accomplished through a variety of physical and movement activities from aerobics to gardening, sport to walking, from exercise to hiking. The positive lifestyle about which we hear so much, and the life worth living so eloquently expressed by Helen Keller are more likely to become realities through such ongoing participation. All of these factors are fundamental factors when planning, developing, and implementing programs that are appropriate for and meaningful to senior citizens possessing disabilities, whether these conditions are sensory, physical, mental, or emotional, and regardless of cause.

Programming Considerations

Often when dealing with older individuals leaders tend to forget a participant's strengths and focus on weaknesses. Leaders forget that participants have had a variety of rich experiences. Leaders must not approach older participants as if they had never learned or participated in anything; and they must not be condescending. Unfortunately, many leaders continue to make similar mistakes in working with senior citizens that were legion in the early days of providing services to persons with handicapping conditions.

In some environments virtually the entire older population can be considered as special with some type of handicapping condition requiring modifications, adaptations, and accommodations to ensure active participation. Aging leads to many conditions which can affect an individual's ability to be physically active. But this does *not* mean that participation should be reduced or neglected. Leisure education and leisure counseling are extremely important techniques to ensure active participation in interesting, challenging, and appropriate activities by aging disabled populations. Appropriate approaches and innovative techniques must be used to help these individuals learn about available opportunities; cultivate and develop new interests in physical, recreational, and sport activities; practice old skills and develop new ones; find out where participation opportunities are available; arrange transportation as needed; and make necessary contacts for active participation. These services are needed whether the individual resides at home, in a community half-way type house; or in a residential facility; whether participation is in a community or special center; or whether integrated (mainstreamed) or separate (segregated).

Personal preferences and opportunities for self-determination are integral, but often overlooked, factors in programming with (not for) senior citizens, with or without handicapping conditions. Previous experiences, interests, abilities, maturity, and ages of these individuals are representative of factors that must be recognized and honored. These are *not* children, and therefore, we cannot permit ourselves to fall into the trap of emphasizing children's games for these older participants, regardless of their ages, handicapping conditions, or severities of these conditions. Other important points to remember include—

- Do *not* be condescending.
- Guide program participants into activities based on their interests and abilities.
- Remember, they have not forgotten everything they have learned so you need to determine where to start when introducing and teaching activities.
- Remember, tone and type of music can be putdowns for these populations.

Program opportunities are sought by the elderly for many different reasons. Program planning and implementation must be approached from perspectives of participants, and not made over complex or sophisticated. Opportunities for individuals to play, have fun, be with others, do things which brought pleasure and satisfaction in earlier years, must not be overlooked as important reasons senior citizens, with and without handicapping conditions, seek activity and participate. This is participation and recreation at their best, and in their purest forms.

Activities and Their Evaluation

While very individual, potential activities for these populations are extremely broad and include:

- Arts and crafts
- Aquatics
- Choral and instrumental musical activities
- Rhythmic activities and dance
- Physical and personal fitness activities
- Individual, dual, and team games and sports
- Outdoor recreation
- Winter activities
- Drama and dramatic activities

- Excursions
- Spectator events
- Television, radio, and phonograph activities
- Quiet and table games
- Special event participation
- Social activities
- Organized groups
- Clubs
- Hobbies and collections
- Community service activities[1]

Many specific activities are appropriate and should be considered for programs involving individuals who are both aging and disabled. Representative, but in no way exhaustive of the many activity possibilities for these individuals include:

- *Aerobics or simply exercise routines done to appealing music.* Rhythm of music and intensity of exercises and activities can be easily adjusted to levels of participants. Individuals in wheelchairs, with walkers, on crutches, or using braces can take part right along with participants who do not use such assistive devices. Each participant should be encouraged to interpret movements in terms of their abilities and what they can do, not be locked rigidly into set movement patterns.

- *Walking.* This is another appealing aerobic activity that possesses many of the same benefits of jogging and running, but without most of the overuse dangers and with much less injury potential. Individuals who must use mobility assistive devices can attain the same benefits from walking as those not needing to use such devices.

- *Swimming.* Although availability of a swimming pool is a necessity for active and regular participation, swimming is another excellent aerobic activity for individuals who are aging and disabled. Natural buoyancy of water enables many individuals to attain mobility and movement in water that cannot be attained on land. Warm water also has a relaxing effect on muscles. For many of these individuals activities in water can be an equalizer since they can take part with nondisabled individuals in ways that mask their handicapping conditions. Other activities in water (i.e., aquadynamics, exercises adapted to the water environment) provide additional appropriate and appealing opportunities for this population. Learning to swim or swim better should not be overlooked along with other recreational aquatic activities such as boating or wading in the ocean.

- *Chair activities.* Individuals in wheelchairs or those who for whatever reason find it difficult to perform exercises and specific activities standing and on their feet can attain an interesting, appealing, and beneficial workout while seated in chairs. Several sources in the reference section of this chapter are excellent resources for such activities. Not only are the activities presented excellent, but they stimulate each reader's initiative and resourcefulness for extension and creative applications. Chair activities can be done to music and with or without auxiliary devices such as frisbees, aluminum pie plates, paper plates, elastic bands, broom sticks, nerf balls, *ad infinitum.*

[1]For additional information, detailed discussion, and specific suggestions of activities related to this listing, refer to *Recreation and Physical Activity for the Mentally Retarded* (Washington, D.C.: Council for Exceptional Children, and American Association for Health, Physical Education, and Recreation, 1966, pages 45 to 66).

- *Traditional recreational activities.* Many traditional recreational activities should not be overlooked or neglected for these populations—i.e., horseshoes, shuffleboard, ring quoits, deck tennis, ring tennis, volleyball, one bounce volleyball, Newcomb, croquet, roque, lawn bowling, Boccia (an adaptation of lawn bowling which can be played indoors), tether ball, table tether ball, golf, miniature or putt-putt golf (can also be adapted for indoor play), tennis, and softball (an increasingly popular sport around the country with seniors). Adaptations can be made so that specifics of the activity are designed and appropriate for individual participants. Do not fall into the trap of believing that the only way to present and play a game is the official way! Be creative and modify rules and approaches so that participants enjoy and derive benefits from the activity. The only limitation is your imagination coupled with that of each of your program participants.

- *Weight training.* Often overlooked in these programs is attention to muscular endurance and muscular strength. Good sense approaches to weight training make this an excellent activity for seniors with disabilities; focus is on low weight and high repetitions. If free weights or various types of machines are available, they can be used. However, benefits may be derived from improvised uses of various easily obtained materials—i.e., bicycle inner tubes, fireplace logs, window sash weights, automobile axles, and homemade weights from tin cans filled with cement or plaster with broom sticks. Active participation in weight training programs also helps in maintaining joint flexibility. Individuals with mobility problems can take part directly from wheelchairs or while leaning on crutches or using walkers for support.

- *Pickle Ball.* This is an adaptation of paddle tennis which can be played on a badminton court with the net lowered so the top is 30 inches from the floor. Paddle tennis or some other type of solid paddles are used with whiffle balls. This is an extremely popular game in programs involving senior citizens and can be adapted further to accommodate those with mobility problems. Information about the official game can be obtained by contacting the supplier listed in the reference/resource section of this chapter.

- *Aerobic Table Tennis.* All that is needed for this interesting, invigorating, and fun game are a table (no net is required and the table does not have to be of an official table tennis variety), a paddle for each player, a table tennis ball, and *three* players. Play is started with two players at one end of the table and the third player at the other end. Serve is by one of the two players. To be legal the serve must hit the table twice, go off the far end, and then be played off the floor on one bounce by the receiver. Upon serving, this player moves to the other end of the table. Returner must play the ball off the floor on one bounce so that it hits on the table; it can go off any side, roll across the table, as long as it hits the table; the receiver must play the ball on one bounce off the floor. Play continues in this way with Player A always hitting to Player B who always hits to Player C who always hits to Player A. . . . After returning the ball—always off one bounce from the floor—the player hitting the ball moves to the other end of the table. If a ball is returned illegally—i.e., does not hit the table—the player hitting the ball must chase and retrieve it which also means all other players must change sides of the table!

- *Competitive opportunities.* Senior Olympics are designed for participants over 55 years of age. Individuals with various disabilities are not precluded from these games and should investigate possibilities in events in which they have interest and ability. Several sport governance bodies for persons with disabilities have introduced master's programs. Additional information about these opportunities can be obtained from Mary Margaret Newsome, Committee on Sports for the Disabled (c/o United States Olympic Committee, 1750 East Boulder Street, Colorado Springs, Colorado).

Although most adaptations presented have dealt with individuals possessing mobility problems, the reader cannot overlook participants with sensory (stimulus), processing, or response problems; refer to the earlier section of this chapter on the *S-P-R Model* for suggestions which can be applied to any and all of these activities for seniors possessing such disabilities.

As a guide to selecting activities and evaluating their effectiveness after use, program leaders should consider the following questions—

- Does the activity offer ample opportunity for achievement and success?
- Is the activity adaptable to the individual or group?
- Does the activity contribute to the need for providing a wide variety of experiences involving many different skills?
- Is the activity practical for the time allotted and the facilities available?
- Is the activity relatively safe for the individual considering the participant's physical and mental abilities and his/her emotional and psychological conditions?
- Does the activity invite response to its challenge?
- To what degree does the activity promote cooperative effort or involve competition?
- Is the activity socially beneficial?
- Is the focus on action and participation? *Recreation and Physical Activity for the Mentally Retarded,* 1966.

Is There a Difference?

Many professionals, for various reasons, look upon working with senior citizens or persons with handicapping conditions as different from working with other populations. Review and observation necessitate asking whether physical, recreational, and sport activities involving different populations are, in fact, different. *If* they are different, are these differences in philosophy? Activities? Methodologies?

From a participant's perspective, philosophies and principles upon which programs are built are little, if any, different, regardless of an individual's age, and with or without handicapping conditions. If differences exist, they are in degree and emphasis, not in basic philosophies or principles upon which programs are built.

Activities, especially when selected appropriately, are no different, regardless of ages or abilities of participants. In reality there are *no* unique or special activities delimited for use by senior citizens, with or without handicapping conditions. Program opportunities for these populations involve tried and true activities for participants of all ages and stages of development. While performance levels may vary among participants of different ages and combinations of handicapping conditions, basic activities found in sound programs are appropriate for the elderly. In fact, programs involving senior citizens with or without handicapping conditions are often broader with more activity opportunities and choices than programs involving younger participants. Contributing factors in this process are ways in which many older individuals lose their inhibitions and find rejuvenated willingness to try new activities.

Methods are really no different either! Methods are on a continuum, simple to complex, concrete to abstract, not separate and distinct for different populations and ages as advocated by many professionals. The key when selecting methods and approaches is relevance and appropriateness for the individual, regardless of activities in which he/she is involved. Methods are matched to individuals, their abilities and functional levels, not used indiscriminately with everyone possessing similar behavioral characteristics. With *no* group is such individualization more important and crucial than when dealing with senior citizens possessing handicapping conditions.

A Final Word

Happiness is not a matter of good fortune or worldly possessions. It's a mental attitude. It comes from appreciating what we have, instead of being miserable about what we don't have. It's so simple—yet so hard for the human mind to comprehend! Happiness is what active participation in physical, recreational, and sport activities is all about for senior citizens, with or without handicapping conditions. As professionals, volunteers, and advocates, our roles, our missions, our responsibilities are to ensure the real happiness of these populations we are dedicated and committed to serve.

Selected References/Resources

Addison, Carolyn, and Eleanor Humphrey. (1979). *Fifty Positive Vigor Exercises for Senior Citizens.* Washington, D.C.: American Alliance for Health, Physical Education, Recreation, and Dance (Unit on Programs for the Handicapped). (*Practical Pointers*, Vol. 3, No. 6).

Best of Challenge—Vol. I. (1974). Washington, D.C.: American Alliance for Health, Physical Education, and Recreation.

Best of Challenge—Vol. II. (1974). Washington, D.C.: American Alliance for Health, Physical Education, and Recreation.

Best of Challenge—Vol. III. (1977). Washington, D.C.: American Alliance for Health, Physical Education, and Recreation.

Challenging Opportunities for Special Populations in Aquatic, Outdoor, and Winter Activities. (1974). Washington, D.C.: American Alliance for Health, Physical Education, and Recreation (Information and Research Utilization Center: Physical Education and Recreation for the Handicapped).

Cordellos, Harry C. (1976). *Aquatic Recreation for the Blind.* Washington, D.C.: American Alliance for Health, Physical Education, and Recreation (Information and Research Utilization Center: Physical Education and Recreation for the Handicapped).

Heckathorn, Jill. (1980). *Strokes and Strokes: An Instructional Manual for Developing Swim Programs for Stroke Victims.* Reston, Virginia: American Alliance for Health, Physical Education, Recreation, and Dance, 1980.

Hill, Kathleen. (1976). *Dance for Physically Disabled Persons: A Manual for Teaching Ballroom, Square, and Folk Dances to Users of Wheelchairs and Crutches.* Washington, D.C.: American Alliance for Health, Physical Education, and Recreation (Information and Research Utilization Center: Physical Education and Recreation for the Handicapped).

Koss, Rosabel. (1981). *The Pensioner's Program from Sweden.* American Alliance for Health, Physical Education, Recreation, and Dance (Unit on Programs for the Handicapped), (*Practical Pointers*, Vol. 4, No. 11).

Peery, Johnette. (1980). *Exercise for Retirees.* Reston, Virginia: American Alliance for Health, Physical Education, Recreation, and Dance (Unit on Programs for the Handicapped), 1980 (*Practical Pointers*, Vol. 4, No. 7).

Pickle Ball: A Fun Court Game. Seattle, Washington (3131 Western Avenue, 98121), n.d.

Practical Guide for Teaching the Mentally Retarded to Swim. (1969). Washington, D.C.: American Association for Health, Physical Education, and Recreation, and Council for National Cooperation in Aquatics.

Recreation and Physical Activity for the Mentally Retarded. (1966). Washington, D.C.: Council for Exceptional Children and American Association for Health, Physical Education, and Recreation.

Reynolds, Grace Demmery (Editor). (1973). *A Swimming Program for the Handicapped.* New York, New York: National Board of Young Men's Christian Associations.

Rhodes, R. "When Senility is the Wrong Diagnosis." *Parade Magazine*, February 9, 1986, page 8.

Stein, Julian U. and Lowell A. Klappholz. (1972). *Special Olympics Instructional Manual. . .From Beginners to Champions.* Washington, D.C.: American Association for Health, Physical Education, and Recreation, and The Joseph P. Kennedy, Jr. Foundation.

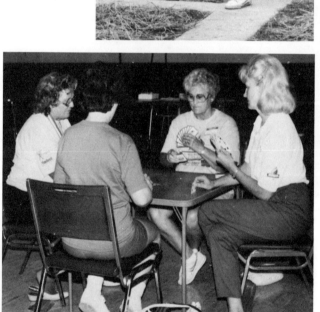

10 Leisure and Recreation Programming

Charles Daniel, Western Kentucky University
Jim Kincaid, Therapeutic Recreation, Inc.
Ron Mendell, Mt. Olive College
Howard Gray, Brigham Young University

The purpose of this chapter is to provide practical guidelines for program design in leisure and recreation for seniors. The guidelines are meant for recreators and professionals who work daily in developing and implementing programs for seniors, and who need a vast amount of knowledge and experience in order to be successful. This chapter provides basic programming information and ideas for all recreators who plan and instruct the many different levels of leisure and recreation programs, from the "super senior" to the "retired senior," to the "home-bound and nursing home senior." The chapter is broken down into three areas of major consideration for the program designer: (1) Physical Considerations in Programming, (2) Activities, (3) Seniors as Participants. The chapter provides an outline for program decisions, recognizing that many times the recreation programmer is not the program facilitator, and that paraprofessionals and other staff (nursing aids, etc.) are important in the actual implementation and participation of the senior in the leisure and recreation program. A model of an in-service program has been included to help in the training of staff for implementation of a leisure and recreation program.

There is no one answer to what leisure and recreation is for seniors, as it takes as many forms as there are seniors themselves.

Leisure and recreation is the personal self-satisfaction and self-realization of the individual senior, based on past experiences and knowledge, and directed by the individual's motivation, interests, experiences, drives, physical needs, social needs, and emotional needs.

Physical Considerations in Programming

The physical health and well-being of the senior must be determined prior to programming. The individual's physical condition can prevent, limit, or suggest the types of leisure and recreation activities in which a senior may be able to participate. Seniors, as a group, are healthier today than in previous years. The problem is that many seniors are seen by the public and perhaps by themselves as unable to perform leisure and recreation activities due to the natural process of aging. Although approximately 5 percent of all seniors reside in nursing homes, and their average age is in the high 70s, the overall majority (90–95 percent) of seniors are living independently and are physically able to care for themselves. The notion that most seniors are physically unable to participate in active leisure and recreation activities is not true. Considerations such as transportation, past leisure/recreation experiences, or financial resources, may be more actual limiting factors to participation in leisure and recreation activities than physical ability.

The recreation programmer must be aware of the significant physical differences between seniors. The recreator who is employed to provide a leisure and recreation program for seniors at a nursing home will be planning programs for a wide range of abilities, from the frail elderly to individuals who are convalescing from an illness. This program will be based on the individual's abilities and may focus on adapted activities. The recreator hired by the Recreation Department, on the other hand, will be programming for a more diverse and larger population of seniors, ranging from the "senior athlete," to the mobile and financially independent senior, to the senior centers, day care programs, and even home-bound programs. From this wide range of physical abilities the recreator must be able to assess status and determine appropriate activities for the seniors, using the individual's physical ability as one of the main considerations in programming.

Assessment of Physical Condition: What is the senior's physical condition?

The following physical conditions can be both limiting factors for senior participation and enabling factors allowing the senior to participate positively. The recreator should always be aware of basic changes in the aging body (see chapters 2–5), aware of the individual senior's physical health, and the relationship of the senior's health to the fitness and skill requirements of leisure activities.

1. Cardiovascular—Heart Disease
2. Respiratory
3. Strength, Balance, Mobility, and Endurance
4. Sight
5. Hearing
6. Other Health Conditions—Diabetes, Arthritis, etc.
7. Medications

The recreator must recognize that what is potentially risky for one senior may not be for another senior. For example: tens of thousands of seniors participate in such activities as senior games, marathons, tennis, racquetball, etc. These activities, however, are high risk, as they can cause significant cardiovascular stress. Only the physically fit senior should participate in such activities. However, the recreator can adapt the activity to the senior's level and reduce the risk-factor allowing the majority of seniors to participate.

Cardiovascular Considerations

Does the individual have heart problems?
Does the individual take medications?
Does the individual have high blood pressure?
Does the individual have low blood pressure?
Does the individual exercise daily?

Activities that cause heart rate and blood pressure to rise suddenly or for a long period of time, can be dangerous. However, the level of possible risk depends on the individual's current physical status. Rising out of bed may cause dizziness and risk for a senior who has been bed-bound or not physically active, while at the same time other seniors may walk miles and/or play tennis or jog. The recreator must know his/her client's physical ability. Activities that can cause a rapid or prolonged increase in heart rate and blood pressure are:

Walking	Tennis	Table Tennis
Jogging	Dancing	Softball
Running	Bicycling	Volleyball
Swimming	Badminton	
	(not complete list)	

The recreator must recognize that the simplest of activities may cause an increase in heart rate and blood pressure based on the individual's present fitness and activity level.

Respiratory Considerations

Does the individual smoke?
Does the individual take medications?
Does the individual have lung disease?
Does the individual have asthma?

Activities that require muscles to generate speed, power, and endurance increase respiratory rate and volume. Lack of oxygen can cause the individual to be light headed or dizzy; this is extremely dangerous. Seniors should always stop exercise if they become light headed, dizzy, have labored breathing, become pale, red to face, or disoriented. These conditions could be caused by lack of oxygen and/or the inability of the respiratory and circulatory system to meet the body's needs for an activity: The recreator must be aware of these signs.

Recreators must recognize that the simplest of activities may cause increased respiration based on the individual's present fitness and activity level.

Activities that cause rapid or prolonged increase of respiratory rate:

Running	Weight Lifting	Badminton
Jogging	Tennis	Table Tennis
Walking	Dancing	Softball
Swimming	Bicycling	Volleyball
	(not complete list)	

Strength, Balance, Mobility, and Endurance

Does the individual have enough strength to perform the activity?
Does the individual have enough strength to walk a required distance?
Does the individual have enough strength to handle the equipment necessary for activity?
Does the individual have mobility and balance to perform?
Does the individual have mobility to walk up and down steps?
Does the individual change direction without balance or motion problems?
Does the individual have endurance to participate in an activity?

The quality and quantity of movement is important to seniors, not only in their daily living routines but as a determining factor in the leisure and recreation opportunities available to them.

The quality of movement determines the skill level and activities that seniors may participate in, while the quantity of movement may limit the possible opportunity and ability to participate.

Seniors who have limited quantity of movement due to physical problems may be skilled (quality of movement) but unable to participate as they cannot get to the event. The inability to walk steps, inclines, long distances, or in crowded areas can limit the senior's participation in leisure and recreation activities.

Lack of strength can prevent seniors from participating in many events as strength is a key factor in many activities. The recreator may adapt activities, equipment, or the environment to meet the present strength levels of the senior.

Balance is necessary for both quality and quantity of movement. Seniors are afraid of falling, and activities which require a quick start or stop, or sudden changes in direction may cause a loss of balance. The recreator must be aware of these activity characteristics and adapt or moderate these activities appropriately.

Activities which have quick change in direction are: dance, aerobic exercise, and sports, such as tennis, softball, bicycling, badminton, table tennis, and volleyball.

Sight

Does the individual have sight problems?
Does the individual have near-sighted problems?
Does the individual have far-sighted problems?
Does the individual have ground figure problems?
Does the individual have "color blindness" problems?

Partial loss of sight can be very limiting to the senior. Activities requiring movement in relationship to moving objects or persons can become very difficult if not impossible to participate in.

Recreators should adapt the activities with such devices as:

1. *Enlarged Equipment*—Cards, puzzles, dominos, books (large print), and balls.
2. *Color of Equipment*—Aware of color blindness.
3. *Slow Down Movement*—Use large balloons instead of balls, or foam, mesh or Nerf balls
4. *Safety*—If playing a game, use safety equipment such as mesh balls, Nerf balls, foam balls, in case the senior does not consistently react in time to catch with the hands.

Hearing

Does the individual have a hearing problem?
Does the individual have a hearing aid?
Does the individual speech read (lip read)?
Does the individual have a balance problem associated with ear damage?
What is the level of loss of hearing?
Does the individual tolerate loud noises?

The senior who has loss of hearing may find many unadapted activities unsatisfying. Attending movies, concerts, plays, and lectures, may not be as fulfilling due to the loss of hearing. Participation in activities where instructions are given (square dancing, bingo, etc.) will not be as enjoyable. Special arrangements by the recreator may help in providing the senior with an opportunity for a more successful experience by:

1. Placing seniors up front in lectures, concerts, plays, etc.
2. Speaking directly to the seniors—don't turn your back while instructing.
3. Providing physical cues and sight cues—bingo, the bingo board; square dancing, hand signals.
4. Eliminating loud noises. Many seniors cannot stand loud noises.

While one senior may need to be close to the speakers, another may not be able to tolerate the sound level and may need to be in the back of the room.

Health Conditions

Does the individual have diabetes?
Does the individual have arthritis?
Does the individual have osteoporosis?
Does the individual have other health conditions that may limit the type of activities?
Does the individual have Alzheimer's?
Does the individual have any physical disability?
Does the individual have sickle cell anemia?
Does the individual have asthma?

Health conditions will have a direct effect upon the activities seniors may participate in. The recreator should be aware of the health status of the seniors and know that this status may change over time. The recreator should notice changes in exercise performance, attitudes, behaviors, and physical appearances. These changes may indicate physiological, psychological, or emotional changes which may be significant. The recreator should take time each day to interact with the seniors so that he/she knows the participants and can many times identify changes prior to problems.

A warm-up (start-up) and a cool-down (ending) period are suggested for all activities, from sing-alongs to exercise classes. Time should also be taken by the recreator to visit and take a mental inventory of each individual participant and to note possible changes or problems that have occurred since their last meeting. Seniors may participate in groups but they are instructed individually.

Some common limiting health problems and adjustments are:

Diabetes—May limit aerobic activities. Care must be taken in the length and severity of exercise.

Arthritis—Many exercises are not recommended for arthritis patients, but exercise is necessary to retain movement.

Osteoporosis—Based on severity, exercise and activities requiring impact to bones and muscles may or may not be recommended—*Adapted Activities*—step dancing, walking, chair exercise.

Alzheimers—Many recreational activities can be used to help in treatment for loss of memory and of daily living skills—card games, board games, fine motor arts, and crafts, etc.

Physically Disabled—Wheelchairs, walkers, most activities can be adapted—horseshoes, golf, shuffleboard.

Sickle Cell Anemia—More common among blacks, an attack of sickle cell can be frightening, painful, and even dangerous. Recreators should be aware of seniors with sickle cell anemia as exercise may bring on attack, also participating in activities where the breath is held. (Swimming is not recommended.)

Asthma—Aerobic exercise may not be recommended. Asthma attack is a real danger. Moderate exercise should be used with caution.

In all these conditions, severity levels for each individual must be considered in recreation programming.

Medications

Does the individual take medications?

How many medications does the individual take?

What types of medication does the individual take?

What is the individual's physical reaction to the medications?

Of the medications taken, are any beta blockers (heart medicines)?

Of the medications taken, are any respiratory medications?

Of the medications taken, are any arthritis related?

Of the medications taken, are any for high blood pressure?

Medications have different physical and emotional effects upon individuals, while combinations of medications may have various effects not evident with the medications alone. Many seniors take a number of different medications and the recreator in planning programs should be aware of the seniors' medical conditions and also the medications that the individuals are taking. The medication regimen (when, how much) as well as the type may have a direct effect not only on the senior, but on what leisure and recreation programs should be offered and when.

Medication may affect physical performance in any activity. Activities of concern include: aerobics, chair exercises, swimming, jogging, walking, dancing, and sports programs

The American Alliance for Health, Physical Education, Recreation and Dance, and the Council on Aging and Adult Development (CAAD) under the direction of Dee Ann Birkley have developed an "Exercise Consent Form" for the purpose of identifying medical problems and medications for seniors who desire to participate in aerobic exercise (Figure 10.1).

Activities

The programmer must be knowledgeable of these eight areas of recreation:

1. Sports/Games
2. Outdoor/Nature Activities
3. Arts and Crafts
4. Dancing
5. Music
6. Literary Activities
7. Social Activities
8. Drama—performance

Each area includes many adaptable activities that the individual senior may find interesting and personally satisfying. Areas of activity include those listed in Figure 10.2.

These suggested activities may be adapted to seniors and to fitness level:

1. *Gross Motor Activities:* Walking, bicycling, exercise class (chair, low-impact aerobics), bicycle erogometer (stationary bike), dancing, aquatics (swimming, exercise), gardening, housework, fishing, nature walks, games—shuffleboard, horseshoes, bocce, croquet, sports—golf, tennis, badminton, volleyball, softball, bowling, flycasting, senior games.

2. *Fine Motor Activities:* Write letters, type letters, sew, paint, cooking, arts/crafts, singing,

AAHPERD
COUNCIL ON AGING AND ADULT DEVELOPMENT
Medical/Exercise Assessment for Older Adults

NAME _____ PHONE _____/_____ DATE _____

STREET _____ CITY _____ STATE _____ ZIP _____

PART I—TO BE FILLED OUT BY PARTICIPANT

A. ACTIVITY HISTORY

    1. How would you rate your physical activity level during the last year?

        ☐ LITTLE—Sitting, typing, driving, talking—NO exercise planned
        ☐ MILD—Standing, walking, bending, reaching
        ☐ MODERATE—Standing, walking, bending, reaching, exercise 1 day a week
        ☐ ACTIVE—Light physical work, climbing stairs, exercise 2–3 days a week
        ☐ VERY ACTIVE—Moderate physical work, regular exercise 4 or more days a week

    2. What exercise and recreational activities are you presently involved in and how often? _____
    _____

B. HEALTH HISTORY

Weight _____ Height _____ Recent weight loss/gain _____

Please list any recent illnesses: _____
_____

Please list hospitalizations and reasons during last 5 years: _____
_____

PLEASE CHECK THE BOX IN FRONT OF THOSE QUESTIONS TO WHICH YOUR ANSWER IS *YES:*

☐ Anemia	☐ Heart Conditions _____
☐ Arthritis/Bursitis	☐ Hernia
☐ Asthma	☐ Indigestion
☐ Blood Pressure _____	☐ Joint Pain in _____
☐ Bowel/Bladder problems	☐ Leg Pain on Walking
☐ Chest Pains	☐ Lung Disease
☐ Chest discomfort while exercising	☐ Shortness of Breath
☐ Diabetes	☐ Passing Out Spells
☐ Difficulty with Hearing _____	☐ Osteoporosis _____
☐ Difficulty with Vision _____	☐ Low Back Condition
☐ Dizziness or Balance problems	☐ Other Orthopedic Conditions (List)

_____

SMOKING: Never smoked   Smoke now (how much? _____)   Smoked in past

ALCHOHOL CONSUMPTION: None   Occasional   Often (how much? _____)

List any existing health concerns: _____
_____

Please list medications and/or dietary supplements you regularly take: _____
_____

FIGURE 10.1 Exercise Consent Form

PART II—TO BE FILLED OUT BY PHYSICIAN   DATE OF LAST EXAMINATION _____

A. PHYSICAL EXAMINATION—Please check if it applies to the patient.

☐ Resting Heart Rate _____   ☐ Resting Blood Pressure _____
☐ Chest ausculation abnormal   ☐ Thyroid abnormal
☐ Heart size abnormal   ☐ Any joints abnormal
☐ Peripheral pulses normal   ☐ Abnormal masses
☐ Abnormal heart sounds, gallops   ☐ Other _____

PRESENT PRESCRIBED MEDICATION(S) _____

_____

B. CARDIOVASCULAR LABORATORY EXAMINATION (Within one year of the present date if recommended by physician)

DATE: _____.

Resting ECG: Rate _____   Rhythm _____

Axis _____   Interpretation _____

Stress Test: Max H.R. _____ Max B.P. _____ Total Time _____

Max VO$_2$ _____ METS _____ Type of Test _____

Recommendation for exercise. MODERATE is defined as standing, walking, bending, reaching and light exercise 3 days a week. Please *check* one:

_____ There is no contraindication to participation in MODERATE exercise program.

_____ Because of the above analysis, participation in a MODERATE exercise program may be advisable, but further

examination or consultation is necessary, namely: STRESS TEST, EKG, OTHER _____.

_____ Becauce of the above analysis, my patient may participate only under direct supervision of a physician. (CARDIAC REHABILITATION PROGRAM)

_____ Because of the above analysis, participation in a MODERATE exercise program is inadvisable.

C. SUMMARY IMPRESSION OF PHYSICIAN

1. Comments on any history of orthopedic and neuromuscular disorders that may affect participation in an exercise

program—especially those checked. _____

_____

2. Message for the Exercise Program Director: _____

_____

_____

Physician: _____   Signature: _____
           (Please Type/Print)

Address: _____   Phone: _____/_____

_____

PART III—PATIENT'S RELEASE AND CONSENT

_____ RELEASE: I hereby release the above information to the Exercise Program Director.

_____ CONSENT: I agree to see my private physician for medical care and agree to have an evaluation by him/her once a year, if necessary.

SIGNED: _____   DATE: _____

FIGURE 10.1. Continued

Sports/Games

Tennis	Swimming	Volleyball	Skiing
Golf	Walking	Softball	Aerobics
Horseshoes	Jogging	Bowling	Exercise Class
Badminton	Bicycling	Billiards (pool)	Aquatic Exercise
Shuffleboard	Disc Golf	Basketball	
Lawn Bowling	Croquet	"Senior Games"—Athletes	

Outdoor/Nature Activities

Camping	Fly Casting	R.V.'s
Canoeing	Skis/Scuba Diving	Recreational Traveling
Cross Country Skiing	Boating	Gardening
Water Sports	Rowing	Flowers/Plants
Fishing	Sailing	Pets
Picnics	Cookouts	

Outdoor and nature activities require fitness and skill unless adapted.

Arts/Crafts

Painting	Sewing	Kits
Tile	Drawing	Canning
Carving	Quilting	Flower Arrangement
Plaster	Pots	Collecting
Crochet	Glass	Baking
Sculpturing		

Arts/Crafts can be adapted for any physical ability or skill level, is noncompetitive, and age and sex are not considerations.

Dancing

Square Dancing	Step Dancing (Adaptation)
Social (Ballroom)	Aerobic Dance (Exercise)
Line Dancing	Ballet
Ethnic Dancing	Performing (Modern) Dancing

Dancing requires fitness level but can be adapted.

Music

Singing (Song Fest)	Recital
Folk	Listening
Instruments	Composing
Band	

Music requires less fitness and skill and is easily adapted all the way to listening.

Literary Activities

Reading	Board Games	Chess	Spades
Writing	Cards	Checkers	Bridge
		Parachesi	
		Hearts	

Literary activities require little fitness or skill level and can be adapted to all levels of service.

FIGURE 10.2. Areas of Activity

Social Activities

Dances	Art Shows	Cards
Sing-A-Longs	Drama Performances	Talent Shows
Suppers	Sporting Events	Concerts
Picnics	Competition	Lectures
Cookouts	Games	Plays
Baking Contest	Parties	Movies
Las Vegas Night	Birthdays	Easter
Banquets	Fashion Shows	Flower Shows
Hobby Shows		

Social activities cross the other seven areas of recreation and are easily adapted.

Drama

Performing Arts	Puppets
Plays	
Poetry Reading	
Readings	

Drama may require fitness and skill but in many forms can be adapted for all seniors.

In planning any activity the physiological condition of the senior must be considered.

Physically Active: High risk factors due to increased heart rate and blood pressure.

Senior Games—Athletics

Jogging	Golf—(if walking in heat)
Bicycling	Water Exercise
Swimming	Hunting
Bowling	Gardening
Dancing	Travel
Softball	Camping
Track	Shopping
Table Tennis	Exercise Classes
Tennis	

Moderate to Low Risk Factors: Based on the individual's fitness level and adaptability of the activity.
Senior Games—"Physically Challenged"

Walking—(Water Heat)
Water Exercise—(Adapted)
Golf—(use care and watch heat)
Bathing
Games—Horseshoes
            Croquet
            Shuffleboard
Billiards
Card Games—Rook, Spades, Hearts, Bridge
Board Games—Monopoly, Chinese Checkers, Checkers, Chess
Fishing
Chair Exercise Class
Arts
Ceramics
Sewing
Quilting
Needlepoint
Puzzles
Singing
Acting
Indoor Gardening

FIGURE 10.2. Continued

pool/billiards, yoga, acting/social plays, table games (cards, checkers, puzzles, dominoes, tiddly winks, bingo, lotto, backgammon) charades, reading, writing, typing, music, skits, pets, dance (see dance chapter), arts/crafts.

Seniors as Participants

Seniors have the same leisure and recreational needs as other age groups. The main difference is how and what services are provided for meeting these needs. Leisure and recreation choices for seniors may be determined by the individual's varied experience, education, environment, skills, fitness level, and personal needs. What is leisure for one senior is work to another. Therefore, a good leisure/recreation program must provide a wide range of various activities as no one program will meet the wide range of needs, interests, and abilities of seniors. (See Figure 10.3.)

Participation in Program Planning

The recreator should always involve the seniors in decisions and planning of activities. This concept of having seniors "buying into the program" by means of being directly involved in planning and implementing the recreation program can provide the big motivation needed to help peak interest and success in participation.

Ways of involving seniors in programming include:

1. *Planning*

* survey of interest (Figure 10.4)
* survey of past experience

Activity	Cardiovascular Risk Factor	Respiratory Risk Factor	Strength	Balance	Adaptation Chair Exercise Floor Exercise
Aerobics	X	X	X	X	
Archery			X		New Compound Bow
Badminton	X	X	X	X	Sitting in Chairs Use Beachball
Basketball	X	X	X	X	Light-Weight Ball No Run Rule
Bicycle	X	X		X	Stationary Bike
Billiards					
Dancing	X	X		X	Walk Dances
Golf	(if using cart)		X	X	Disc Golf Miniature Golf
Horseshoes			X	X	Plastic Shoes & Weight *Physically Challenged
Jogging	X	X	X	X	
Shuffleboard			X	X	Indoor, Lighter Equipment *Physically Challenged
Softball	X	X	X	X	One Baseball
Swimming	X	X	X	X	Bathing, Water Exercises
Walking (based on walk)	X	X	X	X	Slow Down Walk, Distance
Volleyball	X	X	X	X	Chain Volleyball, Beachball

FIGURE 10.3

Sample of a Program Survey

Dear _____.

   Please check the recreation activities you would be interested in participating in, and please feel free to add to or comment.

                                                                Thank you,

                                                                Recreator

Would like to go!

_____ 1. Travel to Ryan Park for lunch and afternoon of cards, horseshoes, and surprises.

_____ 2. Attend the play "The Golden Girls" at the Capitol Arts, Friday, April 22 at 7 p.m.—Cost—Transportation provided.

_____ 3. Visit Centennial Museum.

_____ 4. Visit Horse Cave.

_____ 5. A day trip to Nashville and visit Grand Ole Opry.

_____ 6. Your idea _____

Inside facilities activities should be separate.

Would participate!

_____ 1. Gospel Group—perform and sing-along.

_____ 2. Casino Night—let's gamble.

_____ 3. Square dancing lessons and dance.

_____ 4. Chair exercise (easy does it).

_____ 5. Cards.

_____ 6. Gardening in pots.

_____ 7. Poetry writing.

_____ 8. Class on income tax preparation.

FIGURE 10.4

- planning program survey
- evaluation of programs
- planning committee on activities (separate committees for travel, community activities, and facility activities)

2. *Program Implementation*

- chairperson—in charge of setting up and storage of equipment
- committee for special events (birthdays, parties, etc.)
- committee to develop new programs
- helpers

Interesting and Pleasurable Activities

The senior likes to participate in activities which he/she find to be personally interesting and/or pleasurable. Many activities for the social and emotional needs of friendship and affiliation will be of more interest to the senior than those which address physical needs.

The recreator should provide a wide variety of pleasurable and interesting activities based upon the individual senior and the environment. Activities which the senior is physically unable to participate in successfully will not be pleasurable or interesting.

Activities for physically active seniors include:

Golf	Tennis
Horseshoes	Walking
Croquet	Touring/Traveling
Lawn Bowling	Shopping
Billiards	Plays
Square Dance	Exercise—Low Impact
Bowling	Fishing/Hunting
Special Event Parties	Dancing
Religious Involvement	Gardening
Spectator Sporting Events	Senior Games—Sports
Bicycling	Swimming

Seniors with walkers, wheelchairs, limited fitness, poor balance, loss of Daily Living Skills (DLS) will need less strenuous and adapted activities (physically active can participate in all these activities):

Gardening—in pots, pans, cups
Walking/Wheeling—shorter distance inside
Plays at facility
Senior Games—"Physically Challenged" developed by Tabitha Daniel
Swimming—"flotation device"
Card/Table Games
Chair Exercise Program
Arts—weaving, sewing, crochet, needlepoint, quilting
Ceramics
Film Travel Logs
Parties—birthday, New Year, Independence Day, etc.
Singing—listening, participation
Religious—visitation to the senior facility or help from the religious group to get the
    seniors transported to the church
Cooking/Baking
Decorating
Drama
Movies
Reading
Writing Letters

Other Motivational Concerns

Seniors will be more motivated to participate in activities in which they have had prior successful experience. The use of externally motivated strategies may be appropriate for starting programs and developing initial interest. The goal, however, would be to develop interest to a level that intrinsic motivation keeps the seniors participating.

Internal Motivation—Is much more desirable and can be obtained by identifying interests, values, prior experiences, and physical, social and emotional needs of the senior.

The programmer upon discovering an activity that the individual senior is internally motivated to participate in should encourage that senior to possibly be a leader or to help in motivating other seniors (this does not always work, be careful not to be intrusive and lose that senior). The seniors who are not motivated should be encouraged to participate by external motivation.

External motivation includes information on activity, awards, record, recognition in newsletters, etc., and competition.

Seniors May Have a Need for Curiosity and Exploration Activities

The drives of curiosity will take many different directions from one senior to another, but some of the best examples of seniors participating in new programs that involve curiosity and exploration are the large number of seniors involved in the recreation vehicle (R.V.) craze. Seniors purchase more R.V.'s and camping trailers than any other group in our society. Seniors are the major portion of the business market for touring groups. Many seniors enjoy traveling together and visiting historical and tourist areas. These outings may take a variety of forms, from a two-week trip to a major recreational or historical site, to a one or two-day trip, down to the trip to the park for lunch or a trip to a play or movie.

Elderhostel is another example of a program providing for the curiosity and exploration of seniors. Presently, over 450 universities and colleges nationally provide a summer program for seniors. The seniors travel to and stay on campus and have a wide range of activities to choose from. Each Elderhostel is different, offering a wide program, with historical, geographic, and regional flavors in classes, workshops, visitations, and outings.

Some seniors even go from Elderhostel to Elderhostel during the summer, making a tour of the country using Elderhostel as the basis of the tour. The concept of Elderhostel may be used by the recreator in all senior programs including in the nursing home. A recreator can provide a quality and varied program using historical, geographic, and local flavor. A recreator could schedule visits to local historical areas, recreation areas, colleges, universities, churches, historical houses, parks, libraries, bring into the facility guest speakers, choral groups, musicians, performing arts, poets, women's clubs, flower clubs, and instructors in the varied presentations.

The seniors should be provided the opportunity to be involved in directing and choosing their own program. This can be accomplished by various methods. An activity survey with suggested activities can be developed asking the seniors to indicate in which activities they would like to participate. Seniors should have ownership in the program and participate in selection of activities.

Provide a list of activities for the seniors to choose from or comment on and separate outside activities from activities in the facility.

Transportation

Seniors who are unable to drive or have no vehicles will be limited on choice of activities due to the inability to get to or from activities without intervention. Most large cities have public transportation and even special transportation for the seniors and disabled. The majority of small towns and rural communities have no public transportation. The recreator will need to provide and plan transportation for seniors.

Monetary Restrictions

Many recreation activities require equipment or money for participation. Seniors living on a limited income may find it too expensive to go to the movies, to a play, or bowling. The recreator must plan for the economic situation; sponsors, free activities, and planned fund raisers can make a big difference and be an enabler.

Past Experiences

Past experiences will many times determine the senior's expected outcomes, and if the senior finds the activity to be interesting and pleasurable. Experiences that a senior has had in the past may trigger a positive or negative response.

The recreation programmer should provide the opportunity for the senior to comment and "buy into" his/her own recreation program.

Seniors' Needs

Leisure and recreation programs can provide for the basic human needs of seniors.

1. *Physical Needs:* The senior's physical needs are important in the maintenance and improvement of fitness and movement that enable the senior to do the minimum Daily Living Skills (DLS) and wide range of activities that provide a release from stress while improving the wellness and quality of life.

   While major physical changes occur during aging, research has shown that daily exercise will provide the senior with the needed physical, emotional, and social experiences to maintain a well and happy life experience.

2. *Social Needs:* Seniors need social interaction to provide much needed interaction and communication with other individuals. As the senior loses his/her independence with age, he or she needs to become involved with activities that increase their acceptance and participation with individuals, social groups, and meaningful events.

3. *Emotional Needs:* The senior has needs for love, security, achievement, autonomy, positive ego, and self-esteem. As a senior ages, he or she is slowly deprived of physical ability, social involvement, and lost social integration of wife/husband and friends. Leisure and recreation can provide the needed emotional activities to establish need relations, friendships, and positive feelings.

Summary

The programmer should consider the following steps:

1. Identification of the senior's physical fitness level and skill ability
   A. Disabilities
   B. Medications
   C. Health Concerns (see Physical Considerations)
2. Identification of the senior's needs—physical, social, emotional.
   A. Senior's ability to be successful
   B. Senior's interest

   C. Senior's past experience
   D. Senior's enjoyment/pleasure
   E. Availability—financial, transportation
 3. Identification of the recreational activities that meet the needs of the senior (consideration of adapting the activity to the senior).
   A. Fitness Level
   B. Skill Level
   C. Specific Health/Disability
   D. Interest
   E. Past Experience
   F. Enjoyment/Pleasure

Bibliography

Beard, J. G., & Ragheb, M. B. (1980). Measuring Leisure Satisfaction. *Journal of Leisure Research, 12,* 20–33.

Birenbaum, A. (1984). An Analysis of Factors Influencing Recreation Practitioners' Attitudes Toward Older Adults. M.A. Thesis, University of Waterloo, Canada, Microfiche (109 fr.).

Broderick, T. & Glazer B. (1983, January). Leisure Participation and the Retirement Process. *American Journal of Occupational Therapy, 37,* 1, 15–22.

Buchanan, T., Allen, L. R. (1985). Barriers to Recreation Participation in Later Life Cycle Stages. *Therapeutic Recreation Journal, 19,* 3, 39–50.

Bull, C. N., & Aucoin, J. B. (1975). Voluntary Association Participation and Life Satisfaction: A Replication Note. *Journal of Gerontology, 30,* 73–76.

Caskey, J. (1986). Seniors and Outdoor Recreation: A Case Study of Campers. Ottawa: National Library of Canada, Microfiche (158 fr.).

Crandall, R. (1980). Motivations for Leisure. *Journal of Leisure Research, 12,* 45–54.

Crandall, R. & Slivken, K. (1980). Leisure Attitudes and their Management. *Social Psychological Perspectives on Leisure and Recreation.* Springfield, IL: Charles C. Thomas.

Cutler, S. J. (1973). Voluntary Association Participation and Life Satisfaction: A Cautionary Research Note. *Journal of Gerontology, 28,* 96–100.

Daniel, C. (1986, January). Recreation, Challenge of Aging. *Journal of Health, Physical Education, Recreation, and Dance, 57,* 1, 55.

Federowicz, T. (1984). Factors Associated With Withdrawal From Leisure Activity Participation Among Aging Individuals. M.S. Thesis, University of Oregon.

Flatten, K., Whilhite, B., Reges, E. (1986, March). Outreach: Recreation and Exercise Programs for Home-centered Elderly: Final Report. Ames, IA: Iowa State University, 153 p.

Freemon, S. (1987). Activities and Approaches for Alzheimer's. Knoxville, TN: Whitfield Agency.

Gillespie, K., McLellan, R., McGuire, F. (1984). The Effects of Refreshments On Attendance at Recreation Activities for Nursing Home Residents. *Therapeutic Recreation Journal, 18,* 3, 25–29.

Godbey, Geoffrey, Blazey, Michael (1983). Old People in Urban Parks: An Exploratory Investigation. *Journal of Leisure Research, 15,* 3, 229–244.

Gray, H. (1981 Annual). Activity Enjoyment Model: A Transactional Approach. *Journal of Recreation and Leisure.*

Harding, J. (1985, Spring). Programs in Action, Recreation for the Homebound. *ACHPER National Journal, 109,* 11–12.

Heinemann, A., Colorez, A., Frank, S., Taylor, D. (1988, April). Leisure Activity Participation of Elderly Individuals With Low Vision. *Gerontologist, 28,* 2, 181–184.

Hiemstra, R. (1972). Continuing Education for the Aged: A Survey of the Needs and Interests of Older People. *Adult Education, 22,* 100–109.

Hiemstra, R. (1976). Older Adult Learning: Instrumental and Expressive Categories. *Educational Gerontology, 1,* 227–236.

Hogden, K. (1985, October). Leisure/Recreation Needs of Hospitalized Elderly: A Task Force Report. *Activities, Adaptation, and Aging, 7,* 2, 53–65.

Jarvik, L. F. & Russell, D. (1979). Anxiety, Aging and Third Emergency Reaction. *Journal of Gerontology, 34,* 197–200.

Kaufman, Jane (1984). Study of Leisure Satisfaction, Leisure Participation, and Patterns of Leisure Activity in Relationship to Anxiety Levels in Retirees. Dissertation, Temple University, 125 p.

Keller, M., Turner, N. (1986). Creating Wellness Programs for Older People: A Process of Therapeutic Recreation. *Therapeutic Recreation Journal, 20,* 4, 6–14.

Krewiak, M. (1984). An Analysis of Leisure Facility Preferences of the Urban Elderly. M.A. Thesis, University of Manitoba, Canada.

Krout, J. (1983, Sept.). Correlates of Senior Center Utilization. *Research in Aging, 5,* 3, 339–352.

Kultgen, P., Habenstein, R. (1984, April). Processes and Goals in Aftercare Programs for Deinstitutionalized Elderly Mental Patients. *Gerontologist, 24,* 2, 167–173.

Larson, R. (1978). Thirty Years of Research on the Subjective Well-being of Older Americans. *Journal of Gerontology, 33,* 109–125.

Lawton, M. P. (1978). Leisure Activities for the Aged. *The Annals, 438,* 71–80.

Lawton, M. P. (1982). Competence, Environmental Press, and the Adaptation of Older People. In M. P. Lawton, P. G. Windley & T. O. Byerts (Eds), *Aging and the Environment: Theoretical Approaches.* New York: Springer.

Lawton, M. P. (1982). Time, Space and Activity. In G. Rowles & R. J. Ohta (Eds), *Aging and Milieu,* New York: Academic Press.

Leon, A., Connett, J., Jacobs, D., Rauramar, R. (1987, Nov.). Leisure-time Physical Activity Levels and Risk of Coronary Heart Disease and Death: The Multiple Risk Factor Intervention Trail. *Journal of the American Medical Association, 258,* 17, 2388–2395.

Leviton, D., Campanelli, L. (Oct./Nov. 1984). Have We Avoided the Frail, Aged, and Dying Older Person in HPERD? *Health Education, 15,* 6, 43–47.

MacNeil, R., Teague, M., McGuire, F., O'Leary, J. (1987). Older Americans and Outdoor Recreation, A Literature Synthesis. *Therapeutic Recreation Journal, 21,* 1, 18–25.

Markides, K. S., & Martin, H. W. (1979). A Causal Model of Life Satisfaction Among the Elderly. *Journal of Gerontology, 34,* 86–93.

McGuire, F., O'Leary, J., Alexander, P., Dottavio, D. (1987, Summer). Comparison of Outdoor Recreation Preferences and Constraints of Black and White Elderly. *Activities, Adaptation and Aging, 9,* 4, 95–104.

McGuire, F., Dottavio, D., O'Leary, J. (1986, Oct.). Constraints to Participation in Outdoor Recreation Across the Life Span: A Nationwide Study of Limitors and Prohibitors. *Gerontologist, 26,* 5, 538–544.

McGuire, F. (1985). Recreation Leader and Co-Participate Preferences of the Institutionalized Aged. *Therapeutic Recreation Journal, 19,* 2, 47–54.

McGuire, F. (1985). Constraints in Later Life. Monograph, Charles C. Thomas, Springfield, IL.

McGuire, F., O'Leary, J., Dottavio, F. (1986, April). Outdoor Recreation in the Third Age: Results of the United States Nationwide Recreation Survey. *World Leisure & Recreation, 28,* 2, 18–21.

Miko, Paul (1985, Oct.). Recreation Programming for the Rural Elderly. *Activities, Adaptation and Aging, 7,* 2, 99–102.

Mobily, K., Hoeft, T. (1985, Summer). Family's Dilemma: Alzheimer's Disease. *Activities, Adaptation and Aging, 6,* 4, 63–71.

Mobily, K., Wallace, R., Kohout, F., Leslie, D., Lemke, J., Morris, M. (1984). Factors Association With the Aging Leisure Repertoire: The Iowa 65 Plus Rural Health Study. *Journal of Leisure Research, 16,* 4, 338–345.

Okun, M., Stock, W., Haring, M., Witter, R. (1984, Mar.). The Social Activity—Subjective Well-being Relation: A Quantitative Synthesis. *Research on Aging, 6,* 1, 45–65.

Ovellette, Pierre (1986, Winter). Leisure Participation and Enjoyment Patterns of French and English Speaking Members of Senior Citizens' Clubs in New Brunswick, Canada. *Canadian Journal on Aging, 5,* 4, 257–268.

Pageot, J. (1986, April). The Leisure Patterns of the Aged Canadians. *World Leisure and Recreation, 28,* 2, 26–27.

Palmer, M. (1983, Spring). Music Therapy in a Comprehensive Program of Treatment and Rehabilitation for the Geriatric Resident. *Activities, Adaptation and Aging, 3,* 3, 53–59.

Parnes, H., Less, L. (1985). Variation in Selected Forms of Leisure Activity Among Males. Monograph, Greenwich, CT: J.A.I. Press.

Pierce, R. C. (1980). Dimensions of Leisure: Satisfactions, Descriptions and Characteristics. *Journal of Leisure Research, 12,* 5–278.

Robinson, John (1987, March). Where's the Boom? *American Demographics, 9,* 3, 34–37.

Romsa, G., Bondy, P., Blenman, M. (1985). Modeling Retirees Life Satisfaction Levels: The Role of Recreational, Life Cycle and Socio-Environmental Elements. *Journal of Leisure Research, 17,* 1, 29–39.

Rooney, J. (1985, Fall). One Treatment Approach for the Confused Elderly. *California Parks and Recreation,* Sacramento, CA, *41,* 4, 36–38.

Rubenstein, J. (1987, April). Leisure Participation and Satisfaction in Two European Communities. *Journal of Cross-Cultural Gerontology, 2,* 2, 151–170.

Scates, S., Randolph, D., Gutsch, K., Knight, H. (1986). Effects of Cognitive-Behavioral Reminiscences, and Activity Treatments on Life Satisfaction and Anxiety in the Elderly. *International Journal of Aging and Human Development, 22,* 2, 141–146.

Searle, M., Iso-Ahola, A. (1988). Determinants of Leisure Behavior Among Retired Adults. *Therapeutic Recreation Journal, 22,* 2, 38–46.

Singleton, J. (1985, Fall). Activity Patterns of the Elderly. *Society and Leisure, 8,* 2, 805–819.

Singleton, Jerome (1984, Fall). Outdoor Recreation Participation Patterns Among the Elderly. *Activities, Adaptation and Aging, 6,* 1, 81–89.

Steinkamp, M., Kelly, J. (1987). Social Integration, Leisure Activity, and Life Satisfaction in Older Adults: Activity Theory Revisited. *International Journal of Aging and Human Development, 25,* 4, 293–307.

Thornton, J., Collins, J. (1984). Patterns of Leisure and Physical Activities in Older Adults: Reasons, Attitudes, and Meanings. Research Grant, Vancouver: University of British Columbia, Canada.

Tinsley, H. E., Barrett, T. C. & Kass, R. A. (1977). Leisure Activities and Need Satisfaction. *Journal of Leisure Research, 8,* 110–122.

Tinsley, H. E., & Kass, R. A. (1978). Leisure Activities and Need Satisfaction: A Replication and Extension. *Journal of Leisure Research, 10,* 191–202.

Tinsley, H., Teaff, J., Colbs, S., Kaufmann, N. (1985, March). System of Classifying Leisure Activities in Terms of Psychological Benefits of Participation Reported by Older Persons. *Journal of Gerontology, 40,* 2, 172–178.

Toseland, R., & Rasch, J. (1978). Factors Contributing to Older Persons' Satisfaction With Their Communities. *Gerontologist, 18,* 395–402.

Verduin, J., McEwen, D. (1984). Adults and Their Leisure: The Need for Lifelong Learning. Springfield, IL: Charles C. Thomas, (170 p.).

Wade, C., Anderson, S. (1987). Perceived Levels of Burnout of Veterans Administration Therapeutic Recreation Personnel. *Therapeutic Recreation Journal, 21,* 3, 52–63.

Weisman, S. (1983, Aug.). Computer Games for the Frail Elderly. *Gerontologist, 23,* 4, 361–363.

Weiss, C., Bailey, B. (1985, Summer). Influence of Older Adults' Activity Selection on Their Progeny's Expectations for Their Own Future. *Activities, Adaptation and Aging, 6,* 4, 103–114.

Weiss, C., Kronberg, J. (1986). Upgrading T.R. Service to Severely Disoriented Elderly. *Therapeutic Recreation Journal, 20,* 1, 32–42.

Wigdor, B. T. (1980). Drives and Motivations With Aging. In J. E. Birren and R. B. Sloane (Eds.) *Handbook of Mental Health and Aging,* New York: Prentice-Hall.

Wilson, George (1975). Leisure Counseling, Indicators of Change In the Recreational Environment: A National Research Symposium. Penn State HPER Series Number 6, College of Health, Physical Education and Recreation, State College: The Pennsylvania State University Press.

PART III:

PROGRAM CONTENT

11 Exercise Program Design

David K. Leslie, University of Iowa
John W. McLure, University of Iowa
Illustrations by Rita Tomanek

Medical Concerns

Persons of any age who are considering entering an exercise program that stresses their body in a manner to which they are unaccustomed, should consult their family physician to acquaint him/her with the scope of the program under consideration and to obtain medical advice concerning participation. This precaution is especially prudent for elderly persons due to the combined effects of normal biological aging and the sedentary lifestyle that is common among the elderly.

A number of medical problems may contraindicate or limit involvement in an exercise program, but there are at least five fairly common problems that may be helped *or* worsened by an exercise program, depending upon how well the exercise program is tailored to an individual's status. The problems are: cardiovascular disease, osteoporosis, bad back pain, arthritis, and diabetes. Medical guidance should be sought prior to starting an exercise program if any of the preceding conditions are known to exist. Because many family physicians are not particularly expert regarding the potential beneficial role that exercise can play in the lives of people with the above medical problems, some physicians recommend going to specialists or just getting a second opinion from another physician. A second opinion may be desired for guidance regarding other medical conditions as well.

While much is yet to be learned about the aging process and the role of exercise in optimal aging, there is an apparent consensus among professionals in the field of aging and exercise that regular appropriate exercise has a favorable effect on the well-being of most individuals.

Program Design Guidelines*

There are six basic considerations that should guide the design of an exercise program. Due to the reduced resiliency and limited physical reserve that is characteristic of the aged, and the serious consequences that misjudgment in exercise selection may have for some people, the authors strongly recommend conservatism in choosing and implementing a program. The basic considerations are: specificity, overload, intensity, duration, frequency, and progression.

* For additional information on this topic, see Chapter 7.

Specificity

Specificity refers to such concerns as the kind of fitness (muscular strength, muscular endurance, flexibility, cardiovascular fitness, etc.) or the body part or system targeted by the performance of a particular exercise.

Overload

Overload refers to an increase in the workload beyond what is normally done. The increase in workload is usually designed to achieve a training effect and is usually adjusted in terms of intensity or duration but may also involve frequency.

Intensity

Intensity refers to the amount of work per unit time and is affected by such parameters as the amount of resistance to a movement, the number of movements per unit time, and the duration of the workout period.

Duration

Duration refers to the length of time of a workout. Duration may be lengthened as participants adjust to a workload. For example, 20 minutes may be required to complete a selected number of repetitions in an exercise series or to walk a prescribed distance. Training effect would be experienced by: (1) increasing the number of repetitions so that it takes 25 minutes to complete the same exercise series, or (2) walking at the same rate for a longer period of time.

Frequency

Frequency refers to the number of exercise sessions scheduled per unit of time. The frequency for range-of-motion exercises for an arthritic condition may be two times per day, whereas, the frequency for bouts on an exercycle may be daily or three or four time per week.

Progression

Progression refers to changes in the work load in a systematic manner in order to achieve or work toward a fitness objective. It may involve increasing the amount of resistance to a movement, changing the amount of time involved in the exercise, or, changing the rate of speed at which a movement is executed.

Application of Guidelines

The application of these guidelines to individuals or groups obviously requires judgment and should result in an individualization of prescriptions for participation. An obvious question is how does one know the proper starting speed or number of repetitions or amount of resistance for any given individual. The not so comforting answer is that we typically do not know the best starting points. Consequently it is usually best to make a conservative judgement, proceed slowly and adjust the workouts appropriately.

Participants in a workout should not experience significant physical discomfort, and recovery from exertion should be rapid. Discomfort that lasts more than five or ten minutes or that appears the next day as stiffness or soreness indicates that the exercise session was probably too strenuous.

Several approaches have been developed to guide judgement about the level of stress in an exercise program. Approaches have included heart rate (HR), the use of metabolic units (METs),* rate of perceived exertion (RPE), and subjective judgement based on professional beliefs about the qualities of specific exercises. The functional fitness test described in Chapter 3 should be useful in exercise prescription.

Heart Rate

In programs that address cardiovascular (CV) fitness need in adults, the use of HR has been widely accepted and reported in the literature. The usage of HR among aged adults has not been as widely reported, in part because many, perhaps most, exercise programs for the aged have not been directed towards developing cardiovascular fitness. The medical screening and monitoring of participants in programs focusing on cardiovascular fitness costs more than programs not needing as thorough screening or monitoring and so there has been a tendency to exclude a CV focus in most programs for the aged.

METS

The use of METS involves the rating of various exercises or activities on the basis of METS and using the MET value as a guide for controlling such exercise considerations as intensity and duration. Because METS are based on known characteristics of physiologic function, their usage has gained considerable support in the scientific community. The acceptance of METS has not been as widespread among practitioners and the reasons for this difference need to be identified and addressed.

RPE

The approach to individualizing a fitness program described by Burke involves using the rating scale of perceived exertions (RPE) developed by Borg. Although presented as an alternate/ complementary measure to HR as a measure of exercise intensity, the principles of the system have also been utilized in exercise programs that involve minimal cardiovascular stress, and with alert well elderly it may be the best approach for given situations. (See Chapter 8 for additional information on RPE.)

Subjective Professional Judgement

The last approach is to focus on muscle toning, range of motion exercises, and other activities that minimize cardiovascular stress and are at or close to the level of exertion that occurs in the activities of daily living for most elderly. The intensity and duration of the exercises and activities can readily be adjusted to the current status of the participant with a minimum of risk. A selection of these types of activities and exercises taken from Leslie and McLure follow, and includes exercises and activities that involve most joints and parts of the body that are important to the physical independence of the aged. They are categorized as loosening-up, miscellaneous, and by

* A MET is equal to using 3.5m of oxygen per kilogram of body weight per minute.

body areas, although some exercises could readily be included in several areas. (See Chapter 7 for a list of precautions.)

Loosening-Up and Miscellaneous

A Word of Caution Before You Start

Don't feel that you have to do all the exercises or complete all the repetitions of the exercises. This caution is especially important for beginners. In general, beginners should try fewer than five repetitions, while advanced participants may go to ten. If at any time a participant feels dizzy, short of breath, or experiences unusual discomfort, they should pause and rest. Some aspect of the exercise may need to be adjusted, such as reducing the intensity or avoiding an exercise entirely. It is important that the participant enjoy the exercise.

Ambulatory Participants

Participants who can walk and move independently can loosen up by walking briskly for two or three minutes with erect posture, breathing deeply, striding with arms swinging forward and rearward and crisscrossing in front and back. Use bouncy rhythmic music that has a lilt for background, and if in a group, join in singing or keeping rhythm with a clear verbal beat like tum-de-tum-tum. Chat and visit, make quips, create an enjoyable mood in the group. If there is considerable variance in the speed with which the participants can walk, form two circles with the outer circle for the faster walkers. Try having the inner circle walk clockwise and the outer circle counterclockwise so that some facing and concurrent socializing can readily occur. Vary the directions of the circles in different sessions as an assist to mental alertness. Encourage verbal interchanges during the walk.

Non-Ambulatory and Modified Ambulatory Participants

Participants in wheelchairs or using walkers or canes may wish to join the slow circle. If needed, someone can push the wheelchairs while the persons in the wheelchairs keep time with hands and/or feet, engage in arm swinging and body shrugs, or hunches and twists in rhythm to the music. Such persons may prefer to remain stationary and just keep time to the music and socialize together or with the passing marchers.

Deep Breathing

Stand or sit tall. Breathe in deeply through the nostrils and let air out slowly through the nose or mouth. Repeat periodically throughout the exercise period. Combine inhalations and exhalations with exercises when the movement in an exercise enhances taking a deep breath.

Breathing Stretches and Collapses

Stand or sit tall. Stretch arms toward ceiling. If standing with hands up against a wall for stability, participants may rise on their tiptoes. If seated, bend forward at the waist in a collapsing movement. If standing, let the shoulders and chest sag and shoulders roll forward in a collapsing movement. Let the air out and loosely stretch downward while collapsing. Repeat five to ten times.

Simulated Swimming

Sitting or standing, move arms at shoulders in a swimming crawl stroke motion and then a back stroke motion. Swim for 30 seconds to a minute, dividing the time between the strokes. Try the breast stroke and the side stroke.

Games and Other Activities

Ball games are popular and may be utilized in a variety of ways with a multitude of levels of challenge. Balls of varying sizes, composition, shapes, weights, and colors can be used to vary the stimulation. For many ball games, groups may be formed into a circle with the participants facing the center. The games work well at either the beginning or toward the end of an exercise session. They may be used for loosening-up or for warming-down. Some participants may tend to over-do if the games become competitive, so individual reactions should be monitored. It is usually best if ball games are limited to five minutes or so. Some possible games are described below:

1. *Circle Relay*, seated. Pass one or more balls around a circle with varied passing or handling techniques. This activity helps as reality contact in addition to hand-eye coordination and manipulation skills. If an individual is not paying close attention, the neighbors will urge, "Pass it on," and those helpful verbal and touching cues stimulate the play.

2. *Team Relays*, seated. Divided the circle in half. At the command "go," have the players pass a ball around each semi-circle and back to start. Again different methods of ball handling and passing can be used for variety and challenge.

3. *Pitcher*. Use large, soft, Nerf or rubber balls and have members of the circle bounce-pass the balls to their neighbor or to persons across the circle. It helps if the pitcher calls the name of the intended catcher and so adds a bit of socializing, reality orientation, and zest to the game.

4. *Modified Soccer*. Have the members roll the balls to each other using their feet.

5. *Hit a target*. Set up empty plastic detergent bottles in the center of the circle. Arrange a contest between the circle halves to determine which can knock down the bottles first with balls or bean bags. Be alert to the effects of creating a competitive atmosphere. The urge to "win" is strong and competition can enhance or it can detract from reaching program goals. If you have "winners" in a contest, you also have "losers." People whose skills or lack thereof tend to make them chronic losers, will soon lose interest in the contest.

6. *Volleyballoon*. Keep two or three large balloons bouncing in the air around the circle. Use heads, fingertips, even feet to keep the balloons up.

Marches are popular in some exercise classes. The original TOES (The Oaknoll Exercise Society) class, started by the authors, had a gifted old-time fiddler, John Rugg, who composed marches for the group. He played his tunes at the beginning of the exercise sessions as his friends walked in briskly and he played again before they left. Recorded marches also help.

Music offers as many possibilities for recreation as the imagination can implement. The authors have seen musical games in a circle ("You put your left foot in, etc.") and formal instruction as well. Exercise classes have utilized everything from aerobics to ballroom and folk dancing with good results. See Chapter 12 for additional information on dance and rhythms.

Exercise Selection

A program of exercises should be selected with specific objectives in mind. The objectives may have a wide variety of focuses but, in general, a program should address all the major muscle groups and joints that are important for effective functioning in the activities of daily living. A selection of about two exercises from each of the groups presented below plus a selection of ball, rhythmic, or specialty exercises can be made to create a 30 minute exercise session that addresses range of motion, muscle toning, and balance needs.

Fingers and Hands

Stirring the Fingers: Grasp the end of a finger and make circles with it in both directions. Pretend you are stirring coffee and your finger is the spoon. Stir all fingers, keeping the palm and wrist relatively rigid. (Figure 11.1.)

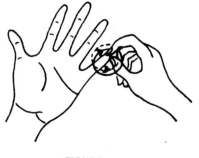

FIGURE 11.1

Exploding Fists: Grasp the hand tightly into a fist, hold one second, then explode the hand fully open, extending the fingers. Repeat five to ten times. (Figure 11.2.)

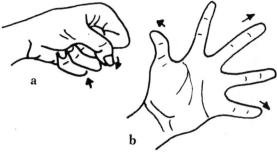

FIGURE 11.2

Finger Extender: Spread the fingers and thumb of each hand and place the fingertips of the left hand against the fingertips of the right hand. Press the palm sides of the knuckles toward each other while keeping the wrists as far apart as possible. Some people will call this exercise "a spider doing pushups on a mirror." Repeat five to ten times. (Figure 11.3.)

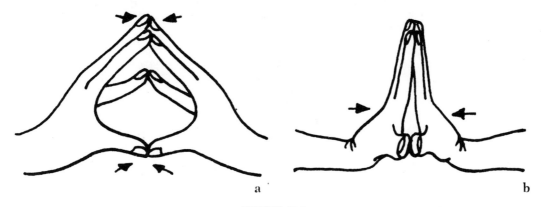

FIGURE 11.3

Grip Strengthener: Take a small rubber ball or tennis ball and squeeze it firmly so that it partially flattens, and then release it. If you cannot do this with one hand, use two. If you have arthritis in your hands, you should check with your physician regarding the suitability of this exercise. Repeat five to ten times.

Palm Stretcher: With elbows bent and hands chest high, clasp the hands and, turning the knuckles toward the chest, move the hands away from the chest by straightening the arms and bringing the elbows toward each other. As the elbows approach their limit of movement, stiffen the fingers and push the palms away from the body. Repeat five to ten times. (Figure 11.4.)

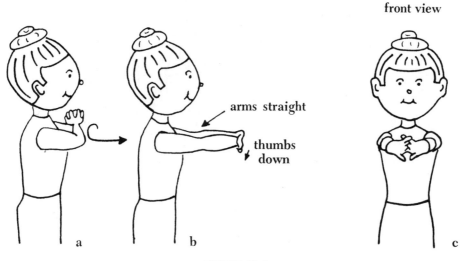

FIGURE 11.4

Wrists

Wrist Flexor and Extensor: With elbows at your side and forearms parallel to the floor, or placing forearms on the armrest of the chair, let the hands hang down. Move hands slowly up and down as far as you can in a slow waving motion without moving the forearms. Repeat five to ten times. (Figure 11.5.)

FIGURE 11.5

Palm Rotator: With elbows at your sides and forearms parallel to the floor, or placing elbows on the armrest of the chair, alternately turn the palms of the hands up and down, twisting the wrist as far as you can in each direction. Repeat five to ten times. (Figure 11.6.)

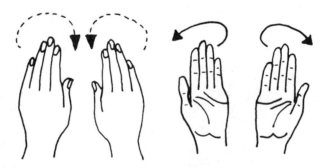

FIGURE 11.6

Wrist Rotator: Extend the left arm out in front of the body, hold the left forearm steady with the right hand, and then rotate the left hand in clockwise circles. Next try counterclockwise circles. Repeat with the other arm and hand. The movement might be compared to wiping out a circular wash basin without moving the forearm. Repeat five to ten times. (Figure 11.7.)

FIGURE 11.7

Elbows

Elbow Extensor: Extend both arms out in front of the body with palms facing up; bend the elbows and touch the shoulders with the fingertips, then fully extend the arms as though you were trying to bend them the wrong way. Repeat five to ten times. (Figure 11.8.)

FIGURE 11.8

Elbow Rotator: Extend the left arm out in front of the body; hold the upper arm steady with the right hand, then rotate the left forearm in a circle from the elbow as though cleaning a large plate glass window (rotate in both directions, clockwise and counterclockwise, and do so with both arms). Repeat five to ten times. (Figure 11.9.)

FIGURE 11.9

Elbows and Shoulders

Elbow Flexor and Shoulder Rotator: Extend both arms out in front of the body with the palms facing up; bend the elbows and touch the shoulders with the fingertips; keep the fingertips on the shoulder and make five to ten large circles with the elbows. Then make five to ten large circles with the elbows in the opposite direction. (Figure 11.10.)

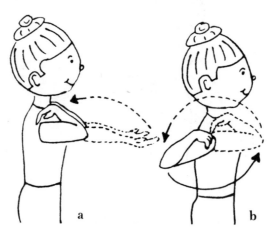

FIGURE 11.10

Breast Stroke: Bring the hands together in front of the breastbone in an attitude of prayer. Turn the fingers in toward the body while raising the elbows. Move the hands forward in a sweeping movement as the arms straighten and move open and outward. Continue sweeping the arms rearward at shoulder height as far as you can and then resume starting position. Repeat five to ten times. (Figure 11.11.)

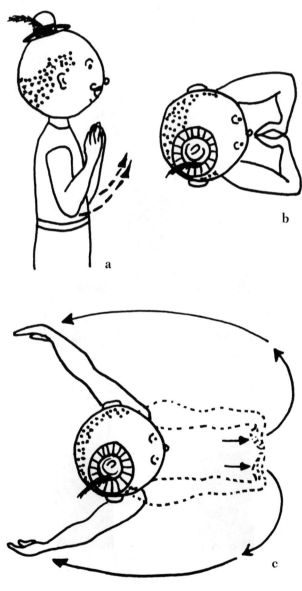

FIGURE 11.11

Hugger: Starting with the arms hanging straight downward and the elbows against the sides, raise the hands to the shoulders. Keeping the finger-shoulder contact, swing the right elbow upward and in front across the chest, reaching the elbow toward the left armpit, and return to position b. Repeat with the left arm. Repeat five to ten times with each arm. (Figure 11.12.)

FIGURE 11.12

Push Away: Standing slightly less than arm's length from a wall you are facing, place hands against the wall at shoulder height. Do not stand so far away from the wall that your feet may slip during the exercise. Bend the arms so that the chest, chin, or nose touches the wall and then push yourself back slowly. If you feel that this exercise is too easy, repeat with the hands approximately at the height of the top of your head. Another advanced version is to repeat again with the hands approximately at the height of the waist. Repeat five to ten times at each position. (Figure 11.13.)

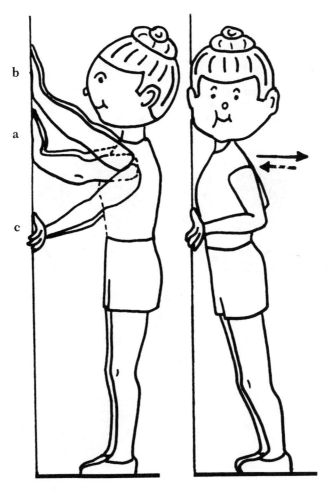

FIGURE 11.13

Chest Stretcher: Standing or sitting, with the palms downward and hands and elbows at shoulder height, touch the tips of the fingers of both hands together about six inches in front of the breastbone. Keeping the hands and elbows at shoulder height, move the elbows rearward as though you were going to touch the elbows behind your back. As your elbows approach the limit of rearward motion, stick out your chest forcefully, hold for a second, and then return to the starting position. Repeat the above movements three times, and on the fourth repetition as the elbows move rearward straighten the arms and inhale deeply. Hold the arms rearward and chest thrust forward position for two or three seconds and then relax. Repeat five to ten times. (Figure 11.14.)

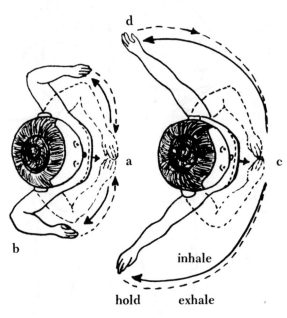

FIGURE 11.14

Shoulders

Shoulder Shrug: Sitting or standing with arms hanging relaxed at your sides, raise both shoulders simultaneously as if you were trying to touch your shoulders to your ears. Then move the shoulders forward and inward toward your chin, then downward, then rearward, and then back to position a. Repeat, reversing the direction of the movement. Repeat five to ten times in each direction. (Figure 11.15.)

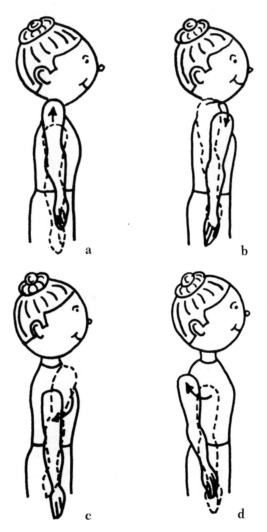

FIGURE 11.15

Back Scratcher: Standing or sitting forward in the chair so that your back is clear of the back of the chair, with the right arm reach over and then behind your head and neck, reaching as far down your spine as you can. At the same time, with the left arm reach under your left armpit and up your spine as far as you can. Hold for three to five seconds. As a challenge, attempt to touch the fingers of your right and left hands together behind your back. Reverse the arm movements so that the left arm goes over the head and the right arm goes under the armpit. Repeat five to ten times with each arm. (Figure 11.16.)

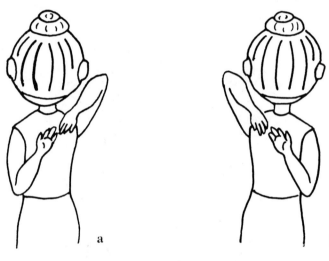

FIGURE 11.16

Toes, Feet, and Ankles

Toe Curlers: Sitting with the heels resting on the floor and the toes elevated, alternately curl the toes toward the floor and upward toward the knees, curling to the extreme positions. Think of simulating a fist with feet when you curl the toes toward the floor and opening the fist all the way when you curl the toes toward the knees. Repeat five to ten times.

Ankle Flexor and Extensor: This exercise may be done with the heels on the floor or with the legs lifted and the heels off the floor. Point toes toward the floor and then move the toes upward toward the knee allowing the entire foot to follow the movement of the toes so that there is flexion and extension at the ankle. You should feel some pull on the rear of the lower legs when flexing and some pull on the front of the lower legs when extending. Repeat five to ten times.

Ankle Rotator: Lift the heels off the floor and simultaneously rotate each foot at the ankle in a circle five times to the left and then five times to the right, making large circles with the toes.

Do not let the legs move. A variation of the ankle rotator may be done by crossing the legs with the right leg over the left and the right foot making circles, then crossing legs with the left leg over the right and making circles with the left foot, repeating five to ten times. (Figure 11.17.)

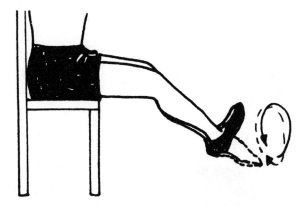

FIGURE 11.17

Ski Exercise: Standing holding onto a chair for balance, with the feet initially flat on the floor, flex the knees and raise the toes and ball of the foot, and pivot on the heels by pointing the toes of both feet to the left at the same time and then to the right. Repeat five to ten times. (Figure 11.18.)

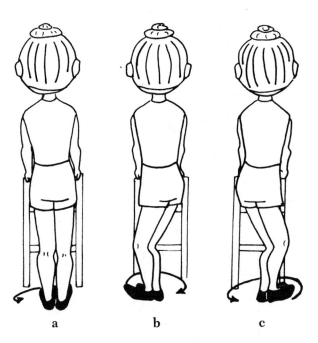

a   b   c

FIGURE 11.18

Toe and Heel Raisers: Standing holding onto a chair for balance, with feet initially flat on the floor, first lift the heels so that you are up on your toes. Next lower the heels and lift the toes so that you are balancing on your heels. Repeat five to ten times.

Knees, Hips, and Abdomen

Knee Extension: Sitting with the feet flat on the floor, lift both legs until the legs are straight out in front of you, as extended as you can make them, then lower the feet again to the floor. If it is too difficult to lift both feet at the same time, do it first with one leg and then the other. Repeat five to ten times. (Figure 11.19.)

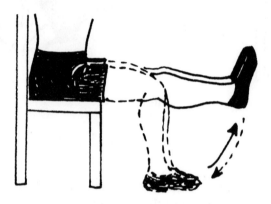

FIGURE 11.19

Knee Rotator: Sitting forward in the chair, raise the right knee so that the foot clears the floor. Make circles in the air with the foot while pointing either the heel or toe toward the floor. Repeat with the left leg. Repeat five to ten times with each leg. (Figure 11.20.)

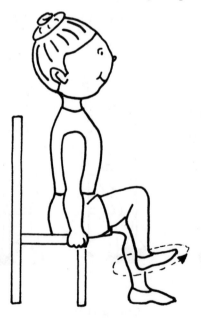

FIGURE 11.20

Marching: Standing holding onto a chair for balance, march in place raising the knees high toward the chest. Repeat five to ten times with each leg.

Leg Swings: Stand with the left hand on the back of a chair to steady yourself (use a heavy chair for stability). Lift the right foot from the floor and slowly swing the leg forward and rearward keeping the body erect. Repeat five to ten times. Then, resuming the starting position, move the leg sidewards as high as you can, keeping the trunk erect and leg straight. Repeat five to ten times. Repeat with the other leg while standing with your other side toward the chair. (Figure 11.21.)

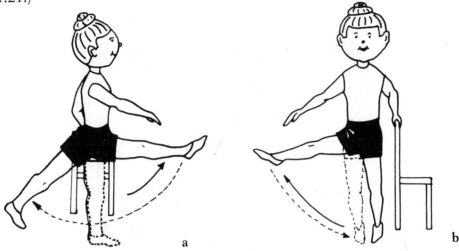

a   b

FIGURE 11.21

Leg Circles: Standing with the left hand on the back of a chair, extend the right leg in front of the body and make five to ten clockwise circles with the leg, making the circles larger and larger. Then stand with your other side toward the chair and do the same thing with the other leg. Repeat with each leg making counterclockwise circles. (Figure 11.22.)

a   b

FIGURE 11.22

Knee Bends: Standing with hands on hips, bend the knees until you have lowered yourself to a quarter- to half-squat position (one-fourth to one-half way down). Hold that position momentarily and then straighten the legs to reassume an erect position. Keep the back straight and erect throughout the movement. Some people will prefer to grasp the back of a chair for balance or have a chair close behind them so they could sit in if needed. You are cautioned not to do a deep knee bend, because of the potential for damage to the knee joint in some people. Repeat five to ten times. (Figure 11.23.)

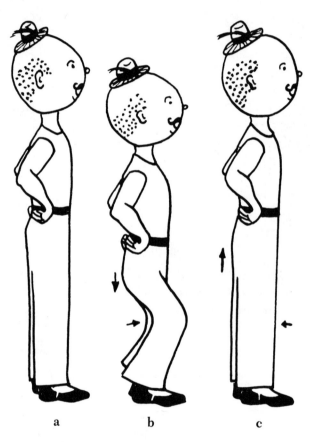

a   b   c

FIGURE 11.23

Leg Lifts: Sitting in a chair with the hips forward away from the backrest and the upper back against the backrest of the chair, keeping the legs straight, lift the legs to an extended position, hold momentarily, then lower the legs. As a precaution before lifting the legs, rotate the hips and suck in the stomach in such a way that you tend to flatten the lower back toward the seat and back of the chair. Failure to flatten the lower back can result in lower back strain. You may need to lift one leg at a time. Repeat five to ten times. (Figure 11.24.)

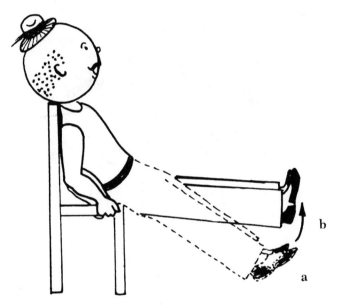

FIGURE 11.24

Back and Trunk

Lateral Bending: Standing or seated with hands either on hips, clasped behind or on the head, or clasped and raised overhead, bend at the waist toward the left, pause, then bend toward the right, alternating in a left-right manner, *always* pausing when reaching the vertical standing position. If seated, spread your feet sufficiently that you are stable when you lean to each side. Repeat five to ten times. (Figure 11.25.)

pause

FIGURE 11.25

Modified Sit-Ups: Sit forward in a chair and simulate a reclining position by leaning backward with legs outstretched. Rotate your hips and suck in your stomach so that you tend to flatten the lower back toward the seat of the chair; lift the left knee toward the chest and return to starting position. Alternate with the right and left legs. Advanced exercisers may lift both knees toward the chest at the same time. Failure to keep the lower back flattened may strain the lower back. Repeat five to ten times. (Figure 11.26.)

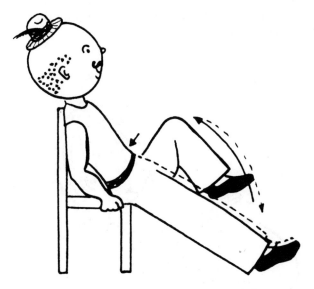

FIGURE 11.26

Spinal Twist: Sitting erect with the right leg crossed over the left, with the left hand on the right knee, and right hand on the left hand, move the right arm steadily to the right until the hand is pointing as far rearward as possible. The movement should require about six to eight seconds. During the movement you should twist your body at the waist and turn your head, keeping your eyes on your moving hand throughout the movement rearward. Then, taking about six to eight seconds, return to the starting position. While moving the hand rearward, inhale; while returning to the starting position, exhale. Take a deep breath between repetitions. Repeat with the opposite arrangement of hands and legs so that the twist is to the left. Beginners may find four-to-six second movement time preferable. Persons with osteoporosis of the spine or other back problems should obtain medical clearance before doing this exercise. Repeat five to ten times in each direction. (Figure 11.27.)

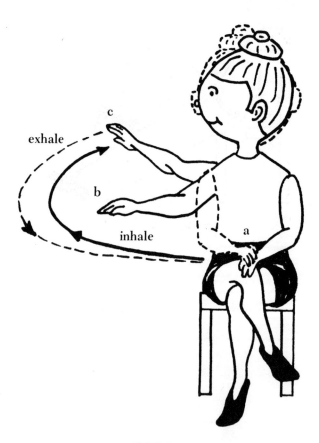

FIGURE 11.27

Flat Back: If while standing with your heels approximately four to six inches from the wall and your hips and shoulders touching the wall, you can slide your hand between the wall and your back, you are in the correct starting position. Suck in the stomach and rotate the pelvis so that the lower back (lumbar region) flattens against the wall. Check the flattened position by placing your hand against the wall and seeing if you can slide it between your back and the wall. If you cannot slide the hand in, you have flattened the back against the wall. This is the movement that is needed to protect the lower back when doing the modified sit-ups and leg lifts. Repeat five to ten times.

Neck Twisting: Alternately turn the head so you face to the left and then to the right, pausing in each extreme position. Keep the chin level and do not tilt the head. Repeat five to ten times.

Scalp and Face

Loosen Tense Scalp: By raising the eyebrows and wiggling the ears and attempting to contract and relax the muscles all over the scalp, try to move the scalp in rearward, forward, and sideward directions. If you are unable to do this, or if you wish to do it in addition, place the fingers on the scalp and massage it pushing the skin across the head in back and forth or circling movements. Exercise for five to ten times.

Funny Face: The object is to exercise the muscles in the face and chin by making funny faces—do just about anything that distorts the features, utilizing the musculature within the face, including smiling grotesquely, grimacing, wiggling the nose, sticking out the tongue, and opening the eyes wide. Suck in the cheeks so that you could chew on them, then close the lips and puff the mouth full of air as if you had walnuts in each cheek. Repeat five to ten times.

Double 88: Standing or sitting tall, with the palms down, place the thumb and forefinger of the hands next to each other, and hold them about a foot and a half in front of your chest. Begin a large figure-8 motion by sweeping the hands downward and rearward just to the left of the left thigh, circle the arms upward above eye level and forward, and then sweep the arms downward and rearward to the right of the right thigh. Continue upward and forward above the level of the right eye. Return downward to the starting position. Let your body twist as the arms sweep past the thighs and flex the knees as you sweep downward. Repeat five to ten times. (Figure 11.28.)

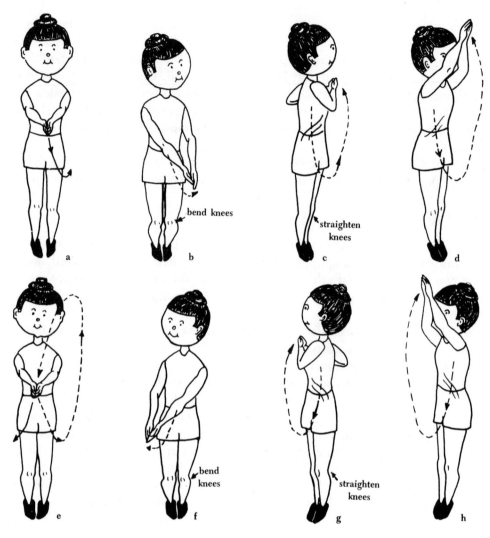

FIGURE 11.28

Eyes

Wandering Eyes: Sitting or standing in an erect position, focus the eyes forward, move the eyes slowly all the way to the left looking leftward as far as you can, then all the way to the right, then up toward the ceiling, down toward the floor, diagonally up left, diagonally down right, diagonally down left, and diagonally up right. Take two to five seconds for each move. Repeat one time and then close and cover the eyes resting them.

Specials

Breathing: This category should be utilized in conjunction with other exercises throughout the exercise period. The basic idea is to fill the lungs as full as possible with air and to exhale as completely as possible in a controlled, regular manner. Attempt to coordinate the breathing naturally with exercises you have been performing. Try several combinations of inhalation and exhalation. One way is to inhale through the nostrils and exhale through the mouth. It is preferable not to inhale through the mouth, inasmuch as the inhalation through the nose provides some screening of any matter in the air due to the hairs in the nostrils. Breath deeply. Fill your lungs more than you normally do in everyday living.

Alternate Nostril Breathing: Sitting erect, place your thumb on the right nostril and first finger on the left nostril. Close off the right nostril and for six counts inhale through the left nostril; then close off both nostrils, hold for four counts; then exhale through the right nostril, hold for four counts; inhale through the right nostril for six counts, hold for four counts; and exhale through the left nostril for six counts. Repeat this five or six times, making your inhalations and exhalations last at least six counts and your holds at least four counts. Between each cycle take a full deep breath, exhale, and relax.

Uddiyana (Pop-Pop-Pop or Regularity with a Laugh): Assume a standing position with feet hip-width apart and toes pointing slight outward. Slightly flex the knees and bend forward at the waist enough to comfortably turn the hands inward on the thighs, with the fingers pointing toward each other and the thumbs on the outside of the thighs. The elbows are up. Exhale as completely as possible, suck in the stomach as far as you can, and then rapidly pop your stomach out as far as you can and suck it back in again. Pop out the stomach five or six times and pause, stand erect, and take a deep breath. Reassume the exercise position and repeat the pop-pop-pop sequence five to ten times. (Figure 11.29.)

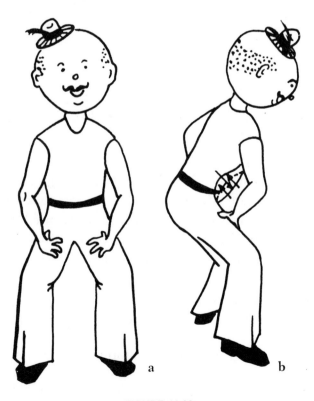

a   b

FIGURE 11.29

Rowing: Sitting as though you were in a rowboat, grasp imaginary oars just above your knees. Leaning forward, push the oars downward and away, then raise the hands and pull the oars toward your shoulders as you lean rearward. Push downward past the knees and lean forward to initiate the second stroke. Repeat 10 to 15 times. For variety, have one hand one-half cycle ahead of the other as though one oar were in the water while the other were in the air. (Figure 11.30.)

top view

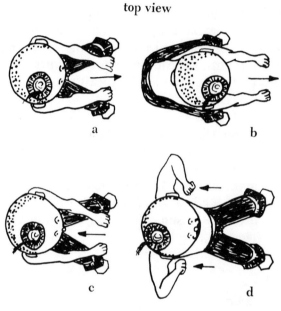

FIGURE 11.30

Evaluation

There are several basic questions which need to be asked before one proceeds very far with an evaluation of an exercise program for the elderly.

1. Was there a pre-evaluation of participant status?
2. Shall the subsequent evaluation be both formative and summative?
3. To what extent is this program designed to yield answers to research questions, if any?
4. Do the program objectives include individualized exercise needs and plans?
5. Are the social and psychological aspects of the program included?
6. What kinds of administrative problems occurred during the program? (See Chapter 2 for additional information on assessment.)

The first question identifies whether or not there is a data-base on which to make comparisons. A measure of program effectiveness can be made by making pre- and post-program test score comparisons.

The second question makes a distinction between formative and summative evaluation. That is, do you want to include suggestions for improvement as the program progresses in addition to some end-of-year reporting? Many of the informal bits of friendly feedback along the way may prove to be fully as useful as a published test or inventory.

Let us consider questions #3 and #4 together. Scientifically validated pre- and post-tests of specific fitness and attitude components could be administered and findings interpreted by trained individuals. The tests selected should measure the qualities that were identified as having high priority by the objectives of the exercise program and they should be administered according to a prescribed plan.

As an example, consider an individual who has recently gained excessive weight and has noted his/her arthritis is causing a loss of movement in a shoulder joint. Such a person may have as primary objectives of an exercise program the loss of 15 pounds and regaining sufficient range of motion at the shoulder joint that he/she can reach the highest shelf in the kitchen without having to climb on a stool. By measuring the weight at the beginning of the exercise program (perhaps accompanied by dieting) and regularly checking the weight to determine progress toward the goal, the individual may claim success when the desired weight is first achieved. A preferred method of determining success would be to retain the desired weight for two or three weeks after first reaching it. An accurate bathroom scale would be an adequate instrument for taking the measures. Range of movement could also be determined by technicians using such instruments as goniometers and rigs using protractors, but such precision is neither practical nor necessary for most people.

Some obvious objective measures of improved fitness would include an increase in the number of repetitions of an exercise performed without fatigue, less difficulty in climbing stairs, and less shortness of breath when walking a given distance. It is easy to keep a record of the number of repetitions of each exercise by listing the exercises and entering the number of repetitions done on each date.

The "Exercise Record Chart" shown in Figure 11.31 can be used by the staff and physicians to monitor the performance of individuals. Certain key exercises may be emphasized due to a particular condition. This kind of chart may be posted for all to see as a motivator, but it may also be counterproductive if posted. People unable to keep up with the group norm may drop out of the program rather than being "spotlighted" as "below average."

A different type of record helps to promote group cohesion and motivates participation. The exercise class can promote a Walking Club with a catchy name, such as the "Tennessee Walkers." Indoor and outdoor routes can be carefully estimated with the use of a pedometer. Participants can enter their names on the "honor roll" chart with the total miles covered to date. Post the chart in a location that is visible for all to see. One example is shown with the "Arkansas Travelers" chart. Note that the chart reads "miles covered" to include residents with wheelchairs also.

Arkansas Travelers
Miles Covered Since *September 1*

Name	*Miles*
1. Ed Keller	125
2. Frances Pugh	251
3. Flo Davies	240
4. Fran Hardy	79
5. Bill Hardy	75
6. Genevieve Hirschhorn	101
7. Aramantha Lewis	116
8. Trudy Wentworth	110

Exercise Record Chart

Number of Repetitions per Day

Name _____

Exercise	M	Tu	W	Th	F	Sa	Su	M	Tu	W	Th	F	Sa	Su	M	Tu	W	Th	F	Sa	Su	M	Tu	W	Th	F	Sa	Su

FIGURE 11.31

The fifth question addresses social and psychological aspects of the program and there are several important aspects of the social and psychological dimensions which are worth mentioning here. Some exercise clubs become an occasion to dress up and perform; they stimulate the participants to greet and enjoy each other. Residents have occasionally begun telephone call networks that enhance involvement in the program and may have a socializing ripple effect apart from the program. "Mabel, today is Thursday. Don't forget the exercise class at 10:00." Those calls also serve as a small piece of reality therapy.

Changes in attitude may also be measured objectively and subjectively. Attitude questionnaires may be developed and administered to oneself or to members of a group who exercise together. A change in attendance patterns at exercise sessions, or participants' comments and behavior during exercise sessions, may be indicative of attitude changes and hence be a source of evaluation.

One word of advice to the evaluator: if you use an inventory before an exercise program begins and then employ it again at the wrong time, the participants could be in a "sore muscle" period. Remember to allow plenty of time between testing. Participants need to be monitored carefully and encouraged in the early stages of an exercise program, so that they will not be frightened and discouraged by unanticipated sore and stiff muscles.

Attendance may be affected by changes in the seasons. In spring and summer, many participants are eager to get about outside and to travel long distances even for extended periods. In the fall, it may be necessary to announce the exercise class again and start it off with a modified design and a new push.

Lastly, there are a variety of administrative concerns which the evaluation can consider. Perhaps foremost among these is leadership. Who is to lead the exercise class? Volunteers are stimulating, yet we believe that a program should not become overly dependent upon them. Some exercise programs have folded when the volunteers quit coming. Activity directors are often quite good at leading the exercises, but what happens when they are sick or away at a meeting? We have looked for leadership among the participants whenever possible. They enjoy the responsibility and share the direction of favorite exercises with their companions.

Other administrative concerns often include the availability of sufficient space for an exercise class, appropriate chairs to sit in while exercising (not soft, cushioned, soporific furniture) and transportation if the program occurs in a centralized senior citizen center. (See Chapter 6.)

Whatever the circumstances, some form of evaluation should be preplanned and carried out. Just knowing that progress will be measured stimulates many people to increased effort and subsequent benefits.

Bibliography

Burke, Edmund J. (1979, November/December). Individualized Fitness Program. *JOPER*. 35–37.

Leslie, David K. and John W. McLure (1975). *Exercises for the Elderly*. University of Iowa, 37.

12 Aquatic Exercise For The Older Adult

Mike Daniel, McMurry College
Dean Gorman, University of Arkansas

Materials in earlier chapters have established that proper exercise is good for people, no matter their age! A senior citizen has much to gain from starting an exercise program, and more to gain from continuing that program through his/her lifespan. Research continues to substantiate that contention, as do the testimonials of participants with a perceived increase in quality of living. The real key, though, is in the *proper* exercise. The principles of duration, intensity, frequency, overload, progression, etc., apply to all exercise and will not be repeated in this section. You are encouraged to review Chapters 7 and 11 in which those principles, their procedures, and their limitations are explained. The purpose of this chapter is to examine a specific mode of exercise—exercise in the water.

Advantages and Disadvantages

Water exercise is unique because its aquatic environment offers advantages which makes it the exercise of choice for a great number of people. Its major advantage is that it provides decreased stress on the joints, and this may be the factor which makes water exercise the only logical exercise choice for many people! The body is lifted to some extent by the water, thereby decreasing the amount of stress on the weight-bearing joints (the extent of lift, or buoyancy, is dependent on the percentage of body fat, body size, and proportion of the body in the water versus out of the water). Many people are not able to walk/jog or participate in other forms of exercise because of ankle, knee, hip, or back problems, but many of these people can exercise in the water painlessly! Those suffering from arthritis may be able to rejuvenate damaged joints while improving cardiovascular, respiratory, and muscular fitness. Nonweight-bearing joints (wrists, shoulders, neck) can be moved against resistance (the water) without the added strain of supporting the total weight of the body part. The American Arthritis Foundation has developed a program of exercises, along with training certification for instructors and facility standards (your local Foundation branch can furnish details). Osteoporosis patients may be able to use this medium for selected exercise benefits, particularly when weight-bearing regimens are contra-indicated due to risk of injury. Regimens that focus on range of motion, muscle toning, and cardiovascular benefits may be safer in the water than on land for people with osteoporosis.

Water therapy has long been a part of rehabilitation programs, but it is only recently that we have begun to capitalize on the uniqueness of the water medium and use it for exercise programs. The decreased stress on the skeletal structure of weight-bearing movements performed in the water and the resultant decreased rate of injury and reduction in chronic pain, compared to when the movements are done on land, should lead to an increased use of water among aging populations.

In the past, many people have believed that water exercise would attract a very limited population because of the necessity of swimming ability. However, swimming ability is not a prerequisite for entrance into a water exercise program. Please notice that the term "water exercise" is used in this section rather than the term "swimming." The benefits of exercise can be obtained in the water without swimming because no swimming skills are required to start a water exercise program. Certainly this is an environment in which certain safety measures must be taken. Lifeguards with training in handling emergency situations should be present at all times, and the pool setting should be controlled so that there is a sense of calm and control around any participant with any doubts about his or her swimming ability. But a great beauty of water exercise is that the benefits of exercise can be obtained while keeping the feet on the bottom in relatively shallow water, or with the hand firmly in contact with the side of the pool. Many a successful water exercise workout has been accomplished with the hair dry and intact and makeup still on!

With the emphasis on "water exercise" rather than "swimming," as many or more people can use a facility at the same time than when people are practicing the lonely art of swimming laps. Further, socializing can be more readily done since the head is out of the water. In fact, water workouts are now being choreographed to music and have the potential for popularity that dance and exercise to music have achieved.

Obviously, water exercise does have disadvantages and unique problems as well. To identify the obvious, a swimming facility is needed. Water exercise is not as convenient as walking/jogging, where very little is needed in the way of a facility, nor is it as inexpensive to purchase the necessary equipment as stationary cycling. But pool availability is not as big a problem as it once was. Many care facilities for the elderly now build pools into their complexes. Many YMCAs, YWCAs, Boys' Clubs, universities and community centers, and private facilities such as health clubs and fitness centers have pools and directors are willing and even eager to make arrangements for exercise sessions. The initial capital outlay for this kind of exercise facility is larger than one would encounter in other forms of exercise. However, the outlay is not one that is usually made by an individual, so this is only a different kind of obstacle, and certainly not one that is insurmountable. Once the facilities are there, the costs are not forbidding for they are shared by many user groups.

One factor which is often overlooked or ignored in other forms of exercise *must* be accounted for in water exercise: support and safety personnel. Lifeguards are a necessity for water exercise. A person engaging in other forms of exercise may be considered to have assumed the risk for accident or emergency. In a swimming pool, that risk is assumed by the pool management. Consequently, lifeguards and supervisory personnel must generally be accepted as another factor to consider in establishing a water exercise program.

Many people enter into exercise programs with fat loss and weight loss as one, if not the primary, motivation. A caloric imbalance caused by any type of exercise will help in a fat/weight reduction program. But one thing must be understood—swimming does not promote the *same degree* of fat and weight loss as do some other forms of exercise. Don't panic! Water exercise will help in a weight reduction program, but it may not cause the extremes of losses that the same amount of, say, walking/jogging on land will cause. The reasons for this are not fully understood. Certainly it is due in part to the fact that water exercise is a "nonweight-bearing" (or at least "reduced weight-bearing") exercise. That is, the buoyancy of the body reduces the burden of its weight as a resistance which must be moved in exercising, so less actual work is done in movement, and less calories are burned per unit of time. Also, the body seems to have a mechanism for retaining some fat as insulation against the cooler environment in the water. Nevertheless, the increased caloric expenditure caused by water exercise, combined with prudent dietary measures, will aid a person in a fat loss and weight loss program.

Before Getting in the Water. . .

A number of safety precautions should be taken prior to beginning any exercise program, whether on land or in the water. The uniqueness of the water environment warrants a review of safety precautions. A basic concern is that participants not place themselves or be placed in a situation that is dangerous to them. The more that is known about a participant, the more individualized the exercise prescription can be, and the potential for optimal benefit is the greatest. Another basic concern is that of the legal liability of the instructor and sponsoring organization. While precautions cannot legally excuse individuals or organizations from a complaint of negligence, the collection of participant information, professional opinions of health status, and the full informing of participants of the nature of and risks in participation will go far to establish that prudent safety measures have been taken.

To elaborate on the first concern, any participant over the age of 35 should have a medical examination by a physician. If that person has had an examination within the previous year, it still may not be adequate if the examining physician did not know that the patient would be undertaking an exercise program. The physician should be informed of the exact nature of the exercise program, so that the degree of stress the patient will face is known. An example of such a notice is given in Figure 12.1.

To the Physician:

_____ has enrolled in a water exercise class. The instructor will lead participants through various exercises in the water, with the intent of allowing the participants to raise their heart rate to 75% of maximum capacity for a period of 10–40 minutes. Each session consists of: (a) a warm-up period, stressing flexibility and muscle tone, along with a gradual rise in heart rate; (b) an "aerobic" period, stressing a monitored heart rate at a predetermined level up to 75% of maximum capability (usually measured as 75% of 220 BPM-age), using dynamic movements of large muscle groups for a period of 10–40 minutes; and (c) a cool-down period, allowing the heart rate to approach resting levels while continuing to move.

Heart rates are monitored by participants; intensity and duration of exercise are voluntary. A lifeguard is present at all times, as well as personnel trained in cardiopulmonary resuscitation.

My examination of _____ has revealed no contraindications to the exercise program described above.

_____

Physician's Signature

_____

Address

_____

Phone

FIGURE 12.1

The physician will then decide the extent of examination called for at that time. Each physician has a preferred base of medical history and areas of examination. The form, which should be kept on file, should provide indications that the physician found nothing to indicate that the patient *should not* participate in the program. (Many physicians are not willing to state that a person *should* participate; only that no reason was found that they should not. The wording might affect insurance reimbursement for the exercise program. Local attitudes and policies will dictate exact wording on the form.)

Second, the instructor and other program personnel need information about the participant. A medical history questionnaire may provide valuable information but one must be careful that the questionnaire is not so cumbersome as to run people off! A form of this type might be used in conjunction with the medical exam. In any case, things such as family history, medications, past exercise habits, injuries, infirmities, and primary risk factors should be known by the program management.

Third, the participant should know exactly what will be expected in the program. An informed consent form is found in Figure 12.2. An informed consent form should include a complete enough description of the activities and the risks and benefits which might result from participation that the participants would be legally considered to have been fully informed. It should be clearly understood by instructor and participant alike that intensity, duration, and even continuation of exercise are purely voluntary. This presents a challenge for the instructor; there is a fine line between motivating participants and removing the voluntary nature of exercise.

Informed Consent for Exercise Program

I, _____, have requested enrollment in a water exercise class. It is understood that the instructor will lead participants through various exercises in the water, with the intent of allowing the participants to raise their heart rate to 75% of maximum capacity for a period of 10–40 minutes. Each session consists of: (a) a warm-up period, stressing flexibility and muscle tone, along with a gradual rise in heart rate; (b) an "aerobic" period, stressing a monitored heart rate at a predetermined level up to 75% of maximum capability (usually measured as 75% of 220 BPM-age), using dynamic movements of large muscle groups for a period of 10–40 minutes; and (c) a cool-down period, allowing the heart rate to approach resting levels while continuing to move.

I further understand that I will be taught to monitor my own heart rate. The intensity and duration of exercise is totally voluntary—I may choose to decrease intensity or totally withdraw from exercise at any time.

Exercise of this nature has the potential for aggravation of cardiorespiratory and/or musculoskeletal problems, including heart attack. Sore, strained, or pulled muscles are also possible. This exercise may also render improvements in functional capacity, respiration, circulation, strength, body composition, and flexibility.

I have read the above information, and fully understand the nature of the water exercise program, the risks and benefits involved, and that I may withdraw from participation at any time.

_____

Signature

_____

Date

_____

Witness

FIGURE 12.2

The Exercise Program

Let me restate that this type of exercise program should adhere to all the principles of exercise prescription and exercise leadership discussed in earlier chapters. What we are about to embark on is a look at some of the water exercises you can use; they should be used in the correct way, as dictated by those principles of exercise.

Also please understand that this will be only a sampling of *some* of the exercises you might use. Your imagination may be your most prolific source. If an exercise fits within the framework of the exercise principles, use it!

The warm-up exercises can also be used as cool-down exercises. For many people in poor physical condition, the warm-up exercises may also serve as cardiovascular exercises. Whatever the case, the instructor and the participant must work together to stay within the guidelines for exercise. All the exercises are designed to be performed in water which is waist deep to chest deep.

A word needs to be added at this point concerning water exercise for the handicapped. The specific exercises which follow can be modified to be accomplished by those with handicapping conditions. Their ability to accomplish these or similar exercises presents less problem than the logistics necessary for them to be in the water. Water depth may be a more critical concern with this population. Depending on the handicapping condition, special facility construction and/or special equipment may be needed for pool entry. Last, and most importantly, a smaller instructor-to-participant ratio is necessary, perhaps one-to-one. While these problems are real and present more work for program management, the work can be done and persons with handicaps may also utilize the water medium.

Warm-up Exercises

Morning Stretch—stand comfortably in waist deep water, feet a shoulder width apart. Reach high above the head, stand on the toes, and stretch as much as is comfortable. Drop down into a relaxed crouched position with the head above water and shake and relax the arms and hands.

Leg Loosener—stand on the left leg and lift the right knee, letting the bottom part of the leg hang loosely. Make circles with the bottom part of the leg for 10 seconds, and then reverse direction for 10 seconds, then change legs and repeat.

Calf Stretcher—stand facing a side wall and lean forward, placing hands on the wall. Keeping the heels in contact with the bottom of the pool and the knees, hips, and back straight, walk with very short steps away from the wall until you feel a stretching in the calf. Stop and hold for 10–15 seconds, relax, and repeat.

Side Stretcher—stand with left side toward the wall, and left arm bracing against the wall. With right arm extended over the head, and with back straight and aligned, lean to the left slowly, stretching the right side. Stretch to the point of discomfort and hold for 10 seconds. Relax and repeat. Do the same for the right side.

Front Thigh Stretcher—stand with left side to the wall, bracing yourself with your left hand. Grasp the right ankle with the right hand, with the heel just below the buttock. Pull and lift the leg to the rear until the point of discomfort. Hold for 10 seconds, relax and repeat. Do for both sides.

Hamstring Stretcher—stand facing the side wall. Place the left foot as high on the wall as possible. Bending at the hips, lean forward to the point of discomfort, keeping the legs straight, and hold for 10 seconds. Relax and repeat. Repeat for right leg.

Hamstring and Lower Back Stretch—hang onto the wall with the feet on the wall, about hip height. Lower the left leg toward the bottom of the pool, against the wall, and press back with the right leg, rounding the back and stretching the right hamstring. Hold for 10 seconds, relax, and repeat. Twice for each leg.

Toe Touch—standing on left leg, lift the straight right leg in front of you, and touch as near the toes as possible with the left hand. Alternate legs (can be done standing still).

Tummy Tuck—hang onto the wall with your back to the wall. Draw your knees up toward the chest while flattening the lower back against the wall. Hold for 3–5 seconds, relax, and repeat.

Tummy Twister—hang onto the side of the pool, with back to the wall. Let the legs float up in front of the body until laid out on top of the water. Twist the trunk to the left, and then twist back to the right. Repeat.

Leg Press—facing the wall, hold onto the wall and float away. Keeping the legs straight and the back straight on top of the water, press the legs down to a standing position. Float back and repeat.

Push Aways—lean forward and place your hands on the wall, keeping the knees, hips, and back straight. Lower the chest to the wall and push away. Repeat as in push-ups (the greater the forward lean, the harder the push away).

Arm Pulls—stand with knees bent so the water is almost shoulder depth. Place one arm straight out in front, the other straight out behind. Pull/push vertically against the water and alternate positions. Repeat.

Kickboard Press—place the hands flat on top of a kickboard directly in front of the body. Maintaining a straight back, press the kickboard under water until arms are extended. Let it rise back to the top slowly. Repeat.

Kickboard Swings—stand with the feet spread comfortably, establishing a good base. With a kickboard to the left of the body, place the left hand at the bottom of the board and the right hand at the top. Pulling with the right arm, pushing with the left arm, and twisting with the body, swing the kickboard around to the right side. Turn it upside down so the right hand is on the bottom, left hand on the top, and repeat back to the left. Repeat.

Cardiovascular Conditioners

Split Jumps—from a standing position, jump slightly and spread the legs (right leg in front, left leg in back). Immediately jump and return to the starting position, then jump and split with right leg in back and left leg in front, then back to starting position. Continue (legs may also split to the side; exercise may be done by alternating the two different movements).

Flutter Kicks—hold onto the side of the pool and brace with one arm. Begin kicking with the legs, swinging them wide apart, and alternating (may be done on front or back).

Ski Slalom—keeping the feet together, jump up and bounce the feet to the right side. Immediately bounce back up and bounce the feet across to the left side. Imagine that you are jumping over a bench. The higher the bench, the greater the work.

Walk/March/Jog—move through the water at whatever pace suits you!

Charleston Kick—stand with feet shoulder-width apart, arms by the sides. Bounce slightly and kick the left heel up to the left hand. Back to starting position, bounce slightly and kick the right heel to the right hand. Continue to alternate.

Cool Down

Wedding March—walk slowly. As the trail leg passes, pause. As you step forward the next trail leg pauses, then steps forward.

Wiggle Through—bend the knees so that the shoulders are under water, then begin wiggling the shoulders and the upper body, and move across the pool.

Easy Kicks—lean back against the wall and let the body float up. Begin doing an easy frog-kicking motion, moving slowly and not pressing the water.

Bibliography

Conrad, Casey (1985). *The New Aqua Dynamics*. Alexandria, VA: NSPI Publications.

Krasevec, Joseph A., and Grimes, Diane C. (1985). *HydroRobics*. Champaign, IL: Leisure Press.

Sholtis-Jones, M.C. (1982). *Swimnastics Is Fun*. Vol. II, Waldorf, MD: AAHPERD Publications.

White, Sue W. (1981). *Feel Good! Look Good! Create a New You Through Aquatic Exercise*. Aquatics Unlimited, 1828 Buffalo Rd., West Des Moines, Iowa 50265.

13 Dance For The Older Adult

Cynthia Ensign, University of Northern Iowa

Introduction

Many references contain ideas for dance activities, and although they may be directed toward the younger adult, they are often just as appropriate for the older adult—with perhaps some modification(s). The dance instructor must understand why and how to choose existing dance activities and why and how to make modifications before using them with the older adult.

Resources for dance activities include references covering such dance forms as folk dance, ballroom dance, square dance, modern dance, ballet, jazz dance, and even tap dance. Many of the dance steps and ideas included in these references can be adapted so that they are appropriate for the older adult. Another resource is that of references covering dance for the young child. Many of the activities contained therein focus on basic movements that are fundamental to all forms of dance activities. It is the dance instructor's manner of presentation that makes the content of these materials appropriate for the older adult.

This chapter includes a discussion of considerations to keep in mind when selecting dance activities, and modifications to make if particular dance activities are not appropriate for the older adult. With an understanding of the benefits of dance, an understanding of why and how to choose and if necessary modify dance activities, and with references available, one should be able to use existing dance materials and to create dance activities appropriate for specific older adult situations. The instructor should remember that dance is often quite vigorous for participants, and the same kinds of precautions need to be taken as for other kinds of exercise programs.

Benefits of Dance

As an exercise form, dance is commonly considered to have a number of benefits for all ages. These benefits can be physical, psychological, or social. A listing of the possible benefits in each of these categories includes:

Physical: Improved flexibility, muscle strength, and endurance; improved cardiovascular-respiratory endurance; improved balance, coordination, and kinesthetic awareness; improved alignment; increased bone mineral content; decreased arthritis difficulties, insomnia, neuromuscular hypertension, stress-related diseases, and low back pain.

Psychological: Increased self-confidence, self-esteem, and stability; increased sense of achievement and acceptance by others; increased expression of feelings and recognition of creative abilities; decreased depression.

Social: Decreased isolation, loneliness, and boredom; increased sharing and support; increased tactile contact, cooperation, and enjoyment.

Selecting and Modifying Dance Activities

For the warm-up or the beginning of a class

1. *Choose dance activities that utilize all parts of the body.* To maintain functional use of the entire body it is necessary to use the entire body. Therefore it is important in each dance class to utilize all or most joints and to perform all or most of the actions possible at those joints. Arthritis may make it difficult for some older adults to perform some of the joint actions. Encourage the older adult to do all of them, but to do so within his/her range of ability. Changing the position of the body in which the joint actions are done, especially so that they are nonweight-bearing, may be helpful.

The beginning of a dance class is a good time to include dance activities requiring many and various joint actions. These movements should be performed slowly enough and with sufficient repetition to bring about increased range of motion and increased joint mobility for activities to be conducted in the later sections of class.

Progressing in order from the feet to the head or vice versa will ensure that all major joints and their actions are included. As an example consider the head. It can be tilted to the right side, lifted to the center, tilted to the left side, and lifted center. It can be rotated or turned to look right, to look center, to look left, and to look center. It can be tilted to look down, to look center, to look up, and to look center. Caution should be taken to lift the head to look up rather than collapsing it back to look up. Such head motions are referred to as "isolations" in jazz dance. "Head rolls" or "head circles" often found in jazz dance classes are not recommended because of the stress to the upper vertebrae, nerve, and blood vessels in that area. (Corbin and Lindsey, 1985: 137)

2. *Include dance activities that will stretch major muscle groups and other muscles that will be used later in class.* Stretching activities should be provided in the beginning of a dance class so that participants may achieve a normal range of motion and therefore, benefit from the rest of the dance class without getting injured. It seems to be most beneficial to perform stretching activities after the body is somewhat warmed up—once the muscle and joint temperature have increased slightly. Also, for stretching activities to be valuable, the position of maximum stretch should be held for a minimum of 10 seconds. Some precautions need to be kept in mind. First of all, bouncing or bobbing into a stretch position is contraindicated. It may cause small muscle tears or result in the muscle contracting rather than stretching because of the stretch reflex. Secondly, pain should not be felt. There may be a slight degree of discomfort from putting the muscle in a stretched position, but there should be no pain. If pain is experienced, the stretch on the muscles should be decreased and/or the position in which the stretch is performed modified or changed. By combining static stretches, particularly for muscle groups that will be used in class, with joint actions a dance instructor can provide his/her participants with a good warm-up.

The last part of a dance class, after the body temperature has been elevated for a while and one's range of motion has been adequately achieved, is the time when flexibility can be improved. The inclusion of static stretches is appropriate here. The same concerns and precautions apply.

3. *Include dance activities that focus on proper placement.* In dance, placement of one's body is important both for safe and efficient movement and because the body is used as the instrument for expression. One focus of placement in dance is that of upright or vertical alignment. In modern dance and ballet good vertical alignment is emphasized because of its aesthetic contributions and

because it is often the center from which other movements emanate. In ballroom dance good vertical alignment is emphasized because of its importance in leading and following. Although the older adult may have difficulty in achieving proper vertical alignment (kyphosis being a common problem), it is appropriate to focus on improved vertical alignment as falling within the realm of dance activities and as beneficial to the older adult's self-esteem. Alleviation of low back pain may be an additional result. Exercises to increase strength and flexibility of muscles necessary for proper alignment in an upright position should be part of a dance class for the older adult.

A second focus of placement in dance is that of the alignment of individual body parts, particularly those of the lower limbs, as important for safe and efficient locomotion. Attention should be given to proper placement at the ankle and knee joints in a dance class for the older adult. The foot should not roll in (pronate) or out (supinate) at the ankle joint. The knees should be in line with the toes in any position in which the knees are bent. Finally, the knees should not lock (hyperextend).

For the activity or the middle portion of a class

In general: Include dances and dance activities that will promote physical conditioning. Physical conditioning—the improvement or maintenance of muscle strength and endurance, flexibility, and cardiovascular-respiratory endurance—is as important to a dancer as it is to an athlete, and, physical conditioning is as important for the older adult as it is for the younger adult and young child. Because the instrument of expression in dance is the body, physical conditioning is important to the ability of the dancer to express him/herself. At the same time, because the medium of dance is movement, dances and dance activities can be specifically selected so that they will provide for the improvement or maintenance of physical conditioning. In addition, dances and dance activities that stress different parts of the body can be selected. These then contribute to the maintenance of bone mineral content which in turn may lead to improved alignment and decreased bone fractures.

Space Considerations

1. *Select dances and dance activities that do not require frequent changes of direction or of body position.* It may be difficult for the older adult to change from moving forward to moving backward, from moving from one side to the other, from moving at a high level to moving at a low one. His/her sensory awareness and coordination (strength, balance, neuro/muscular sequencing) may have decreased and therefore his/her ability to control his/her body may have decreased. Once his/her body is in motion in a given direction, it may take more time for the older adult to counter this motion—especially to do so without injury.

If in other ways a particular dance or dance activity seems suitable, the dance instructor should consider modifying the dance by continuing the direction of movement for twice the amount of time indicated. When a dance is accompanied by a specific selection of music, it may be necessary to modify the dance further so that the movements in the dance fit the phrasing of the music. For example, a portion of the dance may have to be omitted to accommodate the increased movement in one direction.

2. *Select dances and dance activities that require little elevation.* Decreased range of motion, inadequate strength, overweight, decreased sensory awareness, and decreased coordination all

contribute to the older adult's inability to perform locomotor steps requiring elevation efficiently and without injury. First of all it is difficult for the older adult to produce sufficient force to cause his/her body to be lifted off the floor. Secondly, if he/she is successful in doing so, there is the difficulty of returning to the floor or landing without causing stress, perhaps resulting in injury, to various joints in the lower limbs and continuing up through the back.

Fortunately, many dance forms and specific dances and dance steps within them do not require elevation. In folk dance there are many dances from many different countries that utilize a walk as their basic means of locomotion. In ballroom dance a walk is the basic means of locomotion for almost all of the various styles.

Modifications, however, can be made to make other folk dances and ballroom dance steps appropriate for the older adult. These include:

a. changing a hop to just a rise to the ball of the foot
—a step hop thus becomes a walk and a rise;
—a schottische becomes three walks and a rise;
b. omitting a hop completely and pausing for its duration
—a step hop becomes a walk and a pause and a schottische becomes three walks and a pause—both perhaps with a higher knee lift of the free leg during the pause;
—a polka becomes a two-step.

3. *Eliminate turns or spinning in dances.* Because of decreased balance, coordination, and sensory awareness, it is difficult for the older adult to change his/her body orientation quickly. The result may be only a momentary loss of balance, but the result may also be a fall of more serious consequence. The common three-step turn may be modified to three walks and a touch of the ball of the foot of the free leg. Turning and spinning in place may be indicated by circling the arms in some manner such as in front of the body or over head.

4. *Consider the complexity of the spatial patterns of a dance or dance activity.* Because of a probable lack of much movement experience through space in many different ways, plus a limited awareness of one's own body in space, it is usually difficult for the older adult to orient his/her own movement within a complex spatial pattern involving other dancers. Additionally, because the visual sense is so strong and reliance on visual cues so keen, without a good sense of awareness of one's own body in space, it will be difficult to perform dances in which visual cues are limited. In a circle formation some older adults will have difficulty orienting their movements when they are on the opposite side of the circle from the instructor. When instructed to move to their right, some older adults will mirror the instructor and move to their left instead. It will be even more difficult for the older adult to perform dances in which participants are moving in different directions or in different spatial patterns simultaneously. In these dances there are limited visual cues to reinforce one's own movement. Not that older adults cannot perform these dances with more complex patterns. It is just that the dance instructor needs to consider the spatial complexity of the pattern when selecting dances for his/her group. The more complex the spatial pattern, the simpler should be the individual dancer's movements and vice versa.

Time Considerations

1. *Consider the tempo at which the dance steps or movements are to be performed.* Because of decreased coordination and balance, it is difficult for the older adult to execute motor patterns as quickly as younger adults. Being able to decrease the speed on the source of music to

accommodate slower movements is extremely helpful in meeting the needs of the older adult. If slowing down the accompaniment would result in distortion of it, there are a couple of possible modifications. First, attempt to find a different recording of the dance which might have a different tempo. Secondly, try doing all the movements twice as slowly.

In addition, due to decreased motor memory, the older adult will need more time to think while learning a dance movement or combination. Again, the ability to slow down the speed of the music accompaniment is helpful. But as with any age group, remember to consider teaching the dance activity first without music. As the group becomes more comfortable and facile with the steps and/or movements, gradually increase the tempo at which instructions and cues are given before adding music. Once the dance is learned the tempo may not seem so fast.

2. *Select dances and dance activities which involve repetition.* As mentioned in #1 under Time Considerations, the older adult's motor memory is often limited. Therefore, remembering a long combination of steps or sequence of movements may be difficult for the older adult. The continuous repetition of a dance step or short sequence of dance steps in a given direction is helpful. Also, the frequent repetition of that sequence of dance steps is helpful.

If several verses of different movement patterns are contained in a dance, repeating one or a couple of them instead of teaching all of them would be appropriate modification. In square dance, dances in which each couple visits the other couples or those in which the head couples and the side couples perform a pattern are good examples involving repetition.

Force Considerations

1. *Include dances and dance activities that allow for a range in the use of muscle tension—from great muscle tension to total relaxation.* In dance, as in sport, attention is often given to the production of muscle tension necessary to execute a movement or movement sequence. The opposite end of the continuum, however, should be given equal consideration because it is the proper balance between muscle tension and relaxation that results in efficient movement. Including dance activities that provide for a variety in the continuum of muscle tension-relaxation extends the older adult's movement vocabulary and assists him/her in gaining greater control over his/her body. Developing an ability to consciously relax parts of the body should help the older adult relax muscle groups unnecessary to the performance of particular movement sequences resulting in smoother, more coordinated performances. In addition, developing an ability to consciously relax both parts of the body and the entire body should help reduce neuromuscular hypertension.

On the other hand, the opportunity to explore and utilize a wide range of muscle tensions can provide the older adult a means to release or give expression to feelings. The body and mind are very interconnected. Through dance activities the older adult can become aware of differences in muscle tension as they relate to differences in feeling states. He/she can become more in touch with his/her own feelings and then through dance activities have the chance to release or express them. (H'Doubler, 79)

For the cool-down or end of a class.

1. *Include dances and dance activities that allow the heart rate and respiratory rate to return to normal.* It may not take much activity to elevate the older adult's heart rate and respiratory rate. Therefore, the dance instructor needs to provide dances and dance activities that allow the older adult's heart rate and respiratory rates to decrease gradually. Dances and dance activities with

slower tempi, which cover less space, and which use a limited amount of the body are some possible suggestions.

To conclude a dance class, the focus of attention may be on vertical alignment—either in a standing or seated position. Not only does such focus assist in improving alignment, but it also assists in "centering" an older adult—bringing one's attention to rest calmly within oneself.

2. *Include dance activities that will stretch different muscle groups and thus assist in improving flexibility.* The last part of a dance class, after one's body temperature has been elevated for a while and one's range of motion has been adequately achieved, seems to be the safest time to work toward increased flexibility. (Van Gelder and Marks, 1987: 160) The inclusion of static stretches as discussed in the warm-up section is appropriate here. And the same concerns and precautions apply.

3. *Include dance activities that allow for conscious relaxation of the body.* In addition to including dance activities that focus on vertical alignment as possible centering and quieting activities, consider including dance activities that will assist the older adult in consciously relaxing various parts of the body and the entire body as well. A good time to include relaxation activities is toward the end of a dance class when the older adult's heart rate and respiratory rate have decreased to normal. Through relaxation activities the older adult may become more aware of his/her body and the various unnecessary tensions held within it. The end of a dance class is a good time for centering, for quieting, for letting go of unnecessary tensions.

On Your Own

How about making up your own dance or dance activity? Benefits of dance have been listed, precautions in selecting dances and dance activities have been discussed and modifications suggested, and references are provided at the end of the chapter. Now by combining information and suggestions provided in the following section, you should be able to make up your own dances and dance activities.

Basic Locomotor Steps

Dance steps and locomotor dance sequences are combinations of different basic locomotor steps. Below are listed basic locomotor steps from which to choose. These may be arranged and rearranged in many different orders. Although the use of locomotor steps requiring elevation should be kept to a minimum, simulating them as best as possible provides some variety.

1. *Walk*—a transfer of weight from one foot to the other with a moment when the ball of one foot and the heel of the other are both in contact with the floor.
2. *Run*—a transfer of weight from one foot to the other with a moment when neither foot is in contact with the floor.
3. *Leap*—a transfer of weight as in a run but with more spring/suspension in the air.
4. *Hop*—a transfer of weight from one foot to the same foot.
5. *Jump*—a transfer of weight onto two feet.
6. *Skip*—the combination of a walk and a hop in an uneven rhythm.
7. *Slide*—the combination of a walk and a leap in an uneven rhythm and usually sideward.
8. *Gallop*—the combination of a walk and a leap in an uneven rhythm and usually forward.

Traditional Dance Steps

Traditional dance steps are just combinations of the basic locomotor steps listed above. Below are listed some of the more common traditional dance steps along with their rhythmic patterns from which to choose when making up one's own dance. They are categorized according to dance style.

Folk Dance

Step-hop—the combination of 1 walk and 1 hop in an even rhythm.

counts:	1	2
	♩	♩
steps:	walk	hop

Schottische—the combination of 3 walks and 1 hop in an even rhythm.

counts:	1	2	3	4
	♩	♩	♩	♩
steps:	walk	walk	walk	hop

Grapevine—the combination of 4 walks taken sideward crossing one foot alternately in front and then in back of the other in an even rhythm.

counts:	1	2	3	4
	♩	♩	♩	♩
steps:	walk R to R side	walk onto L crossed in front of R	walk R to R wide	walk onto L crossed behind R

Two-step—the combination of 3 walks with the first two being taken twice as fast as the last.

counts:	1	&	2
	♩	♩	♩
steps:	walk	close opposite foot to the first	walk on first foot

Polka—the combination of 3 walks as in a two step and 1 hop in an uneven rhythm.

counts:	1	&	2	a
	♩	♩	♩.	♩
steps:	walk	walk closing opposite foot to first	walk	hop

Square Dance

Grand right and left—Give partner right hand as if shaking hands. Then move past partner passing right shoulders. Give left hand to next person similarly; then move past passing left shoulders. Continue alternately giving right and left hands.

Elbow swing—hook right or left elbows with person indicated and turn once around.

Do-sa-do—walk forward toward person indicated, passing right shoulders, move around each other back to back, and return to original position walking backward.

Forward and back—walk forward toward person indicated or center of circle; then walk backward back to original position.

Ballroom Dance

Except where indicated, the direction for the steps is not indicated because there is such a variety of dance steps based on changes in direction for each ballroom dance style. Consulting references on ballroom dance listed at the end of this chapter will provide more specific steps.

Waltz—the combination of 3 walks evenly in time in a meter of 3.

counts:	1	2	3
	♩	♩	♩
steps:	walk	walk	walk

Foxtrot—the combination of 3 walks to 4 counts of music in a meter of 4.

counts:	1	2	3	4
	♩		♩	♩
steps:	walk		walk	walk
	slow		quick	quick

OR—the combination of 4 walks to 6 counts of music in a meter of 4.

counts:	1	2	3	4	5	6
	♩		♩		♩	♩
steps:	walk		walk		walk	walk
	slow		slow		quick	quick

Jitterbug/Swing—the combination of 4 walks in place or 6 counts of music in a meter of 4.

counts:	1	2	3	4	5	6
	♩		♩		♩	♩
steps:	walk		walk		walk slightly	walk
	slow		slow		backward	quick
					quick	

OR—the first two walks may be varied to a toe-heel action of one foot and then the other.

counts:	1	2	3	4	5	6
	♩	♩	♩	♩	♩	♩
steps:	toe	heel	toe	heel	walk slightly backward	walk

Cha cha cha—the combination of 5 walks to 4 counts of music in a meter of 4.

counts:	1	2	3	&	4
	♩	♩	♩	♩	♩
steps:	walk slow	walk slow	walk quick	walk quick	walk slow

Charleston walk—the combination of 1 walk and 1 touch forward and then 1 walk and 1 touch backward in an even rhythm. The touch may be varied and become a small kick forward and a lunge backward.

counts:	1	2	3	4
	♩	♩	♩	♩
steps:	walk forward	touch/ kick	walk backward	touch/ lunge

Aerobic Dance

Step-kick—step on one foot and kick the other diagonally across in front in an even rhythm.

counts:	1	2
	♩	♩
steps:	walk	kick

Step-close-step-touch/kick—the combination of 3 walks sideward and 1 touch with the ball of the free foot beside the opposite in an even rhythm.

counts:	1	2	3	4
	♩	♩	♩	♩
steps:	walk R to R side	walk L closed beside R	walk R to R side	touch ball of L beside R

This step may be taken to the right (as described) or the left. A small kick may be substituted for the touch. The degree of difficulty may be increased by changing the first 3 walks to a grapevine step.

Slap the thigh—step on one foot and lift the opposite knee and slap it with one or both hands in an even rhythm.

counts:	1	2
	♩	♩
steps:	walk	slap thigh

Elbow-to-knee—with the hands on the shoulders step on one foot and lift the opposite knee to touch it with the opposite elbow in an even rhythm.

counts: 1   2
                 ♩   ♩
steps: walk   elbow to
                              opposite knee

Formations

There are several formations of dancers that can be used as structures for dance activities. Utilizing these various formations can be helpful in meeting the different social, psychological and emotional as well as physical needs of the older adult. The basic formations include: circle, circle with partner(s), partner(s), forward facing, and free.

Circle—a formation in which all the dancers face the center of a circle. They may or may not join hands or make similar contact—joining forearms, putting arms around neighbor's waist or on shoulders. (Figure 13.1.)

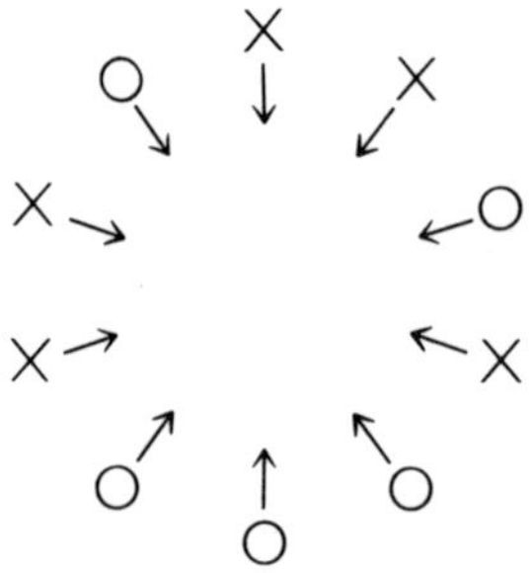

FIGURE 13.1

In a circle formation dancers feel a sense of belonging to a group and as they move together as a group gain strength and support from one another. Visual facial contact can be made resulting in recognition of one another as important and unique individuals.

Circle with partner(s)—formations which include a double circle in which partners stand beside one another (Figure 13.2)

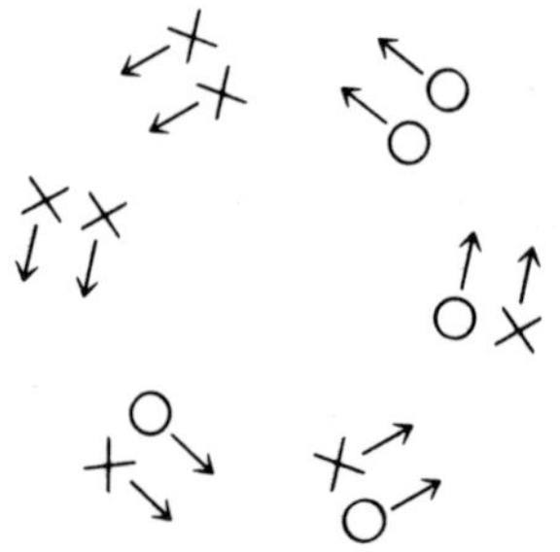

FIGURE 13.2

or face one another (Figure 13.3)

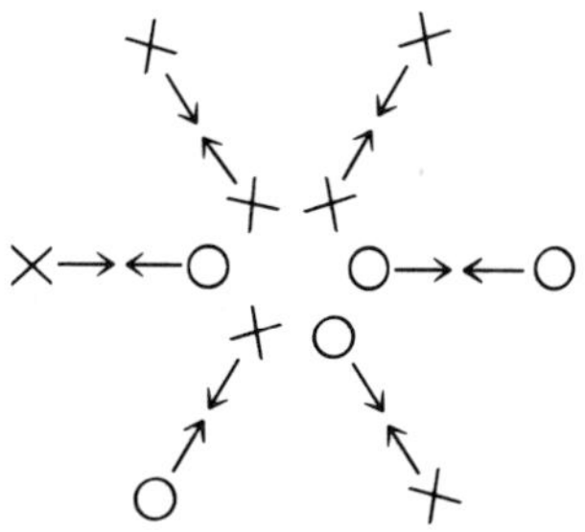

FIGURE 13.3

or a triple circle in which partners stand beside one another (Figure 13.4)

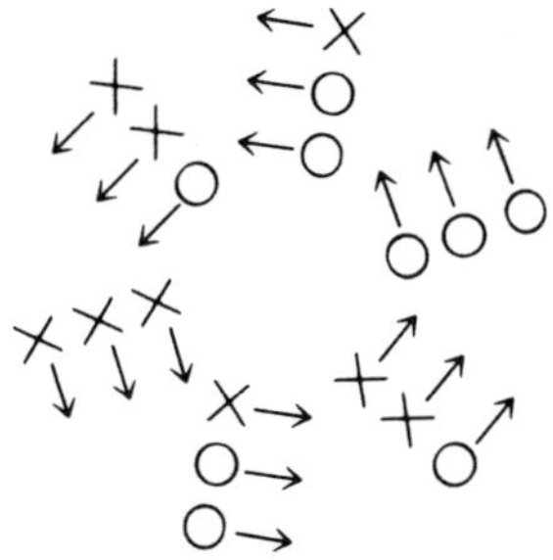

FIGURE 13.4

or a group of three faces another group of three (Figure 13.5.)

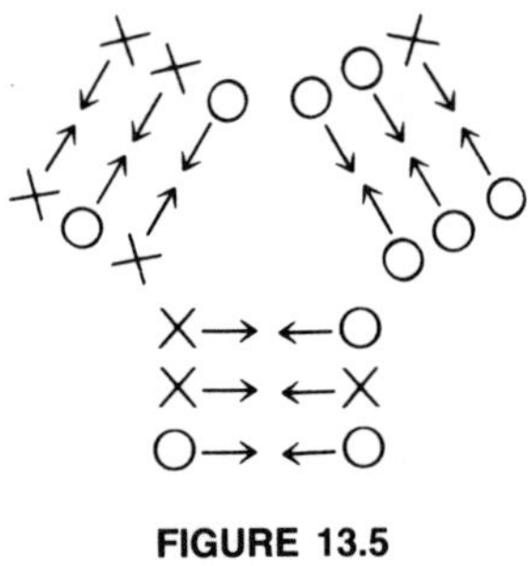

FIGURE 13.5

In circle with partner(s) formations, dancers not only gain a sense of belonging to a group but also make special contact with others which allows for more specific recognition of others as well as of themselves. In addition, changing partners in circle with partner(s) formations permits one to make special contact with more than one person which allows for the development of ties with several others within the group.

Partner—formations which include arrangement with a partner other than in a circle and include partners facing one another in two parallel lines (Figure 13.6)

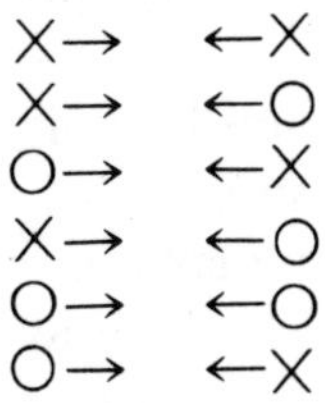

FIGURE 13.6

or partners facing one another and distributed randomly in the available space (Figure 13.7)

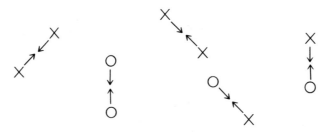

FIGURE 13.7

Although partners may be randomly arranged, it may be advisable because of the direction of movement to have partners face one another with their sides to a specific wall. (Figure 13.8.)

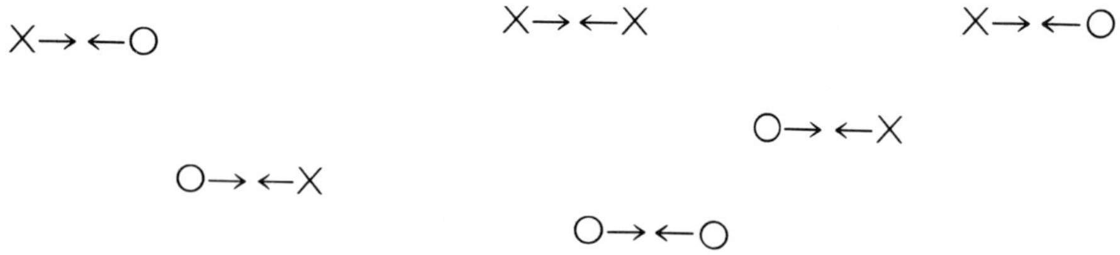

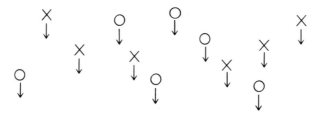

FIGURE 13.8

In partner formations one's focus is primarily on one's partner. Each recognizes the individuality of his/her partner through cooperating and possibly adapting one's own movement.

Forward facing—a formation in which dancers face the same way in the space and are usually arranged randomly within it. (Figure 13.9.)

FIGURE 13.9

In a forward facing formation dances can be more complicated because no one is dependent upon another. If someone is slower or makes a "mistake," no one else is disrupted. For some persons the challenge to execute more complex sequences of steps is enjoyable. The forward facing formation accommodates this need.

Free—a formation in which dancers may move anywhere in the available space. Although specific instructions are given as to how to move through the space, exactly where to move is left up to the individual.

In a free formation more individual responsibility is given. Dancers have the responsibility of choosing where to move. They have the responsibility of cooperating with one another to share the given space. Moving in a free formation may improve one's spatial awareness of one's body in relationship to others and to space in general—how one can/cannot move with a given set of directions. In addition, for some dancers the sense of freedom to move through the available space rather than being restricted to a given spatial formation feels good.

Improvisation

Improvisational dance activities are ones which allow participants to explore movement within a given structure. They allow the participants to do so within their own abilities. They are valuable because they allow the participants to experiment and to discover their own movements and to express themselves through movement. Through improvisational activities participants may gain an appreciation not only of their own individualities but recognize the individuality and uniqueness of each of the other participants.

Suggestions when conducting improvisational dance activities include:

1. Participate with the group. Participants will feel more at ease and less inhibited if they feel that they are not being watched.
2. Assure your participants that there is no right or wrong way of responding to movement directions.
3. De-emphasize "technique" or how exactly one does a movement.
4. Give clear, objective instructions but ones which do have more than one possible movement solution.
5. Eliminate or limit demonstration when giving instructions. Allow participants to discover their own movements rather than being influenced in any way by demonstrations.
6. Encourage spontaneity rather than planning ahead. Thinking will often interfere with imagination and result in ordinary and stereotypic responses.
7. Try to make the environment as nonthreatening as possible.
8. Introduce improvisational activities gradually—especially to groups in which individuals may feel embarrassed or self-conscious.

Suggestions for Improvisational Activities

There are many references to which one can turn for improvisational or new ideas for movement experiences. The bibliography at the end of the chapter lists several of these. In the following section are some suggestions for starters. They are divided into three categories: small hand equipment or props, word imagery, and body movement explorations.

1. *Small Hand Equipment/Props:* This category focuses on ideas for movement stimulated by small hand equipment or props. Items such as scarves, light weight material, stretch material, parachutes, yarn balls, frisbees, bean bags, shoes, towels, and percussive instruments fall into this category. Use of such props as a source for movement can be advantageous because a participant's attention is focused on something other than him/herself as the mover. For many older adults it has been a long time since they moved with any degree of creativity and for some to move creatively is almost an entirely new experience. In addition, the older adult often has limited movement background of any kind and therefore feels self-conscious about his/her movement to begin with. Having to deal with an external object places the focus of attention on the movement of the object rather than on the movement of the participant. For the object or prop to move appropriately, however, the participant must move in a certain way(s). Because of the difference in weight, size, shape, and material of different props, different kinds of movements are possible or more likely to occur while each of them is being used. The dance instructor can thus extend the older adult's movement vocabulary by his/her choice of props.

The following are some suggestions for the use of some props:

Frisbee

a. as a hat (has potential for working on alignment, but a frisbee can be balanced on one's head with all kinds of postures beneath!)
   - walking
     normal
     high on balls of feet and with arms stretched over head
     low by bending knees
     lifting knee and slapping thigh with one or both hands
     lifting knee and clapping hands underneath
     placing hands on shoulders and touching elbow to opposite knee
   - doffing hat (be sure to use with each hand)
     with exaggerated arm motion remove frisbee/hat from head and bow or curtsy and then replace
     greet others as you walk around room with above gesture

b. as a tambourine (be sure to use with each hand)
   - shake frisbee as if tambourine
   - hit/clap frisbee with free hand anywhere in space
     high over head
     low to floor
     wide to side
     behind back
   - hit other parts of the body with frisbee
     hip
     head
     knee
     foot
     shoulder

c. as a steering wheel
   - walking
     in front
     exaggerate turn for curves
     high over head to go up a hill
     low toward floor to go down a hill
     behind for reverse

d. as a pillow

e. as a fan

f. miscellaneous
   - twirl on index finger—clockwise and counterclockwise
   - for over shoulder stretch—hold frisbee behind back with one arm over shoulder and down back and the other arm under opposite shoulder and up back

Shoes

a. on the hands as

- mittens/gloves
- scrubbing mitt
- another pair of feet

b. as extensions of the arms as
- hands
- fly swatter
- racquet
- back scratcher
- eating utensils
- tools (saw, hammer)

c. as different kinds of
- cowboy
- fireman
- ballet
- tap
- galoshes
- moon boots

Light-weight Material

a. to float
- cloud
- autumn leaves

b. to glide/soar
- bird
- kite

c. to wave
- flag

d. as extension of arm(s)
- paintbrush
- baton

Towels

a. to dry off various parts of the body
b. as a coat, cloak, or shawl
c. as a scarf, veil, or other head piece
d. as a bull fighter's cape
e. to wring out as if wet
f. as a rope in tug-of-war
g. as a whip
h. to toss in air and get under
- on top of head
- in a given shape

2. *Word Imagery:* This category focuses on improvisational activities and new ideas for

dance/movement experiences that are stimulated by the imagery of words given by the instructor. The underlying structure or stimulus is provided by the instructor while the responses originate with the participants. The varying responses are the result of the interpretations of the individual movers. Because attention is focused on the mover's own interpretations of the structure and his/her resulting movement response, activities listed below may be more difficult for a person lacking in creative movement experience to do than those activities with small hand equipment or props. In these activities the individual expresses some of him/herself in his/her movement response. However, there is safety in the knowledge that the movement response is stimulated or triggered by an outside source which provided the structure.

The following are some suggestions for the use of Word Imagery:

Move as words suggest

a. verbs
   - search
   - squirm
   - push
   - ooze
   - stomp
   - tilt
   - wander

b. adjectives
   - frantic
   - sticky
   - frisky
   - limp
   - cold
   - happy

Choose words so that they will call forth contrasting movement responses. "Search" and "push" will probably result in fairly different movements whereas "frantic" followed immediately by "frisky" may not result in much different movement for beginners with this activity. Also, consider varying the space over which the movement responses take place, the time in which they occur, and/or the force with which they are performed. Thus one could "wander" in a very large area or a confined area, "stomp" in slow motion, and "push" a heavy object or a light one.

Move as in sports activities

a. swimming (in place or with some kind of locomotion) with arms doing various swimming strokes
   - forward crawl
   - backward crawl
   - breaststroke
   - elementary back stroke
   - tread water
   - float!

b. tennis (be sure to try with "racquet" held in each hand)
   - forehand

- backhand
- serve
- smash
- lob

c. skating (attempt to do various movements with the feet; sticky floors which are generally good for traction will not allow a good imitation of forward skating)
- forward
- backward
- cross overs
- glide on one foot
- play hockey

d. basketball
- dribble with each hand
- deceive an opponent
- steal a ball from another
- shoot for imaginary baskets
   lay-up
   foul
   jump

e. cross country skiing
f. golf
- teeing off
- drives
- putts

Choose different sports and activities within each so that they will call forth contrasting movement responses. Also, consider varying the space, time, and force components of the natural movement responses. For example, vary the time component by performing tennis strokes in slow motion or racing swimming strokes. Vary the space component by playing a basketball game with opponents (other participants) but without balls, baskets, and court markings.

Move as in daily activities

a. brushing teeth
b. getting into car
c. typing
d. eating
e. scrubbing bathtub
f. applauding/clapping

Indicate ways of changing the natural movement responses by varying the space, time, and/or force components of these. For example, perform the movement with an exaggerated range of motion from very large to very small; in slow motion or as fast forward; with a lot of strength or very softly; with another part(s) of the body.

Move as if driving a vehicle (through space with any of the following variations)

a. curves on the road

b. on a freeway

c. up a hill

d. down a hill

e. it rains (put on windshield wipers)

f. stop sign

g. in reverse

h. car pool

Arrange the above variations and any other additional ones so that there will be a contrast in movement responses.

Move as if playing musical instruments

a. piano

b. accordion

c. slide trombone

d. cymbals

e. drums

f. violin

g. castanets

Again, alter the natural movement responses by varying the space, time, and/or force components.

3. *Body Movement Explorations:* In this category improvisational activities and ideas for dance/movement experiences come from the exploration of the wide range of body movements possible within structured situations. Often the older adult will find the first two examples easier to do because the activities are quite structured, are fairly familiar to them, and do not require much self-expression. Usually, the older adult at first will be less comfortable with the other examples because the activities are not as tightly structured, will be unfamiliar, and will require more involvement of one's own ideas.

The following are some suggestions of Body Movement Explorations:

Basic Locomotor Activities

a. anywhere in room with following changes
   • direction: forward, backward, sideward, diagonal
   • level: from high to low
   • range: from large to small

b. across the floor in lines
   • with changes as in a. above
   • varying floor pattern: zig-zag, scallop, half-boxes, half-circles

Traditional Dance Steps

a. with spatial variations listed under Basic Locomotor Activities

Body Parts

a. dance instructor indicates which part of the body leads the participant through space
   • hand
   • elbow

- hip
- back
- chest
- nose

Although the older adult may extend the part of the body indicated, actual "leading" with that part will probably be limited due to a decreased kinesthetic awareness of what it takes for the entire body to let that part "lead."

    b. write one's name or draw a picture in space with a selected body part. The space utilized may be varied from the small, personal space immediately around the participant to the large, general space of the entire room.

Shapes

a. freezing in shapes
- round
- long
- square
- twisted

b. create shapes with other(s)
- in close proximity
- attached to

c. move in shapes
- as individual
- while connected to partner or small group

d. move from shape to shape
- as individual
- with partner or small group

Mirroring
In this activity, participants face either the dance instructor or a partner and move if they were facing themselves in a mirror. Initially it is helpful for the dance instructor to be the leader for the entire group. The dance instructor can then introduce a wide variety of movement possibilities utilizing many body parts, ranges of movement, and tensions in the movements. Beginners with this activity tend to limit their choices to calisthenic movements.

Follow the Leader
Anywhere from two participants to the entire group are in line single file and perform the same movement as the leader. Although this activity is readily accepted, the variety in movement responses will probably be limited in the beginning.

Choreography and Performance—A brief word

Ideas that develop from improvisational activities may be organized into a dance and performed by the older adult. The selection of the ideas to be used and their organization should come from the group. The opportunity to bring together many related ideas and to give them form is satisfying. It provides a sense of achievement.

Performance, then, completes the process. The opportunity to perform for others is valuable. It is the chance to share, to express oneself, to communicate with others. Performance within the dance class is all that is necessary. Although performance may be extended further to a larger audience, perhaps family and friends, it is not necessary.

Bibliography

Beal, Rayma and Berryman-Miller, Sherrill, eds. (1988). *Focus XI: Dance and the Older Adult.* Waldorf, Maryland: American Alliance Publications.

Caplow-Lindner, Erna, Harpaz, Leah, and Samberg, Sonya (1979). *Therapeutic Dance/Movement Expressive Activities for the Older Adult.* New York: Human Sciences Press.

Corbin, Charles B. and Lindsey, Ruth (1985). *Concepts of Physical Fitness with Laboratories.* Dubuque, Iowa: Wm. C. Brown Publishers.

Corbin, David E. and Corbin, Josie-Metal (1983). *Reach for It! A Handbook of Exercise and Dance Activities for Older Adults.* Dubuque, Iowa: eddie bowers publishing company.

Harris, Jane A., Pittman, Anne M. and Waller, Marlys S. (1988). *Dance A While.* New York: Macmillan Publishing Company.

Hayes, Elizabeth (1964). *An Introduction to the Teaching of Dance.* New York: The Ronald Press Company.

H'Doubler, Margaret N. (1959). *Dance: A Creative Art Experience.* Madison, Wisconsin: The University of Wisconsin Press.

Hypes, Jeannette, ed. (1978). *Discover Dance: Teaching Modern Dance in Secondary Schools.* Washington, D.C.: AAHPERD.

Lockhart, Aileene and Pease, Esther E. (1987). *Modern Dance Building and Teaching Lessons.* Dubuque, Iowa: Wm. C. Brown Publishers.

Murray, Ruth Lovell (1975). *Dance in Elementary Education.* New York: Harper and Row, Publishers.

Stenger, Leslie A. and Smith, Christel M. (1985). *Healthy Moves for Older Adults.* Washington, D.C.: Clearinghouse on Teaching Education.

Van Gelder, Naneene and Marks, Sheryl (1987). *Aerobic Dance-Exercise Instructor Manual.* San Diego: International Dance-Exercise Association Foundation.

Index